BEHAVIORAL SCIENTISTS IN COURTS AND CORRECTIONS

BEHAVIORAL SCIENTISTS IN COURTS AND CORRECTIONS

James T. Ziegenfuss, Jr., Ph.D.

VNR VAN NOSTRAND REINHOLD COMPANY
_____ New York

Manufactured in the United States of America

Published by Van Nostrand Reinhold Company Inc.
135 West 50th Street
New York, New York 10020

Van Nostrand Reinhold Company Limited
Molly Millars Lane
Wokingham, Berkshire RG11 2PY, England

Van Nostrand Reinhold
480 Latrobe Street
Melbourne, Victoria 3000, Australia

Macmillan of Canada
Division of Gage Publishing Limited
164 Commander Boulevard
Agincourt, Ontario M1S 3C7, Canada

15 14 13 12 11 10 9 8 7 6 5 4 3 2 1

Library of Congress Cataloging in Publication Data

Ziegenfuss, James T.
    Behavioral scientists in courts and corrections.

    Bibliography: p.
    Includes index.
    1. Social sciences—Research—Law and legislation—
United States.   2. Courts—United States.   3. Correctional
law—United States.   4. Psychology, Forensic.   5. Social
psychology.   6. Corrections—United States.   I. Title.
KF9674.Z44   1985   347.73'1'0724   85-3294
ISBN 0-442-29390-9   347.30710724

To Margee, Kate, Sarah and Jamie
with love

PREFACE

I have been involved with law and behavior issues since 1973 when I staffed a task force studying the attitudes of criminal justice personnel toward addictions. Since that time my work has been in what my advisor Professor Eric Trist has defined as the domain of law and society—that is, social systems. Behavioral scientists need to select a problem area in which to work that is of major significance to society, and certainly the difficulty in building a court or correctional social system that meets both human and legal needs is a critical problem. For the past twelve years I have worked in this broad domain, focusing my attention on law and medicine, particularly the rights of institutionalized persons—both patients and prisoners.

This book represents my views of where behavioral scientists can contribute in subsets of the law and society domain—courts and corrections. It is a linkage of law and behavioral science through the organizational systems perspective. And, most important, it links theory with practice and practice with theory toward the end of developing better criminal justice systems by addressing their organizational systems problems.

A key point must be made here about the nature of the problems in courts and corrections when defined from the organizational systems perspective. These are complex social systems problems that are interdisciplinary and transdisciplinary.The work on the problems involves two or more disciplines, *and* they go beyond any single discipline or group of them. Discipline-bound thinkers will find the book's perspective somewhat discomforting. It is not a book just for psychologists, or sociologists, or organization behavior scientists. They are all involved in the organizational systems problems of courts and corrections. Each perspective is needed, but each is not of itself adequate to address the problem. A single discipline or two is necessary but not sufficient for solving these complex problems. "Behavioral scientist" (in some sense, at least) is becoming a transdisciplinary label that will continue to experience growth under the new perspective of the interrelatedness of aspects of complex problems.

This is clearly and purposefully an attempt to *extend* the opportunities for, and the work of behavioral scientists. It is an analysis of behavioral science activities, not a study of courts and corrections work per se. The latter is left for the criminal justice experts. Undoubtedly I have left out some key points that courts and corrections experts would think should be identified.

The book presents five primary functions of behavioral scientists. These functions are defined, described, and related to court and correctional organization parts in order to enable professionals to match their skills with management and service needs in courts and corrections. The term "behavioral scientists" broadens the readership target beyond psychologists to include others involved in the human behavior field (e.g., organizational and social science professionals). However, it will be apparent to the reader that there is a clear and dominant link to such individual disciplines as psychology. The book identifies key areas of courts and corrections and presents examples of how behavioral scientists have contributed or could contribute to organizational problem solving.

Using standard courts and corrections topic outlines as a guide, each subject is considered in terms of how one or more of the five primary functions of behavioral scientists could be employed (assessment and diagnosis, treatment, education and training, research, and consultation). The introductory chapter defines this view of courts and corrections as a system. Subsequent chapters match this functional set against various court topics to illustrate how behavioral scientists *can* contribute by looking at how they *have* contributed. The idea is to extend the reader's thinking about the variety of ways to get involved.

The readership for the book includes any behavioral scientist seeking new areas or problems in which to test his/her skills. These persons might include professionals just beginning their careers and others looking for new areas of interest to add to established practices and directions. It will be particularly useful to students in psychology, psychiatry, criminology, social work, organization behavior, and sociology, as it will provide examples of future career activities. Finally, lawyers and law firms will find it useful, not for telling them about law and legal process but for illustrating how they can use behavioral scientists in a wide range of court and correctional activities.

The "reports" that are cited here are used as cases to be examined in terms of how behavioral scientists work. They are of necessity greatly simplified "summaries" of the true research and practice reports published by the authors. There has been no attempt to provide process and procedural detail. That is left for those readers interested in a specific study requiring more detailed examination. The "research examples" are used for the purpose of illustrating the problem areas as a whole, and the specific issues that can be addressed by behavioral scientists. There is little if any discussion and analysis of their individual findings or of the methodological issues. That would require a doubling of the size of the book and would distract readers from the intended focus on the breadth of opportunities for work.

It is important to note also that these problems are defined as *problems*. This is so because behavioral scientists are too often (most often) brought in when difficulties arise, not as part of a problem-prevention strategy. The problem orientation is not meant to overlook the fine and successful organizational work that is already provided in both courts and corrections.

Last, this is a macro view of both court and correctional organizational systems. That is, it focuses on topics showing the range of these areas, but not their depth, which is quite extensive for each area. Depth in functional areas such as clinical psychology or assessment is appropriately the topic of behavioral scientists with a special interest in subtopics such as competence for trial or jury selection. This overview with illustrations is designed to help behavioral scientists to think of a greater range of applications of their skills. A reader thinking creatively should be able to find topics of interest, as well as a good match of skills/experience and a problem to work on. The book is offered as a means to encourage more behavioral scientists to apply their knowledge and skills to our social system problems. In courts and corrections these problems involve the core values of the American social system—liberty and justice provided in organizational systems that work.

Harrisburg, Pennsylvania   JAMES T. ZIEGENFUSS, JR.

ACKNOWLEDGMENTS

My thinking about the ways in which behavioral scientists could contribute to courts and corrections has been assisted by many persons. A psychologist, Dr. David Lasky, first helped me to see the behavioral and process consultation aspects of evaluation and planning. At Penn State, Dr. Rupert Chisholm helped me to connect behavioral science with organization behavior and sociotechnical work. This introduction was reinforced and extended in my program in Social Systems Sciences at the University of Pennsylvania's Wharton School. The influences of Professors Eric Trist and Russell Ackoff are here, particularly with respect to sociotechnical interests and a total belief in wide-ranging organization development and planning strategies. Social systems scientists are intimately involved in and contributing to both. I appreciate this teaching.

The book was produced with tireless support from several persons. I thank especially Yvonne Harhigh for help in digging out the "facts" of the reports and for bibliographic work. Virginia Fossi and Debbie Langdon also assisted in "fact" gathering. Typing was done by Jean Billet, Daria Sessamen, and Wendy Kauffman, for which thanks are extended. I am also grateful for support from The Pennsylvania State University and from Dr. Christopher McKenna.

Last, but especially, I am grateful for the encouragement and support of my editor at Van Nostrand Reinhold, Susan Munger.

LIST OF CASES

CONTENTS

BEHAVIORAL SCIENTISTS IN COURTS AND CORRECTIONS

1
BEHAVIORAL SCIENTISTS AND THE ORGANIZATIONAL SYSTEMS VIEW

Chapter 1 describes an organizational systems view of court and correctional organizations in order that readers may have a common understanding. This view considers the organization to be comprised of five subsystems: goals/values, technical, structural, psychosocial, and managerial. These subsystems are the areas of work for behavioral scientists; whose functions are defined and described under five headings: assessment and diagnosis, treatment, education and training, research, and consultation.

This book identifies various ways behavioral scientists can contribute to two organizations that are common to all our communities: courts and corrections. The book has several purposes: (1) to define five common functions of behavioral scientists in organizations generally, including court and correctional organizations; (2) to illustrate how these five functions contribute to the diagnosis of problems and to the planning, actions, and evaluations of court and correctional organizations; and (3) to provide behavioral scientists (psychologists, psychiatrists, sociologists, anthropologists, and others) with a greater understanding of the wide range of their potential functions in the two types of organizations. This last purpose is achieved through analysis of specific examples of how other behavioral scientists have made contributions to both courts and corrections.

To achieve these purposes, several things must be done. First, we must identify the nature and characteristics of an organization in a "generic" sense (the common systems view). For if organizations are to be the subjects of extensive behavioral scientist activity, we must have a somewhat mutual understanding of what it is that they are. Therefore, one goal of this first chapter is to define one view of the "organization in general," the "every organization" as in "everyman." This view will then allow us to think in common about how behavioral scientists affect the various structures and processes in both courts and corrections, which are defined as subtypes of the organization in general.

The second goal of the first chapter is to develop a clear presentation of the five primary functions of behavioral scientists. This is done by collecting and analyzing a wide range of behavioral science activities, clustering them according to their similarities in purpose, process, and outcome. In the model to be presented here, the five functions are: (1)

assessment and diagnosis, (2) treatment, (3) education and training, (4) research, and (5) consultation. In this chapter, these functions are defined in detail, with illustrations of behavioral scientists' activity in each of the functional roles. Examples of role activity subsequently appear throughout the book in the case examples.

Building on this first chapter's work, the third task is to collect and briefly analyze examples of what behavioral scientists actually do in both court and correctional organizations. We do not want to direct our thinking toward the theoretical areas (i.e., to what behavioral scientists potentially can do) because in some views the options are limitless. Instead, case examples outlining selected activities of these scientists' contributions to both courts and corrections attempt to present a realistic picture. Chapters 2 through 5 include case examples, which cover a wide range of activity from technical service to management and clinical care. The examples are categorized according to their relation to the various elements of the organization. For example, organization planning work is in the management area.

The first section of this first chapter presents a systems view of the organization, one that will give us a shared understanding for the organizational categorization of the case examples.

THE SYSTEMS VIEW OF ORGANIZATION

In a book concerning organizations (such as courts and corrections) we might ask,'' why do we need to have a common understanding of the nature of organizations? ''There are several reasons. The organization theory literature is quite diverse and still developing. This means, in effect, that there are both competing and conflicting views of what an organization is. To ensure that our consideration of what functions behavioral scientists play in the organization is comprehensive, we need some understanding of these competing and conflicting views. An analysis of these views leads us to an understanding of what the organization is, and at what points behavioral scientists might contribute.

After a brief review we can select one model for the nature and working of organizations in general, and use it as our basis for understanding the functions that behavioral scientists can play in an organization. Without a common model of the nature of the organization, readers would consider the behavioral scientists' functions from different points of view. Knowledge and understanding of an organization is in part derived from each individual person's perception of what the organization is. By providing a common conception of the organization, we will help to diminish conflicts and debates regarding the potential and proper behavioral scientist roles within organizations such as those in courts and corrections.

A second reason for using a common model is my belief that the organization theory perspective used in this model is a leading candidate to become *the* point of consensus in the future. As we are attempting to consider the most modern behavioral scientist functions, it is important to use one primary candidate for organization theory leadership as the framework for the organization analysis. The view chosen here, that of Fremont Kast and James Rosenzweig, has been quite well accepted in universities, and has been the basis for the training of many executives and managers in all types of public and private organizations.[1] The use of this model makes it possible for behavioral scientists offering their services to courts and corrections organizations in the future to have a mutual understanding with those organizations' executives and managers. It is certainly helpful for them to start from the same conceptual perspective as those to whom they will offer their services, executive teams trained in public and private management.

In summary, as behavioral scientists we first need to know what organizations are. Second, we need to have some common understanding of a common model of organizations. Third, to as great an extent as possible, we need to have the same understanding of the organization as those managers and executives to whom we will be proposing our services. The organizational systems view of Kast and Rosenzweig, our model for this analysis, is derived from a short but vigorous history of organization theory. A brief review provides an introduction to the theoretical base on which the Kast and Rosenzweig view rests.

What is the current status of organization theory, and what does it tell us about the design and operation of courts and correctional organizations? In summarizing the developing thoughts on organization theory, particularly the reviews of William Scott[2] and my own histories,[3,4] one theme seems to be outstanding: *The conception of organization is continuing to expand and develop so that we have ever enlarging views of the organizational system.* Three groups of organization theorists have advanced the knowledge about organizations in their own respective "schools of thought" over a period of some fifty years. As we mastered each school of theory, it was found to be inadequate.

Beginning with the classical school, there was an orientation toward traditional organizational functions and structures (tables of organization, written procedures—the formal organization). The human relations school followed, with special concern for individual and group behavior, and particularly for informal systems within the organization. Importantly, neither the "classical emphasis" on formal organization charts, job descriptions, and formal structure nor the "human relations" concern for people, status, job satisfaction, morale, and commitment was considered to be sufficient to define what an organization is and how it works. The more modern "systems theory" school attempts to integrate both the original thinking of the classical organization theorist and the human relations school's concern for people. The two are combined to create a dynamic view of the organizational system that includes both formal structures and functions and informal group behaviors, norms, status, and other less "visible" aspects.

The early thinking about what constitutes an organization focused on the formal structures and the technical work of the organization. In the courts, for example, organizational analysts were concerned with types of jobs and their arrangement in levels or hierarchies. When the human relations theorists came on the scene with their interest focused on human behavior, the basis for developing an understanding of the organization changed to a concern for people. Using courts again as the example, human relations theorists would "explain" the organization by examining and reporting on the relations between judges and prosecutors and public defenders and between plaintiffs and defendants and the jury. This too was a limited perspective that did not account for other relevant components of the organization.

In the 1980s the work in organization theory presents a strong integrationist concern. This involves defining and understanding the organization in a way that includes persons with traditional formal concerns and those interested in the more informal aspects (e.g., group relations theorists). There are other new topics as well. The modern systems school includes the organization's environment as a needed subject for study. Activities and variables outside the organization are now brought into models of organization in recognition of their effects on both the formal and the informal systems. In brief, the most modern views of what organizations are and how they work include a wide range of internal organizational effects/elements and effects/pressures from outside the organizations' boundaries. This modern systems theory view of the nature of the organization will be used to define the organizational subjects of the behavioral scientist's work. We need only to know more about the systems view.

What is organizational systems theory? The following summarizes some of the basic characteristics of this view of organizations:

Modern organization theory, which emphasizes integration, describes the organization as a system with diverse interrelating elements that all contribute to the whole organization. It involves the study of these elements, their purposes, their interrelationships, and the processes used to integrate them. This theory, known as the systems approach, builds on the functional and human relations concepts. Its holistic orientation and emphasis on environment and interrelatedness are significant new developments and represent a third dimension of reality (for organization thinking).

Systems theory states that there are general principles which are the formative guidelines of all organizations. These general principles are either characteristics (e.g., the concepts of feedback, purpose, environment, hierarchy, and boundary) or actions (e.g., adaptation, exploration, differentiation, and integration). Although some of these terms have been utilized by other theories, they are viewed by modern organization theorists as primary elements in understanding the nature of organization. In sum, modern organization theory views the organization as a dimension of generalized design principles, interacting subsystems and the processes of integration with constant emphasis on the whole.[5]

This is an introduction to the thinking of modern organization theory as represented by many different writers. We need to identify and select one particular theoretical approach presented by one writer (or group of writers) to guide our developing understanding of the nature of organization. The theoretical approach/writer will both exemplify and extend our brief history while combining the diverse schools of organization theory into one integrated perspective that can be used to probe courts and corrections organizations.

Kast and Rosenzweig have developed an integrated systems view of the organization that will serve as the framework for our analysis of elements of courts and correctional organizations. The basis of the Kast and Rosenzweig model is their belief that organizations are composed of five linked subsystems that are in constant two-way interaction with the environment. The five subsystems are defined as follows:

1. Goals and values system: the ends or desirable future of the organization with high relative worth or importance.
2. Technical system: the knowledge required for the performance of tasks, including the techniques used in the transformation of inputs and outputs.
3. Structural system: the ways in which the tasks of the organization are divided (differentiation) and coordinated (integration). In the formal sense, structure is set forth by organization charts, by position and job descriptions, and by rules and procedures.
4. Psychosocial system: the individuals and groups in interaction. It consists of individual behavior and motivation, status and role relationships, group dynamics, and influence systems. It is also affected by sentiments, values, attitudes, expectations, and aspirations of the people in the organization.

5. Managerial system: spans the entire organization by: relating the organization to its environment; setting the goals; developing comprehensive, strategic, and operational plans; designing the structure; and establishing control processes.[6]

These five subsystems are the essence of all organizations, whether they are court organizations or correctional ones. The systems are pictured in the Figure 1-1. No detail is provided as to how the individual subsystems interrelate one with the other or even what the elements are within them. It is sufficient to begin to think of these five subsystems as the major elements of organization.

How does this view of the nature of organization relate to our interest in identifying points in the organization that could use behavioral scientists? A further elaboration of the detail of the systems will help. For example, in the courts, there are goals and values that "produce" the court's philosophy (e.g., conservative vs. liberal) and a technical system of work that describes how the judicial process, the public defender, and the prosecution system interact to complete their primary work tasks. The courts also have a structure beginning with the lower courts and their types of cases, and continuing through the state and federal courts. This structure includes ways in which this whole judicial system is differentiated according to levels and coordinated in terms of, for example, the intergration of the legal system from higher to lower levels of appeal. At the same time, the court system has a whole set of individual and group behaviors and relationships (psychosocial aspects), which involve the individual personalities, attitudes, and related personal characteristics of judges, attorneys, and court administrators. The psychosocial system involves the sentiments, values, motivations, and expectations of those persons participating in the judicial subsystem. Last, there is a managerial element. This subsystem is involved in setting the goals for the judicial process, in developing strategic and operational plans, and in creating a structure whereby all of these will be achieved.

Figure 1-1 helps us to conceptualize both the court and the correctional organization in terms of the five subsystems—goals, technical, structural, psychosocial, and managerial. Each court and correctional organization has the basic elements of these systems. This perspective enables us to discuss the functions of behavioral scientists in terms of different but related and co-contributing building blocks of the organization—the five subsystems.

For example, suppose that a warden is considering the possible use of a behavioral scientist to design and develop a training program for inmates in a correctional organization. Since the training program would be thought

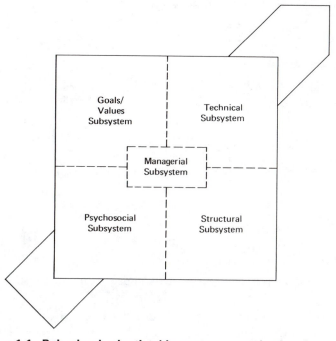

Figure 1-1. Behavioral scientists' impact on organizational systems.

of as a core aspect of the technical work of corrections, the training task employing the behavioral scientist in this situation would be essentially a *technical* subsystem intervention. However, during the process of the work, the behavioral scientist would need to consider, as a part of his/ her primary task, the relation of the training to the *goals* of the organization; the way in which the current training program is *structured;* and the attitudes, values, and expectations of the staff now involved in inmate training *(psychosocial* aspects). There is multiple subsystem impact, as demonstrated in Figure 1-2. This example illustrates that the language of the organizational systems discussion of Kast and Rosenzweig enables us to discuss various aspects of the organization with a common set of terms and a common perception of the organization's basic nature. With this reference we can examine a multitude of behavioral science functions within both court and correctional organizations.

This very brief introduction to organization theory and to one organizational view does not provide very much detail as to the exact nature of the variables within each of the systems. There are a wide spectrum of elements that constitute each of the organizational systems involved. The case examples throughout the book will illustrate how these elements

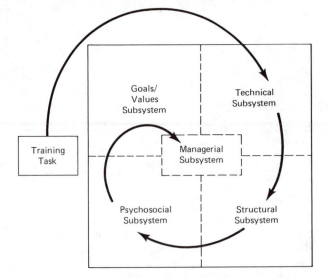

Figure 1-2. Multiple systems impact of training task.

are the organization. These are the internal elements that both create and respond to the organization's behavior. There are external influences as well.

If the organization were considered to be a closed system, that is, completely contained within its boundaries, there would be no external influences. However, that is very unlikely to be the case in theory, and it is especially not true with regard to judicial and correctional systems. They are subject to many forces outside their respective organizational boundaries. Again, Kast and Rosenzweig have given us a convenient list, for what they have called *environmental characteristics*. This group of nine elements should not be considered absolute or exhaustive, but they are basic categories to help us to organize our thinking about the diverse external pressures on both courts and correctional agencies (i.e., those pressures coming from outside the organization's boundaries). These so-called organization environment characteristics have been defined as a series of clustered elements, as identified below:

1. Cultural
2. Educational
3. Economic
4. Legal
5. Political
6. Sociological
7. Demographic

8. Natural resource
9. Technological

The presence of this wide diversity of environmental influences on the organization means that each court and correctional organization must contend with a significant range and depth of pressures from outside its boundaries.

It is important to recognize that both courts and correctional organizations are in constant interchange with this environment. The presence of the elements does not mean only one-way influence. Organizations shape their environment as they are being shaped. Thus behavioral scientists operating in one or more functions within either organization need to consider the effects of various environmental influences on their work. For example, within the courtroom it often appears at first examination that the judicial sentencing process depends primarily and/or almost solely on the individual boundaries established by the law and the discretion allowed to the judge and jury. However, the sentencing process exists within a cultural value set that may demand at varying times in our history different kinds of sentences. There may be a period of time in our court system during which sentencing is considered to be relatively light, with much in the way of a "second chance offered" (e.g., the 1960s and 1970s). Recent thinking regarding sentencing and punishment has resulted in an "environmental pressure" for harsher sentences (the pressure originates from outside the boundaries of the court decision system). Judges and juries are now expected to respond to this cultural pressure by handing out longer sentences for a wide variety of crimes. This example illustrates the environmental-characteristics nature of organization, and it suggests a point of involvement. Behavioral scientists could be asked to study state, regional, or national trends in sentencing for a set of crimes. Any findings that purport to provide guidance to judges would need to take cognizance of this cultural change.

Correctional agencies experienced similar changes in cultural pressures. During the late 1960s and 1970s many innovative criminal justice programs were tried, often as "alternatives to prison." These programs allowed increasing discretion in programming and internal restrictions, as well as early release for inmates who could demonstrate that they were seriously attempting to correct an inappropriate life pattern. However, the conservative cultural pressure that is supporting longer sentences in the court system is now operating on correctional organizations. There is intense lobbying to restrain early releases and to restrict the number and kinds of experimentations with alternative-to-prison programs. What would be needed if behavioral scientists were asked to assess the degree to which a correctional agency's programs are meeting the public's current goals?

Would there need to be consideration of this external environmental pressure? Yes, because society's goals for its publicly funded correctional organizations have changed. Society now favors increased punishment over further exploration of treatment-oriented alternatives. The example indicates in a simple and obvious situation that there is always a need to assess the environmental context of the organization.

This brief introduction to the systems view of the organization provides the base on which to build our examination of the functions of behavioral scientists within court and correctional organizations. We now have some sense of the various systems toward which behavioral scientists would be directed. We have a common set of terms for referring to these systems and a sample of their individual variables. Now we need to consider just exactly what the behavioral scientists' functions are that would be applied to the organizational systems problems of courts and corrections.

FIVE BASIC FUNCTIONS OF BEHAVIORAL SCIENTISTS

As preparation for our discussion of the five basic functions of behavioral scientists, we need to know first what behavioral science is. Bevelson offers the following as an introduction to the field:

> The behavioral sciences study human behavior by scientific means; as a preliminary approximation, they can be distinguished from the social sciences as designating a good deal less but, at the same time somewhat more. The term "social sciences" typically includes the disciplines of anthropology, economics, political science, sociology, and most of psychology. As a case in point, the scholarly associations in these five disciplines—along with history and statistics—provide the core membership of the (American) Social Science Research Council. The behavioral sciences, as that term was originally intended and as it is usually understood, include sociology; anthropology (minus archeology, technical linguistics, and most of physical anthropology); psychology (minus physiological psychology); and the behavioral aspects of biology, economics, geography, law, psychiatry, and political science. The edges of any such broad concept tend to be fuzzy—as are the edges of the social sciences themselves—but the center seems to be reasonably clear.[7]

As indicated, the disciplines are fairly diverse with considerable intersection at the edges of each group's boundaries. This is important because this analysis of functional possibilities is directed at the larger, broader group, not just a selected subgroup.

Bevelson continued with an abstract of the history of the development of the behavioral sciences. He identified the Ford Foundation's (1953) plan for a behavioral science program as a key point in the history, as it provided both a base and a clear path for development. The seven points of the plan will complete our introduction to the field.

1. It refers primarily to a program of research. A major part of Program Five is conceived as a program for research on human behavior, not as an "action program." Furthermore, it is not expected that the staff of Program Five will itself conduct behavioral research; rather, it will help to initiate and to support such activities.

2. It refers to the scientific approach. It encourages the acquisition of behavioral knowledge under conditions which, so far as possible, ensure objectivity, verifiability, and generality. It calls for conformity to high standards of scientific inquiry.

3. It refers to the acquisition of basic knowledge of human behavior and thus it is considered as a comparatively long-range venture. Basic study of the tremendously complicated problems of man cannot be expected to yield significant results in a short period of time.

4. It refers to the interest of the Foundation not in knowledge of human behavior as such but rather in knowledge which promises at some point to serve human needs. The program is thus oriented to social problems and needs.

5. It refers to an interdisciplinary approach and not to any single conventional field of knowledge or a single combination of them; traditional academic disciplines as such are not included or excluded. The program's goal is to acquire scientific knowledge of human behavior from whatever sources can make appropriate contributions. Social scientists, medical scientists, and humanists, singly and in combination can be engaged in the program. The intention is to use all relevant knowledge, skills, concepts and insights.

6. It refers to a broad and complex subject matter since the program aims at a scientific understanding of why people behave as they do. "Behavior" includes not only overt acts but also such subjective behavior as attitudes, beliefs, expectations, motivations and aspirations. The program seeks knowledge which is useful in attacking problems of an economic, political, religious, educational or personal nature by studying the behavior of human beings as individuals or as members of primary groups, formal organizations, social strata, or social institutions. The program is vitally concerned with the cultural heritage by which men live, the social structures they have devised to organize their societies, the goals they pursue and the means with which they pursue them.

7. Finally, it is definitely not considered as a cure-all for human problems but rather as a contributor to their solution, along with other sources of knowledge and judgment. The goal of the program is to

provide scientific aids which can be used in the conduct of human affairs; it seeks only to increase useful knowledge and skills and to apply them wherever appropriate.

In short, then Program Five is conceived as an effort to increase knowledge of human behavior through basic scientific research oriented to major problem areas covering a wide range of subjects, and to make such knowledge available for utilization in the conduct of human affairs.[8]

With this as a brief historical base the functions of this science within courts and corrections can be introduced.

This section builds on both the behavioral science history and the organizational systems view just presented, identifying five common functions of behavioral scientists within organizations generally. That is, the functions are theoretically of generic use in organizations of all types. As we continue through the book, it is necessary to keep in mind that these functions are most often not applied to the whole of the organization but are usually targeted specifically at one of the five organizational subsystems.

The five common functions now defined are not to be considered an all-inclusive presentation of the full set of behavioral science activity options. Instead, they are a shorthand way for identifying some major functional activities of behavioral scientists in courts and corrections. Derived from an inspection of hundreds of published reports of behavioral scientists' work, they are listed as follows:

1. Assessment and diagnosis
2. Treatment
3. Education
4. Research
5. Consultation

The key point is that most of the major activities of behavioral scientists in courts and correctional organizations can be placed under one of these five functional "labels." They are not mutually exclusive categories; there is considerable overlap. But the labels are useful for identifying the differences in activities of a wide variety of psychologists, psychiatrists, sociologists, and other behavioral scientists.

Each of the functions can be further differentiated, offering more detail as to the definition of that particular activity. For example, the assessment and diagnosis function can be further differentiated in terms of educational, vocational, or psychological activities. Each further definition of activity is a specific subtype of the more general class of assessment and diagnosis.

The other functions can be subdivided as well. The research function can be discussed in basic, applied, and/or action research terms. The education and training function is further defined as either preparatory or continuing.

The selected examples of behavioral science work have been categorized according to these five functions in order to provide readers with as broad a picture as possible. Potential functions for behavioral scientists in court and correctional organizations are highly variable and bounded only by the imaginativeness of the scientist and his/her client. Utilizing the organizational systems model presented, these five functions can be matched with the five organizational subsystems to provide a function by organization subject matrix. For example, behavioral scientists can become involved in research designed to examine the court's goals and values, technical services, or management subsystems. Simultaneously, other behavioral scientists can examine the court's structure and the attitudes and job satisfaction levels of certain of the employees (e.g., public defenders). The relationship between the five functions identified here and the five organizational subsystems is presented in Figure 1-3.

Several examples will further demonstrate. The functions and some sample work topics of behavioral scientists may be classified as follows:

Assessment and diagnosis: provision of psychological testing in a pretrial competency determination process for the court.

Treatment: provision of therapy to individual and inmate groups within the prison.

Behavioral Scientist Functions / Systems Parts	Assessment and diagnosis	Treatment	Education and training	Research	Consultation
Goals/values					
Technical					
Structural					
Psychosocial					
Managerial					

Figure 1-3. Behavioral scientists/organizational systems relations.

Education and training: design of a training program for prison counselors on conflict resolution.

Research: investigation of the job satisfaction levels of public defenders.

Consultation: provision of assistance to management in organizing a corrections program planning process, department by department.

As these five functions are the means for identifying the nature and breadth of behavioral science work, we need to be further informed about each of them. The following discussion more fully defines the functions, providing examples of the work, function by function.

Assessment and Diagnosis

Assessment is defined as "those procedures by which a behavioral scientist evaluates an individual's strengths, weaknesses, problems and needs."[9] Diagnosis, a closely related procedure, is here defined as the collection and analysis of the data derived from the assessment procedures. These data are used to create a concise technical description of an individual's strengths, weaknesses, problems, and needs. The combined assessment and diagnostic process can be further differentiated according to the nature of the problem in which the assessment and diagnosis is used. That is, assessment and diagnosis can concern the individual's educational, vocational, or psychological aspects. While there are some parallels in assessment purpose, process, and outcome, the educational, vocational, and psychological assessment functions will be individually introduced in this section.

There is a need also to differentiate assessment and diagnosis of individual needs from the assessment of a program or organization. The latter is more often identified as program evaluation and is linked to either research or consultation. Posavac and Carey have made the distinction as follows:

> Educational psychologists, personnel workers, counseling psychologists, and others have traditionally provided diagnostic information for human service organizations. These people have served by administering intelligence, aptitude, interest, achievement, personality, and other tests for the purpose of "evaluating" an individual's need for a service or higher qualifications for a job or for advancement. These activities are not involved in the program evaluator's role.[9]

They are more considered to be individual assessment activities, with the subject the individual, not the organization or program.

The assessment and diagnosis function is divided into three separate activities (functional subdifferentiation):

- Educational assessment and diagnosis
- Psychological assessment and diagnosis
- Vocational assessment and diagnosis

Educational Assessment and Diagnosis.   This is the function of behavioral scientists that is directed at the educational aspects of participants in the court and correctional organizations. Page and Thomas defined educational assessment as follows:

the process by which one attempts to measure the quality and quantity of *learning* and teaching using various assessment techniques, e.g. assignments, projects, continuous assessment, objective type tests final examinations and standardized tests.[10]

Depending on the subjects within court and corrections organizations, the assessment may differ. Courts could be interested in the current level of education of a young offender, while corrections officials may be interested in the progress of offenders in an educational program. Both subjects would be included in the above definition of the assessment function.

Page and Thomas further link the assessment work to diagnosis: "Tests are diagnostic when they are used to identify strengths and weaknesses in school attainment, most commonly in basic skills of literacy and numeracy or where remedial education is required." It is therefore a review of the current situation, whether it be of a defendant in court or an inmate in prison. The whole educational assessment and diagnosis function is a part of the field of testing. Testing in the education area will not be further elaborated here, other than to enumerate several types of tests to indicate the wide range of potential topics of concern for behavioral scientists. The Health, Education and Welfare Department identified the following test titles as a part of their glossary:[11]

- Achievement test
- Advanced placement
- Attitude
- Basic skills
- Reading diagnostic
- Health
- Mental ability
- Norm referenced
- Psychomotor

- Audiometric
- Reading readiness
- Scholastic aptitude
- High school equivalency

This list is illustrative of the testing aspects of this function. As noted, some may involve psychological testing, which is also an activity under a separately defined behavioral science function.

Psychological Assessment and Diagnosis.   Psychological assessment is the process of evaluating clients' individual status with regard to the behavior, attitudes and emotions, motivations, values, and other aspects that constitute their "psychology." By psychology we mean both the clients' mental processes and their behavior as individual persons and as they interact with others in groups. Assessment is quite simply the making of a determination of the status of a person's mental processes or his/her behavior. Psychological assessment may also include a social assessment. This assessment is directed at generating an expanded view of the client and is defined as: "the process of evaluating each patient's environment, religious background, childhood history, military service history, financial status, reasons for seeking treatment, and other pertinent information that may contribute to the development of the individualized treatment plan."[12] This type of evaluation is frequently done through testing. Psychological testing services that include assessment and diagnosis have been defined by HEW as: activities concerned with administering psychological tests, standardized tests, and inventory assessments of ability, aptitude, achievement, interests, and personality and the interpretation of these measures for pupils, school personnel, and parents.[13] These can be added to the educational and vocational assessments to gain a well-rounded sense of the person. Psychological assessment is thus one "subset" of the more general assessment and diagnosis function, which also includes vocational reviews.

Vocational Assessment and Diagnosis.   Vocational assessment and diagnosis is defined as: "the process of evaluating each patient's or client's past experience and attitudes toward work, present motivations, or areas of interest, and possibilities of future education, training and/or employment."[14] This is a whole process and procedure by which behavioral scientists attempt to identify essential strengths and weaknesses in a client's working life by reviewing his/her "work-attainment-to-date." Central to this process are traditional testing procedures as well as in-depth interviewing that is designed to establish a "picture" of the client's "best match," both with work in general and with a specific kind of work. In the sociotechnical sense this assessment includes measures of the social and psychological aspects of the individual with relation to work tasks and work organizations.[15] It also includes the individual's match with the task requirement aspects of the work; for example, whether the client has appropriate skills and abilities to enable him/her to complete the job successfully.

The outcome of the vocational assessment and diagnosis process might mean the recommendation of certain activities designed to lead to greater occupational proficiency. For clients of courts or correctional organizations, these could include the following examples resulting from the assessment/diagnostic work:

- Apprenticeships with subsequent review
- Guidance by a counselor
- Training programs
- On-the-job training and review
- Career orientation
- Specific skill training
- Specific job placement

In summary, vocational assessment and diagnosis analyzes the client's current vocational status, making recommendations for future development. Since a successful working life is often a prerequisite for avoiding court and correctional involvement, its importance has been recognized and is now supported more than ever. Recommendations such as those above sometimes involve treatment for contributing personal problems, a subject for the next behavioral science function.

Treatment

The second behavioral science function in court and correctional organizations is labeled the treatment function. Treatment is here defined very simply as the action of applying remedies to a defined problem of a client (e.g., the use of therapy; the design and carrying out of a whole treatment plan; the use of behavioral modification and behavioral change techniques to alter client behavior). The behavioral scientist is seen less frequently in a treatment function in the court organization than he or she is in corrections.

In the courts, the treatment function of behavioral scientists follows closely on and is very much related to the assessment and diagnosis function. In court cases, particularly those that concern addicted or mentally disabled offenders, alternative treatment approaches are identified, evaluated, and recommended, based on whether or not they will support the case for the prosecution and/or for the defense. For example, consideration would be given to whether mentally disordered offenders and drug addicts could receive treatment in a hospital or therapeutic program instead of punishment in a jail or prison.

In correctional organizations, however, the treatment function is the very traditional one of applying remedies to psychological or other personal or social problems of the offenders. For example, clinical psychologists offer therapy and counseling to individuals and groups. Behavioral scientists may design and develop a treatment program for a county prison that is directed at diminishing inmates' feelings of frustration and anger. Quite frequently a behavioral scientist is found in the role of key service provider in the correctional institution—at all levels, county, state, and federal. There has been a long and rather vigorous history of behavioral scientists providing direct clinical services to offenders in both residential institution and outpatient-oriented community programs. This has frequently created a conflict with the security goals of the criminal justice system so that an uncertain peace often exists. Behavioral scientists are now serving that function within more organizations; however, this is not a new or innovative step, but one representing increased intensity and acceptance of all types of services.

There are far too many definitions and types of treatment to be reviewed here in real detail. But the term treatment is a bit too general. Thus for purposes of further differentiation, the treatment function is defined rather simplistically as being of three types: short-term treatment, long-term treatment, and crisis intervention. The distinction here is primarily that of length of time, but it is acknowledged that a number of criteria can be and are used, as noted below:[16]

> The term "brief psychotherapy" attempts to define the process of treatment purely in terms of its overall length, but it is not possible to do justice to its complexities solely in terms of its duration. Actually, brief psychotherapy is often used to refer to one or more of the following somewhat overlapping variables: (1) the length of the treatment, from inception to termination; (2) the frequency of the therapeutic sessions and the duration of each session; (3) the intensity of the treatment, which depends on item 2 as well as on the particular techniques employed; and (4) the goal of treatment, which is often expressed in terms of polarities, even though, in reality, various blendings of the following alternatives are the common occurrence: "supportive" or "suppressive" as contrasted with "insight-oriented," "expressive," or "exploratory."[17]

The intent here is not to undertake an analysis of clinical treatment types, but instead to note that there are different approaches to and types of treatment. It should be remembered that the three types listed here are illustrative of a wide set of alternatives, with this distinction based on one criterion primarily.

The types of treatment are described next, using these labels. By way of introduction, crisis intervention services are defined as the "action of stepping in or interfering in a situation so as to affect its course or issue." This is an early service that successfully achieves an interruption of a crisis that may have led to a serious short-term or long-term treatment need. If the crisis is unable to be short-circuited, the offender's need for short-term treatment may arise, creating a plan of from ten to perhaps ninety days' duration. Any treatment lasting longer than ninety days is defined as long-term. For example, the type of service offered by therapeutic community specialists may require up to one or two years for full treatment by a team including one or more behavioral scientists. Under this classification system, time is the primary differentiator, and is sufficient for demonstrating behavioral science opportunities.

The following sections will define in more detail the types of treatment functions that behavioral scientists can offer.

Short-Term Treatment.   With regard to this simplified presentation of treatment in general, a distinction on the basis of only one criterion is made. This function is therefore identified as short-term treatment, a service that is brief in its total length or duration. This function involves those behavioral scientists who are providing services (in prisons primarily) in a program format that may last up to ninety days. These programs may be targeting the specific behavioral or personality needs of inmates, including aggression, attitudes toward incarceration, or resistance to authority. Clearly these sample problems can be treated on a short-term or a long-term basis, depending on the theoretical model of problem causation and treatment. Along with duration, a medical versus a nonmedical approach has significant implications for the process of the treatment itself.[18–20] For example, short-term treatment may use a behavior modification approach to alter acting-out type aggressive behavior. Some visible results could be expected on the prison ward very quickly, perhaps in several weeks. Alternatively, the aggressive tendencies could be addressed through a long-term psychoanalytically oriented approach. This might necessitate years of treatment designed to alter basic personality formations. In short, there are a wide variety of approaches to, and types of, short-term treatments that involve behavioral scientists.

Long-Term Treatment.   Behavioral scientists may also provide long-term treatment, defined here as that treatment which requires an extended term of client–therapist interactions over a relatively long period of time (i.e., over ninety days). Long-term treatment, much like the short-term work, is more likely to be provided in prisons or jails than in a court-related setting, although treatment in "alternative-to-prison" programs under court sponsorship is now quite common. As in the review of short-term approaches, there are a wide variety of techniques based on various theoretical positions. One example will illustrate.

The therapeutic community has been developed and described by Maxwell Jones over more than three decades.[21-25] Its basic concept is that troubled clients such as offenders require a long-term interaction with a "treating culture" that is able to alter inappropriate mental processes and behaviors over an extended period of time. Since the total culture and the social system interactions are both the *basis* for treatment and *are* the treatment, months and sometimes years are required for change. Several weeks will not be enough time to enable the culture's effects to work. Behavioral scientists have long been involved with designing, developing, and operating these programs. This concept and practice represent only one type of long-term treatment.

Some clinical needs are closer to "emergency" situations, as discussed below.

Crisis Intervention.   In contrast to the long- and short-term treatments, behavioral scientists must sometimes provide treatment that is needed to manage an acute crisis.[26] Defined as crisis intervention,[27] it is not an extended program over months or years, or even several weeks. Instead this function addresses acute feelings of distress that may be related to a new or particularly troublesome situation. For example, waiting for a jury to decide one's guilt or innocence may certainly bring on feelings of anxiety—an anxiety attack, perhaps. This attack can be coped with, or it can result in acting-out aggressive behavior. The clinical psychologist may help the accused through this time with supportive counseling. The counseling may be only one or two sessions of active listening and/or positive reinforcement, but that is all the treatment needed for this situational problem.

Alternatively, an offender committed to a long prison sentence may suggest to a guard that he is going to commit suicide. Here the crisis is very acute, with the possibility that death will result if quick intervention is not forthcoming. The task is to avert the suicide, allowing the client eventually to be directed into a short- or long-term treatment that will address the more significant personality and adjustment problems likely to be present.

Both examples illustrate the behavioral science function in managing a crisis. The crisis can be a response to an isolated situation that will end, or it can be another crisis in an ongoing pattern that the client generates. The latter eventually produces an ongoing need for continued treatment in a short- or long-term program.

These treatment functions are allied to and often overlap with education. This is particularly the case when treatment is viewed as consisting mostly of education as its basic substance. The education function is described next, and the reader should keep this linkage in mind.

The Education and Training Function

The third function of behavioral scientists in court and correctional organizations is an education and training one. Behavioral scientists can provide either preparatory or continuing education for either staff or client participants. Education is defined as including training, and is meant to signify in total the systematic instruction given to individuals or groups to prepare and/or update them for a life's work. Very simply, behavioral scientists can help to prepare employees for their initial jobs; or they can provide additional education and training to continue the development of those employees who are already a part of court and correctional organizations. In some cases, programs similar to staff development sessions can be provided for clients.

In courts, for example, changes in the law regarding the insanity defense have recently created a need for additional training for judges. While judges have long been accustomed to hearing cases involving the insanity defense, this defense has sometimes resulted in the accused being judged "not guilty by reason of insanity." Some states have now changed the law in this area to signify that the accused may be regarded as guilty but insane. This requires treatment followed by punishment through a prison term. In this "training need," judges do not require preparatory information about the general issue of the insanity defense; they are already employed judges. They understand the traditional aspects of the law in this area. However, new developments in the law have given rise to the need for continuing judicial education.

Behavioral scientists such as psychiatrists and clinical psychologists as well as attorneys working in the mental disability area would be particularly suited for this function. The behavioral scientist would be able to present an analysis of the various advantages and disadvantages of this finding, and the likely impact it would have on the psychosocial health of the accused, while attorneys discussed the legal aspects.[28-31] There are several organizations that now take this interdisciplinary perspective of the problem, promoting, for example, law/medicine and psychiatry/law collaboration (e.g., The American Society of Law and Medicine, The American Academy of Psychiatry and Law, and The Law and Psychology Society).

In correctional organizations, behavioral scientists may become involved in assisting with the preparatory training of new corrections officers. For example, several community colleges and many regular colleges have criminal justice departments that are used to train correctional officers.

In these departments, psychologists and sociologists and others provide course work on the culture of the prison, the various treatment methodologies involved, and the general nature of prison work as it contributes to the rehabilitation function. Other professionals might provide the punishment and security-oriented perspectives.

The following information will further define the preparatory and continuing education functions individually.

Preparatory Education Function.   To educate is defined by Webster as "to develop mentally or morally." Preparatory education is simply the basic or first development of a person in relation to a specific job or to a new occupational situation. Behavioral scientists provide preparatory education in prisons when they make a contribution to the development of basic inmate learning, both in the intellectual sense and for individual skills. The distinction between preparatory and continuing education establishes recognition of the organizational purpose of the educational function. As a further example, behavioral scientists may become involved in providing basic job readiness training for delinquents who are soon to be released from prison. Very young inmates may never have held a job. At this time in their life they are in need of primary preparatory education that teaches them about work attitudes, scheduling, attendance, and productivity requirements. Additionally, they will need to learn and practice such basics as interviewing in preparation for their first encounter with the employment process. The behavioral aspects of employment are increasingly being recognized as critical to the offenders' chances of securing a job.[32]

Those offenders with previous work experience may need to further develop or change their work attitudes, a continuing education function of the behavioral scientist.

Continuing Education Function.   A second aspect of this general education/training function is identified as continuing education. If some learning and experience in a field has already occurred, establishing a base to build on, expansion and further development of that base are needed. Shortell's comments are adapted to our topic below:

We define continuing education as the planned learning beyond the basic professional education, of generic . . . skills relevant to the topic. Planned learning refers to learning oriented to stated objectives, and to the evaluation of both the process and outcome of the learning experience. Although valuable, purely informational programs designed to bring practitioners up-to-date (for example, on the latest legislation in the field or the latest funding developments in Washington) would not constitute continuing education as we have defined it. Continuing education must be relevant to today's problem but must also transcend it . . . the problems of today are not the problems of tomorrow; consequently, we emphasize the development of generic skills, knowledge, and value orientations which can be useful . . . in a variety of circumstances.[33]

Shortell's points are directed at administrative and management skills, but they are also generally true in defining the continuing education intentions of this behavioral science function. By addressing current needs, behavioral scientists can assist both clients and staff of courts and correctional organizations to prepare for and be capable of addressing their future problems.

Shortell follows up those introductory comments with the following further explanation of this function:

Broadly defined, continuing education . . . could include any educational activity through which systematic learning opportunities are provided, including formal and informal courses, conferences, conventions, symposia, seminars, institutes, and workshops. In an even broader sense, any daily experience from which an individual is able to obtain a new skill, a new idea, or a new insight which can be generalized to future situations can be considered continuing education. In defining continuing education in somewhat more circumscribed terms, this report does not question the obvious value of a broad view of continuing education. Rather, it reflects the need to develop a working definition of continuing education upon which specific programs and activities can be built.

Behavioral scientists provide continuing education and training on an almost unlimited number of topics. The job and work experience examples for prison offenders are just one of the types of activities. Each type is most significant for the individual. At one Offender Development Service Program, specific job and interviewing skills were identified as a significant need for most of the inmate-client group.[34] But these were provided in a total program context that also included individual clinical and family treatment work.

Education and training may require research either before or after the services are provided. The research function is closely related to education and training in that it is one mechanism for providing the data for education and for monitoring the effects of the education and training activities.

The Research Function

The fourth function of behavioral scientists in courts and correctional organizations is the research function. Without attempting to review the many and varied definitions of and presentations on the research function, a brief introduction gives us an understanding of the diversity of purposes, processes, and outcomes.

Kerlinger defines research as: "systematic, controlled, empirical, and critical investigation of hypothetical propositions about the presumed relations among natural phenomena."[35] It will be evident from discussing three different types of research—basic, applied, and action research—that this definition is oriented toward the scientific notion of basic research. Two further points made by Kerlinger are particularly relevant to all of the research activities that concern behavioral scientists:

> First, when we say that scientific research is systematic and controlled, we mean, in effect, that scientific investigation is so ordered that investigators can have critical confidence in research outcomes. As we shall see later, this means that the research observations are tightly disciplined. Among the many alternative explanations of the phenomenon, all but one are systematically ruled out. One can thus have greater confidence that a tested relation is as it is than if one had not controlled the observations and ruled out alternative possibilities.
>
> Second, scientific investigation is empirical. If the scientist believes something is so, he must somehow or other put his belief to a test outside himself. Subjective belief, in other words, must be checked against subjective reality. The scientist must always subject his notions to the court of empirical inquiry and test. He is hypercritical of the results of his own and others research results. Every scientist writing a research report has other scientists reading what he writes while he writes it. Though it is easy to err, to exaggerate, to overgeneralize when writing up one's own work, it is not easy to escape the feeling of scientific eyes constantly peering over one's own shoulders.[36]

These points are made with respect to research in general, *and* they apply to behavioral scientists' functions in court and correctional organizations, whether these functions involve basic or applied research.

For the purposes of this book, a further distinction must be made that will enable us to match the types of research work with our organizational subjects. The research function includes three types of research activity—basic, applied, and action research. There are no universally accepted definitions of these types, as debate is still vigorous as to the purposes and processes of each as compared to the others. Basic research is often considered to be the very theoretical and/or empirical work that occurs mostly in university and specialized research settings. Applied research is an activity that attempts to link the methods of basic research with problem solving in the organization or community as a whole. It is research methods applied to "real world day-to-day problems." Third, action research is an activity taken by one organization to solve one problem without especial concern for whether those research results will generalize to the greater scientific community. In some views, action research is a subpart of the more general notion of applied research work. The workers in the research field give us a further indication of the differences. Academics are the behavioral scientists involved in basic research, while practitioners and various entrepreneurs (such as consultants) provide the applied and action research (see, e.g., Bernstein and Freeman[37]). These distinctions are breaking down as more behavioral and social scientists recognize that all good theory requires practical testing, and all practice has theoretical assumptions and feedback for future theory development.

The following sections discuss in more detail the basic, applied, and action research functions of behavioral scientists.

Basic Research Function. How do we distinguish the basic research function from that of other types? As a first step we can take a simple explanation that might be offered by commonly available dictionaries:

> Basic research is an unrestrained search for new knowledge. Basic researchers follow their own directions and interest in learning without the need to justify their purpose, process or outcome. Other than its contributions to the expansion of knowledge they can be contrasted with applied researchers who are guided by a given problem and a need to find the practical application.[38]

Basic research is simply a search for new knowledge without boundaries, without the necessity of finding some immediate or even future application for the work. For example, some researchers examine the behavior of juries as a representation of the behavior of transient, short-term groups. The research relates the juries' actions to those activities predicted or expected in various theories of human decision-making. With this basic-research orientation, there is little (or no interest) in how this research would help to make a jury more efficient, or more fair in its judgments.

Almost all court and correctional organization topics that have been studied (if not all) could be contributors to fundamental knowledge development in the behavioral sciences. Some research, however, is directed at solving practical problems. This practical problem-solving orientation is another aspect of the behavioral science research function.

Applied Research Function. How do we distinguish the applied research function from basic research? Psychologists as a core group of all behavioral scientists are good indicators of mainstream views of what this function is, as noted below:

> Since applied psychology follows the same fundamental procedures as basic psychological research, how can the two be differentiated? When the applied psychologist is engaged in research—as is true much of the time for many applied psychologists—the distinction hinges on the difference between basic and applied research. This difference is one of degree. Although examples can be found that fall clearly into the basic or the applied category, some research can be classified in either one. One determining factor is the reason for choosing a problem: to help in theory construction (basic) or in making administrative decisions (applied). For instance, is the investigation concerned principally with the nature of learning or with the most effective method for teaching children to read?
>
> Another difference pertains to the specificity or generality of the findings. The results of basic research can be generalized more widely than those of applied research. The latter typically yields results pertaining only to narrowly limited contexts. Similarly, applied research permits less analysis of casual relations, since situations are likely to be compared in their totality rather than being broken down into more elementary components. For example, applied research may demonstrate that one of two training procedures—in all their operational complexities—yields better results than the other in a particular situation. But it may not be possible under these circumstances to specify why the one method was superior.[39]

This quotation illustrates key functional distinctions between basic and applied behavioral science research. Applied research is practical, of limited generalizability, and directed at a specific problem(s) confronting an individual organization; that is, applied research is not a constraint-free search for new knowledge. These two research functions represent the bulk of the work, except for one increasingly popular approach—action research.

Action Research Function. Action research is undertaken by behavioral scientists in courts and correctional organizations for a purpose specific to the organization. A formal definition is provided by Gray and Stark: "the process of identifying the organization's specific problems, gathering and analyzing organizational data, and taking action to resolve the problems constitutes action research."[40] Gray and Stark further distinguish between action research and the basic and applied research functions just described. "It is in sharp contrast to 'hypothesis testing research' (basic research; some applied research) which deals with problems or situations that are of interest to organizations generally but which may or may not be relevant to a specific organization."[41] This statement requires some further discussion, as much of the work cited as court and correctional research cases would be categorized as applied and action-oriented research.

There is a very keen interest in action research among organizational systems-involved behavioral scientists, particularly those engaged in organization development work. Gray and Stark use both the research subject and the researcher to make the distinction between action research and hypothesis-testing research, or what we are labeling basic (academically oriented) and applied (practitioner-oriented) research. They identify the following as distinguishing characteristics of the respective approaches:

For many years there has been disagreement between practicing managers and academics about the approach that should be used to solve organizational problems. Many academics lean toward the "hypothesis testing" approach. This involves gathering and analyzing data about common organizational problems (e.g., turnover, motivation, conflict, etc.). Once this has been done in many companies and in many settings, general guidelines and conclusions are developed which are then applied to specific companies.

Many managers object to this approach, arguing that "our company is unique and what worked in another company won't work here." These managers are really arguing for the "action research" approach. This involves analyzing a specific company's problems and then taking action to correct them. By focusing on only one company, actions can be taken which presumably will directly solve its problems.

This disagreement about approaches may be unnecessary, since each of these approaches has merit. The hypothesis testing approach is beneficial because it discovers basic patterns of human behavior across organizations and then proposes ways to solve problems that may arise from this behavior. The action research approach is beneficial because it tailors solutions to specific problems being experienced by a given company. Thus, the approach can be complementary, not contradictory (i.e., specific action research builds on the general knowledge of people and organizations that has been generated through the hypothesis testing approach). Likewise, the hypothesis testing approach can utilize the data generated during action research for further analysis of typical organizational problems.[42]

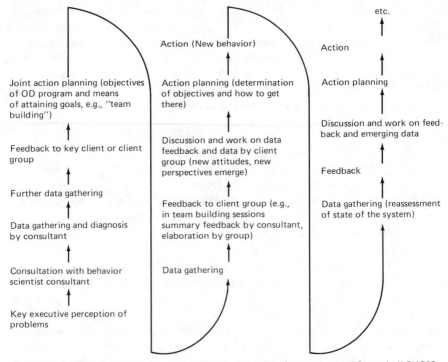

Source: Wendell French, "Organization Development: Objectives, Assumptions and Strategies" © 1969 by the Regents of the University of California. Reprinted from *California Management Review* 12, no. 2 (1969): p 26 by permission of the Regents.

Figure 1-4. Action research model.

This comparison of action research with the hypothesis testing approach identifies the linkage between the two that researchers often overlook in their debates about which is more important and appropriate. Importantly, it reinforces the position that there is a need for behavioral science research of both types in court and correctional organizations.

Figure 1-4 identifies an example of an action research model that is used for organizational development, a special purpose within the whole set of action research purposes.[43] With this purpose in mind the action research function of the behavioral scientist means that he/she investigates "a specific problem, formulates and possibly implements recommended solutions, and then monitors and evaluates the effectiveness of the recommended strategy."[44] It is part of a diagnosis–planning–action–evaluation cycle that is directed at organizational problem solving in a way that promotes long-term development of both the people and the organization.

When researchers use scientific methods to attack organization-specific problems, they are frequently not identified as researchers. This is a close parallel to consultation. The parallel becomes clear overlap when researchers are called in as consultants to work on one organization's problems by conducting action research.

Consultation Function

Behavioral scientists may be called on to act as consultants to court and correctional organizations. The consultation function is the fifth and final one. There are a wide range of consulting activities and an equally wide range of practitioner definitions. The following definitional summary was offered by Meyers, Alpert, and Fleisher:

> There seems to be agreement that consultation is a joint effort at problem solving and that consultation involves indirect assistance to a third party. While there is agreement around these general issues, the models differ with respect to such issues as the role of the consultant, the problems to be addressed in consultation, and the means to go about helping. The theoretical framework and assumptions underlying each particular type of consultation naturally lead to these differences.[45]

There is no convenient classification system for the varieties of models, but they all involve some form of joint problem solving. After the problem-solving commonality, the models differ, with some focused on content or substance of the problem and others on the solution process. As noted by Meyers et al.:

> The goals of . . . behavioral consultation are (1) to help solve specific client-oriented problems and (2) to extend the consultee's overall knowledge base, thus contributing to a client-specific remedial process and to a broad-ranging preventive community mental health process. While these models share goals, their methods for realizing these goals differ. In fact, . . . behavioral consultation work(s) to help consultees to become more resourceful, self-reliant and effective contributors in the future.
>
> While other models are content oriented, organization development is form-oriented. Thus, its goal is not content specific; rather, it is, as Schmuck (1981) notes, to help train members of organizations to be able to make the changes they democratically see fit to make on a system, not individual, level. Through fostering increased understanding of interpersonal communication, the uncovering of conflicts and interdependence, the increase in the desire and the ability to establish collective goals and make decisions, the OD consultant facilitates the development of a self-renewing system.[46]

This distinguishes between two approaches: a content-focused one and an organizational development form-oriented one.

In practical terms these types have been differentiated by the Organizational Development Institute for the benefit of their members' clients. Because these definitions have been fairly widely disseminated, they will be used here. Three types have been differentiated: the "purchase of service" consultant, the "expert advice" consultant, and the "process consultant." The first is defined and described below:

The Purchase of Service Consultant is either an individual or a group who provides a specific program, usually an "off the shelf" item. For example, almost every executive has received fliers and brochures in the mail that invite participation in a management program of one kind or another. It may focus on "team-building", "conflict management", "time management" or any one of a number of management concerns. Such programs are frequently available through colleges and universities and are often designed and conducted by selected staff of the institution. Other programs are also offered by private groups or practitioners.

Most of the time these fliers will include a description of the program being offered, the names and backgrounds of the people who will conduct the program, and other information relative to fees, locations, and registration. Such programs are often very helpful when the registrants are certain that the contents of the program are directly related to their professional or organization needs. The major advantages to purchase of service are relative low cost, opportunities to meet people from other organizations with similar needs, and concentration of effort (most seminars are designed to be 2 or 3 day intensive learning programs). A major disadvantage to such programs is that they cannot, by virtue of their target audience, be system specific. That is, they are rarely designed to deal with each participants' particular or unique problems. Further, participants have no way of being sure that the program being offered will be addressed to their own perceptions of the company's problems. Another disadvantage is that it is often difficult for the participant to apply the learnings gained in the "back-home" setting. No follow-through exists, and there are no ongoing maintenance features or long-term evaluation of results. Finally, many pre-designed programs lack flexibility. The sequence, contents and activities that were planned for the program are usually—although not always—"locked in", and there is little participants can do to change the program if it does not meet their expectations.[47]

This model assumes that behavioral scientists have a set of "packages" that can be applied in generic fashion to a large group of organizations.

These might include sensitivity training, management by objectives systems, decision making and planning models—whole packages delivered in almost identical fashion to different organizations. While there are some consulting services that can be offered in this way, not all can be. Expert advice on a problem specific to only one organization may be needed on an individual basis.

The Organizational Development Institute defines and describes the expert advice consultant as follows:

> The second type is the *Expert Advice Consultant*. Again, this may be a professional group or individual found in the yellow pages of the phone book under "Management Consultants". These consultants are asked to visit the organization and diagnose its "state of health" or illness. This is usually done through observations of staff meetings and worker activities and through interviews with employees and managers. After gathering the necessary data a comprehensive report is prepared, typically containing a description of the corporation, an analysis of its needs and problems, a listing of recommendations and suggestions for action, including a suggested cost analysis, and, in the better reports, a recommended set of procedures or strategies for effecting the recommended changes. The major advantage to such consulting services is that they are objective and therefore minimize internal biases. Planning is deferred to acknowledged experts in the field of organization and management and their experience and ability can help. The major disadvantages are that such studies can be very expensive, and they often include many suggestions and recommendations for change that could have been provided by talented in-house staff. And, since there is little internal "ownership" of the suggestions and recommendations, the results of such studies often never get implemented.[48]

The Institute's bias against these two types of consulting approaches should be quite apparent. They reject the first because organizations have specific, not general problems. Each organization is considered to be an individual. The second approach uses an outsider to solve the organization's problem. This approach is not favored because, unless the organization happens to learn the problem-solving process inadvertently, it will have to call in the expert each time the problem comes up. However, both approaches are widely used and will continue to be used.

The third type of consultation is the Institute's preferred consulting approach:

> The third consultant type, the Process Consultant, is again a professional group or individual who focuses attention on how work is ac-

complished. This is the usual model espoused by the Organization Development professional. In this consultant model, an organization diagnosis is made, the results of the diagnosis are shared with staff and management, and the needs of the organization are identified, clarified, and put in perspective. Next, the consultant determines, in collaboration with the organization, which problems are most immediate and what has to be learned or done in order to correct these. The consultant, again in concert with staff, will create an intensive learning program especially designed to meet the individual organization's needs. After the program is planned, conducted and evaluated, new learning programs are created and the cycle begins anew. The major advantages of the process consultant model are moderate cost, the establishment and maintenance of a long-term relationship between the consultant and the client system, and a mutual vested interest in the success of the outcome.[49]

This process consultant is the organizational development consultant referred to by Meyers et al., defined in detail by Schein,[50] and illustrated by Hirschhorn and colleagues.[51] Process consultants concentrate on examining and reworking the way organization problems are defined and addressed. This problem-solving capability is the target.

While this is not an extensive comparison of the models, the overview does highlight significant differences in the approaches to this function. As a conclusion to this review (and a statement of the author's bias) the Organization Development Institute further commented on the differences and the strengths of the process approach:

In the purchase of service model, it is the participants who must determine the value of what was learned. If they are satisfied, they wait for some sort of "follow-up program" to provide the next level of learning; and such follow-ups are relatively rare.

In the expert advice model the client system must determine the value of the information and recommendations provided. They must also take responsibility for putting these recommendations to work. The problem here is that many client systems often lack the skills necessary to do that and, consequently, these "best-laid plans" never materialize.

In the process consultant model, the implementation of action plans is typically a mutual effort between the consultant and the client system. The client system wants the plans to work because it developed them. The consultant wants the plans to work because consultant success is very closely tied to the success of the client system. The major disadvantages of the Process Consultant Model are that client systems may have to share with the consultant in the investment of time and energy during all phases of the project. Organization development (OD) projects are long-term efforts, usually taking 2 years or more, and OD requires a learning commitment on the part of the organization as well as a financial investment.[52]

The stated advantages/disadvantages inform us about each model's applicability. The above statement favors process work. But it is the view here that *all* three types are in constant use by behavioral scientists in all types of organizations. This situation will continue. The task is to match the type of consultation approach with the appropriate organizational need. The remaining chapters contain case illustrations of that situationally contingent use.

SUMMARY

This chapter introduced a common model for understanding organizations based on the work of Kast and Rosenzweig. This systems model integrates both the classical and human relations schools of organization theory. It provides a framework for analyzing the interactions of the functional and human relations aspects of an organization. The approach considers the organization to consist of five subsystems: (1) goals and values, (2) technical, (3) structural, (4) psychosocial, and (5) managerial. A sample topic of interest to behavioral scientists in courts and corrections would be the structure of the court system itself.

How are the various elements of the court arranged? These subsystems also have internal elements that are interactive in nature. For example, a shift in values might require new or different technical equipment or methods, and the technical changes might then necessitate a change in organizational structure or management. Thus three subsystems would be affected by one change in the internal elements of one system.

Organizations are also affected by their environment. Kast and Rosenzweig list nine environmental influences: cultural, educational, economic, legal, political, sociological, demographic, natural resource, and technological. Relating these characteristics to the example above, a shift in organization values might easily be the result of a shift in a cultural value set. A specific courts and corrections example can be seen in the cultural shift toward stricter sentencing as reflected by the interest in standardized sentencing.

After examining the common organization model, this chapter examined the five basic functions of behavioral scientists. Behavioral science is the scientific study of human behavior, including a wide set of disciplines from anthropology to psychology. The five basic functions of behavioral scientists were defined: (1) assessment and diagnosis, (2) treatment, (3) education and training, (4) research, and (5) consultation.

The assessment and diagnosis function consists of the collection and analysis of data about human behavior and the forming of a judgment about current status. Data are collected by means of educational, psychological, and vocational testing. Educational testing can be used to show levels of current education for placement in programs, or to see if educational programs are actually educating. Psychological tests look at the status of mental processes or behaviors. Vocational testing looks at both work experiences and aptitudes of individuals in any part of court or correctional organizations.

Treatment is simply the application of remedies based on the information collected and analyzed in assessment and diagnosis. For the purposes of courts and correctional organizations, treatment can include a whole range of problems from individual treatments to plans for remedying treatment program problems. In corrections, the traditional treatment role for behavioral scientists has been divided into short-term (less than 90 days), long-term, and crisis-intervention treatment for offenders.

The education and training function covers both preparatory and continuing education for either staff or clients. The topics for education and training are practically unlimited, as they relate to both job preparation and skills expansion.

The research function of behavioral scientists also has an almost unlimited topic potential. The research done is divided into three types: basic, applied, and action. Basic research is controlled empirical testing of theories and hypotheses. Applied research is more practical and uses basic research findings to address organization-specific problems. Action research studies similar specific organizational problems, but does so in terms of a diagnosis–planning–action–evaluation cycle that includes monitoring of research-stimulated change.

For the consultation function, diversity is again a key element. Consultation is essentially joint problem solving by the behavioral scientist and the organization. Consultation is defined to include purchase of service work or expert advice. The former often means a "packaged" approach to problem solving or providing services such as training. Organization development or process consultation is defined as an individualized cooperative problem-solving effort with the organization. It is designed to help the organization grow by seeing—with the consultant—the problem, its sources, possible resolutions, and an evaluation of the success of the resolution.

The common organization systems model provides a framework through which behavioral scientists can understand court and correctional organizations. The five functions defined can be applied to organizations both in traditional and in new and creative ways. The functional types are not necessarily all-inclusive. Nor are they an exact academic taxonomy of the behavioral scientist function in the organization (i.e., there is some ambiguity, overlap and redundancy). The set is designed as a practical and convenient way for us to understand the kinds of activities that behavioral scientists can provide to a court or correctional organization, in a general sense. The functional types help us to identify some of the activities that will be discussed as examples of functions that actually have existed or do exist in court and correctional organizations.

The next chapters will identify specific organizational elements and the types of behavioral scientist functions that have been used to address key needs and problems in those organizations.

REFERENCES

1. Kast, F. E., and Rosenzweig, J. E. (1979). *Organization and Management*. New York: McGraw-Hill.
2. Scott, W. G. (1961). Organization Theory. *Journal of the Academy of Management, 4* (1).
3. Ziegenfuss, J. T. (1982). Do Your Managers Think in Organizational 3-D? *Sloan Management Review, 24* (1).
4. Ziegenfuss, J. T. (1985). *Patient–Client–Employee Complaint Programs: An Organizational Systems Model*. Springfield, Illinois: Charles C. Thomas.
5. Ziegenfuss, J. T. Op. cit., see note 3.
6. Kast, F. E., and Rosenzweig, J. Op. cit, p. 109.
7. Bevelson, B. (1968). Behavioral Sciences. In D. Sills (ed.), *International Encyclopedia of the Social Sciences*. New York: Macmillan.
8. Ford Foundation, Behavioral Sciences Division (1953). Report. New York: The Foundation.
9. Posavac, E. J.; Carey, R. G. (1980). *Program Evaluation: Methods and Cases* Englewood Cliffs, New Jersey: Prentice Hall.
10. Page, G. T., and Thomas, J. B. (1977). *International Dictionary of Education*. New York: Kogan Page Ltd.
11. HEW. *Combined Glossary* (1974). Washington, D.C.: National Center for Education Statistics—HEW, U.S. Government Printing Office.
12. Joint Commission on Accreditation of Hospitals. Op. cit.
13. HEW. Op. cit.
14. Joint Commission on Accreditation of Hospitals. Op. cit.
15. Susman, G. (1976) *Autonomy at Work*. New York: Praeger.
16. Arieti, S. (ed.) (1966). *American Handbook of Psychiatry*. New York: Basic Books.
17. Knight, R. P. (1952). An Evaluation of Psychotherapeutic Techniques. *Bulletin of the Menninger Clinic., 16*, 113–24.
18. Ziegenfuss, J. T. (1983). *Patients Rights and Organizational Models: Sociotechnical Systems Research on Mental Health Programs*. Lanham, Maryland: University Press of America.
19. Goldstein, M. S. (1979). The Sociology of Mental Health and Illness. *Annual Review of Sociology, 5*, 381–409.
20. Blaney, P. H. (1975). Implications of the Medical Model and Its Alternatives. *American Journal of Psychiatry, 132* (9).
21. Jones, M. (1953). *The Therapeutic Community: A New Treatment Method in Psychiatry*. New York: Basic Books.

22. Jones, M. (1962). *Social Psychiatry in the Community, in Hospitals and in Prisons,* Springfield, Illinois: Charles C. Thomas.
23. Jones, M. (1979). Therapeutic Communities, Old and New. *American Journal of Drug and Alcohol Abuse,* 6 (2), 137–49.
24. Jones, M. (1968). *Social Psychiatry in Practice.* Harmondsworth: Penguin.
25. Jones, M. (1976). *Maturation of the Therapeutic Community.* New York: Behavioral Pubs.
26. Ziegenfuss, D. G., and Ziegenfuss, J. T. (1984). *Health Information Systems: A Bibliography.* New York: Plenum.
27. Caplan, G. (1968). *Principles of Preventive Psychiatry.* New York: Basic Books.
28. Roesch, R., and Golding, S. L. (1980). *Competency to Stand Trial.* Urbana: University of Illinois Press.
29. Roesch, R. (1978a). A Brief, Immediate Screening Interview to Determine Competency to Stand Trial: A Feasibility Study. *Criminal Justice and Behavior,* 5, 241–48.
30. Roesch, R. (1978b). Competency to Stand Trial and Court Outcome. *Criminal Justice Review,* 3, 45–56.
31. Roesch, R. (1978c). Fitness to Stand Trial: Some Comments on the Law Reform Commission's Proposed Procedures. *Canadian Journal of Criminology,* 20, 450–55.
32. Shenk, G., Williams, J. and Ziegenfuss, J. T. (1983, May). The Offender Development Services Program: Cost Savings and Benefits in a County Prison. National Conference on Social Welfare. Houston, Texas.
33. Shortell, S. M. (1978). *Continuing Education for the Health Professions.* Ann Arbor: University of Michigan, Health Administration Press.
34. Shenk et al. Op. cit.
35. Kerlinger, F. N. (1973). *Foundations of Behavioral Research.* New York: Holt, Rinehart & Winston.
36. Ibid.
37. Bernstein, I. N., and Freeman, H. E. (1975). *Academic and Entrepreneurial Research.* New York: Russell Sage Foundation.
38. Kerlinger. Op. cit.
39. Anastasi, A. (1968). Applied Psychology. In Sills, D. (ed.), *International Encyclopedia of the Social Sciences.* New York: Macmillan Co. and The Free Press.
40. Gray, J. L., and Starke, F. A. (1980). *Organizational Behavior.* Columbus, Ohio: Charles E. Merrill.
41. Ibid.
42. Ibid.
43. French, W. (1976). Organization Development: Objectives, Assumptions, and Strategies. *California Management Review,* 12 (2).
44. Page and Thomas. Op. cit.
45. Meyers, J., Alpert, J. L., and Fleisher, B. (1983). Models of Consultation. In J. L. Alpert and J. Meyers (eds.), *Training in Consultation.* Springfield, Illinois: Charles C. Thomas.
46. Ibid.
47. Organization Development Institute (1981). *Improving Profits through Organization Development.* Cleveland, Ohio: Organization Development Institute.
48. Ibid.
49. Ibid.
50. Schein, E. (1969). *Process Consultation.* Reading, Massachusetts: Addison-Wesley.
51. Hirschhorn, L., and Krantz, J. (1982). Unconscious Planning In A Natural Work Group, *Human Relations.* 35(10), 805.
52. Organization Development Institute Op. cit.

PART I
THE COURTS

Part I will examine the functional opportunities for behavioral scientists in the court organization. It matches the five functions of behavioral scientists (assessment and diagnosis, treatment, education and training, research, and consultation) against the five subsystems of the court organization (goals/values, technical, structural, psychosocial, and managerial). Each subsystem is explored, with cases of completed work and suggested follow-up topics identified.

2
THE COURTS' TECHNICAL SYSTEM WORK OF BEHAVIORAL SCIENTISTS

Chapter 2 begins the analysis of functional opportunities, focusing on the technical aspects of court work. This includes a review of behavioral scientist functions with respect to the following core aspects of court work: intake and detention, screening and diversion, negotiations, pretrial proceedings, competency, trials, testimony, jury process and outcome, commitment, sentencing, punishment, parole and probation, and discretion.

Chapter 1 introduced the organizational systems view and model for examining behavioral scientist activities in both courts and correctional organizations. This chapter examines opportunities for behavioral scientists in the court organizational systems, beginning with the area of most interest—the technical system. It is only one of five subsystems, as noted in Figure 2-1. As noted in Chapter 1, the technical system is "the knowledge required for the performance of tasks, including the techniques used in the transformation of inputs and outputs."[1] The technical system of the "organization" is that set of core activities that are engaged in by participants in the court organization in order to fulfill their primary mission; to complete their critical tasks. The question to be addressed here is: how would behavioral scientists be of use in the technical system of the courts? Chapter 1 also identified the core behavioral scientist functions as: assessment and diagnosis, treatment, education and training, research, and consultation. In order to know how these functions would be utilized in this area of the organization, we need to create a list of technical processes and procedures that represent some, or at least the main, activities of the court system.

The following items are considered primary activities of the court system and prime candidates for behavioral scientist work. The list is not exhaustive; certainly others could be added. However, it is sufficiently inclusive to give us a sense of the range of court activities that behavioral scientists could and do become involved in. These are the key technical procedures and processes of the court's organizational system as a whole that may utilize behavioral scientists in one or more of their functional capacities:

- Intake and detention
- Screening and diversion

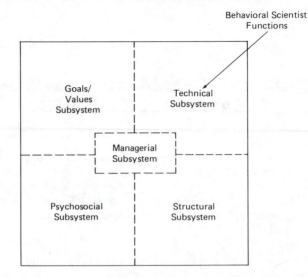

Behavioral Scientist
Functions

Goals/
Values
Subsystem

Technical
Subsystem

Managerial
Subsystem

Psychosocial
Subsystem

Structural
Subsystem

Figure 2-1. Behavioral scientist functions in court technical subsystem.

- Negotiations
- Pretrial proceedings
- Competency
- Trials
  - Evidence
  - Instructions to the jury
- Testimony
- Jury process and outcome
- Commitment
- Sentencing
- Punishment
- Parole and probation
- Discretion

These technical procedure and process topics will be matched with the behavioral scientist functions in order to create a work opportunity table.

The work opportunity table is a matrix that helps the reader to understand the fit of topics and functions. In theory, all topics that comprise technical procedure and process (the list above plus others that may have been missed) make up the left side of the matrix, while the core behavioral scientist functions are placed across the top. It is then possible to proceed to examine how each of the functions could contribute in each of the technical procedure and process areas. Obviously not all of the functions would be appropriate to all topics. For a humorous example, it would be difficult to conceive of how a behavioral scientist could offer clinical

Table 2-1. Court technical subsystem: Work opportunity table.

TECHNICAL TOPICS \ FUNCTIONS	ASSESSMENT AND DIAGNOSIS	TREATMENT	EDUCATION AND TRAINING	RESEARCH	CONSULTATION
Intake and detention					
Screening and diversion					
Negotiations					
Pretrial proceedings					
Competency					
Trials					
Testimony					
Jury process and outcome					
Commitment					
Sentencing					
Punishment					
Parole and probation					
Discretion					

treatment that would be related to jury process and outcome. However, it is completely conceivable that some type of treatment function could be provided to a client during parole and probation following the jury process. Table 2-1 illustrates these relationships.

To illustrate the diversity of behavioral scientist functions within each of these court activities, examples have been collected from the published literature of behavioral science and criminal justice. These "case reports" describe the work of behavioral scientists who have provided service in these technical procedure and process areas. The balance of the chapter introduces each technical topic of the court, providing a case report example of one behavioral scientist function for each. First, the technical procedures and processes are briefly explained, with a summary of key components. Following this introduction, a problem is presented along with the response of a behavioral scientist that is indicative of one of the primary functions. A brief analysis follows each case report.

INTAKE AND DETENTION

The first contact with the criminal justice system involves intake and possible pretrial detention. This aspect of the judicial system is important because it represents the first critical encounter that the suspect is likely to have with the formal organization of the system. At this point, a person is accused of a crime and has been engaged by an agent of the criminal justice system as part of the formal organizational process that signifies entry. Several steps in this formal intake process appear to highlight the accused's movement through the system. The following are six of the key steps in the intake procedure:

1. Arrest
2. Processing
3. Release
4. Imprisonment
5. Magistrate appearance
6. The plea

At any one of these steps, or at several of them, problems can and do develop that impede the court's workings. For example, there may be conditions of the arrest process that raise the question of the suspect's right to counsel during the very first of the proceedings; or the imprisonment of the suspect while awaiting trial may raise questions of fairness and appropriateness of the detention. This latter problem is particularly acute with juveniles.

It is not the intent here to provide full discussion of each of these steps individually. Their explanation is already included as a topic in many books on court organization and process. The point is that any of these procedural steps can become problems that might require the assistance of the behavioral scientist in one or more of the primary functions introduced in Chapter 1. The several cases that we have in this area illustrate some of the ways that behavioral scientists have made contributions to problem solving of intake and detention dilemmas.

CASE ONE: PRETRIAL PSYCHIATRIC COMMITMENT.   A common problem at the intake and detention point is the question of whether or not the accused will require pretrial psychiatric examination. Although this becomes a critical decision during pretrial proceedings, it first arises at the intake point. Since many accused persons do require pretrial psychiatric examinations, the question is: what are the guidelines that determine an assessment of competency and possible commitment? The problem for the behavioral scientist is: what are the processes and individual criteria for criminal commitment of the psychiatrically disabled defendant? This problem raises the issue of all of the guidelines for and activities of the behavioral scientist in a diagnosis of psychiatric disability that may subsequently lead to commitment of the individual. These are most significant problems for a society that values individual freedom and a fair process of determining imprisonment/institutionalization. The first case examines this problem.

In 1971, the Massachusetts Legislature passed an act that revised its laws on the admission, treatment, and discharge of mentally ill individuals.[2] The intent of the act was to "rectify the misuse of civil and criminal commitment, safeguard the civil rights of the individuals and avoid the potentially destructive effects of commitment."

The revisions mandated that alleged defenders were first to be examined at the jail or courthouse by a forensically qualified psychologist. The examination could be requested by the judge, the prosecution, the defense attorney, or the accused. The purpose of the examination was to aid the court in determining competency to stand trial and/or criminal responsibility. Following the review the alleged offender was either brought to trial or committed to an inpatient facility for further examination. If the individual was committed, the staff of the facilities were asked to give the accused an in-depth examination and to report on several points: the presence of mental illness; competency to stand trial; criminal responsibility; and recommendations for treatment.

Comments and Follow-up Work.   This problem leads to consideration of the question: what is the behavioral scientist function in terms of assessment and diagnosis in this part of the intake and detention process? The function could be a direct service one through the provision of assessment (e.g., psychological tests); it could be one of training relative to new procedures; or it could be research or consultation related to process improvement. The following are examples of some further activities:

1. Conduct an analysis of the pretrial psychiatric commitment policies and procedures used, examining effectiveness, fairness, efficiency.
2. Comparatively analyze two courts' approaches to pretrial commitment, including purpose, process, and outcomes.
3. Examine the current procedures to determine whether they are consistent with recent legal changes protecting the rights of the disabled.
4. Provide assessment and diagnostic assistance to the courts to assist them in making commitment decisions.
5. Create a directory of current experts on types of tests and analytical methods.

Psychiatric examinations are an important area and warrant a second case, particularly because of their close ties to clinical psychology work.

CASE TWO: PSYCHIATRIC EXAMINATIONS.   The whole area of psychiatric commitment has been a troublesome one for the courts and for outside advocates. The nature of psychiatric examinations and the tests themselves have been questioned. As the next study indicates, the examination problem is closely allied to pretrial proceedings issues in this area.

In 1975, Geller and Lister conducted a study to determine how revised commitment procedures affected criminal commitment for pretrial psychiatric examinations.[3] Before the revisions, there were no consistent medical or legal guidelines for commitment, no specified time limits, and requests for psychiatric intervention were ill defined. Geller and Lister found that behavioral scientists participating in the assessment and diagnostic process (specifically involved in the psychiatric examination aspects) were working under very ambiguous conditions.

The study was conducted at Worcester State Hospital. The organization's commitment procedures and the affects on the patients were examined. The eighty-seven cases in the sample represented those patients committed to Worcester under pretrial status in 1975. The authors examined psychiatric data, including the evaluation by the court psychiatrist; the report of the hospital psychiatrist; legal data (including the charges against the accused); and the disposition of the cases when they were returned to the court. Finally, they compiled statistics from hospital records to examine the use of pretrial commitment over the preceding ten years.

As a result of the study, the authors found that the legislation did not bring about the desired effects. They concluded that pretrial commitment, regardless of its intent, serves to control and seclude deviants. Both this study and other literature supported this conclusion. The study found that most of those committed were isolated, were resourceless, and were charged only with minor crimes. Although these clients were originally sent for evaluation of competency, and/or responsibility, only two of the eighty-seven were committed in the final disposition. The authors found very little consistency between the questions asked by the court and the answers given by the psychiatrists. They also noted that there was resistance on the part of the psychiatrists to declaring patients criminally responsible. Finally, they found that the number of pretrial commitments remained relatively fixed, despite steadily declining admissions and civil commitment.

Comments and Follow-up Work.   The findings of this analysis of pretrial psychiatric examination indicate that behavioral scientists performing the examinations (their assessment and diagnostic function) were struggling under most difficult conditions. Additionally, the study indicates that the organizational change that was initiated by the state did not achieve the desired effect. The behavioral scientist function through the completion of the study was an analytical one. The researchers examined the assessment and diagnosis process, a subpart of the intake and detention procedure of the system. Behavioral scientists acting in a research mode analyzed another behavioral scientist function of the court technical procedure and process. They found it wanting, suggesting that alternative processes need to be designed, developed, and tested in the future.

Several other activities were suggested as a result of the first case. Three more are offered below:

1. Analyze the population that is given psychiatric examinations, looking for bias in selection and effects on subsequent trial outcomes.
2. Analyze the psychiatric examination process to determine reliability of reviews using different reviewers and different methods.
3. Offer assessment services as part of the psychiatric examination process (i.e., become a service provider) and consider establishing a group practice with a number of colleagues who also offer this service.

The assessment process often leads to screening and diversion. Our next topic is client movement into the system.

SCREENING AND DIVERSION

A second step in entering the criminal justice system involves a set of screening and diversion activities. Screening and diversion is the activity of examining a group of persons brought through intake to determine whether they should be continued in the criminal justice system or diverted to an alternative means of handling. One very clear outcome of screening and diversion, which is a benefit to the accused, is a cessation of prosecution. Halting prosecution occurs for example through plea bargaining or assignment to a community service facility as an alternative to further involvement with the criminal justice system.

There are two problems with this aspect of the court system that appear to surface quite frequently. First, there are police reactions to halting prosecution in general and to plea bargaining specifically. For example, police officers who have gone to considerable trouble to track down the accused become very angry when the accused persons are dismissed or diverted. The anger pushes them quickly to the position of "Why bother to arrest if the courts will only screen and divert without punishment?"

Second, there is a reaction to halting prosecution from the community. When informed of plea bargaining or other diversion processes, the community quickly generates the same kind of anger, following up with questions of "Is this justice?" and "Is the community safe?" When the court system is perceived to be simply picking up accused persons and quickly diverting them to alternative noncorrectional facilities, or even outright freedom, citizens ask, "Who is protecting us?" In response to these perceptions (whether they are correct or not), there is the question of what are the criteria for making the decisions? Can behavioral scientists help to improve the accuracy or fairness of the decision to halt prosecution;

and/or can they help in mediating the anger of both police and community? The answer to both of these questions is clearly yes.

First, the psychosocial history of the accused is a key topic, an area in which behavioral scientists have expertise. Second, there is the question of whether judges can make a decision independent of outside advice; or, are they in need of behavioral consultants to help them with the decision-making process? This latter point is addressed by examining the motivation and the criteria for taking the accused out of the system, diverting them to alternative services. First, prisons are crowded so that the judge is forced to decide whether to add to the crowding or to alleviate it by screening. This decision is often an individual one based on the facts of the case and the current status or the capacity of the facilities involved. There are additional outside influences such as political motivations, as well as the individual client's history of previous contacts with the criminal justice system.

How can behavioral scientists contribute to this aspect of the court system? There are several ways such as assessment and diagnosis during the screening process; administrative consultation to improve the efficiency of the procedural steps; research into the nature of diversion relative to its clinical and developmental purposes for the system; and analysis of its structure and its long-term effects on both the clients and the community (i.e., do clients return to court, and is the community more or less safe?). The following examples illustrate.

CASE THREE: A SCREENING AND DIVERSION PROBLEM. A community's judicial advisory group expresses concern for finding out what kind of families may be most likely to do well as a result of screening and subsequent diversion to a community service. When expressed, this community's concern is found to match the interest of a court administrator and a judge in reducing the workload of the family court. Both are also interested in trying to find out what families will do well, as this knowledge will inform their decision making regarding alternatives for clients. This is a fairly common workload/outcome problem for many court systems throughout the country. A team of behavioral scientists could make a contribution toward solving this problem. Their work would be needed and welcomed by many communities. An attempt of this kind has been made.

Kohn and Sugarman presented the results of their contribution addressing this problem, with specific relation to the family court service.[4] The family court service was established to provide unified services to, and when possible divert cases from, the family court of Staten Island, New York. The service collects and analyzes data on all cases, both "persons in need of supervision" and delinquents who come into the court. The court service is directed at two groups. PINS (persons in need of supervision) are juveniles brought into court for behavior that would not be considered a crime if done by an adult. Delinquents, the second group, are charged with acts that would be considered crimes if committed by an adult. The family court service offers both groups an alternative to standard formal proceedings.

The family court service collects data on its clients for three purposes. First, it wants to know the frequency of case types and the percentage of cases adjusted at intake. Second, it wants an analysis of the background and demographic characteristics of those the court deals with, including their geographic distribution over sections of Staten Island. Third, it wants to be able to identify problem areas where the court service can direct its efforts to intervening in fully developed problems and preventing new ones. Behavioral scientists could help the service to achieve these purposes.

In 1975, Kohn and Sugarman studied the information collected by the service. Analyzing the different characteristics of PINS and delinquents, they attempted to identify the areas or cases that could best be handled by the court service in place of the standard court proceedings. From the data analysis, the authors found that PINS are more involved in serious family conflicts, while delinquents are more involved in community conflicts. In PINS cases, the conflict many times involved all of the family members, even though the juvenile was the focus of the complaint. PINS cases showed more overt parental rejection than delinquents. And, although delinquents had more deviant role models, PINS were more confused about role expectations.

In their conclusion, the authors suggested that PINS cases are suitable for clinical intervention by the family court service. In this way, "the family can get help in resolving the crisis, the juveniles can be spared the stigma of having a record and precious court time can be devoted to more serious cases."

Comments and Follow-up Work.   Here we find behavioral scientists evaluating the caseload of one part of the total court process to determine what kinds of persons might do well as a result of careful screening and diversion to an alternative service. This analytical service has an administrative advantage for the court system as well as a clinical benefit. This dual payoff means that there are actually two clients for the behavioral scientists. Both the accused delinquents and PINS (client one) and the court administration (client two) stand to gain from the work of the scientists.

Although this was research, the behavioral scientists also acted in the role of consultants to the court with some elements of the assessment and diagnostic function. That is, they made assessments of individual cases, creating a diagnosis of those persons likely to do well in diversion (in terms of both individual cases and the aggregate). This assessment and diagnostic function assists the delinquents, PINS, and the administrative system. The system's workload is reduced, while the needs of the delinquents and PINS is better addressed in terms of how they are likely to achieve progress for themselves and for the community.

Several other work possibilities are presented, again with an interest in program design/redesign.

1. Examine the screening procedure, offering assistance in redesign; or update it, integrating new developments in the field.
2. Offer services to the court or to private attorneys e.g. assessment, preparatory to formal screening or as a part of the formal process.
3. Analyze the set of diversion possibilities used by a given court, offering to develop a directory of possible alternatives for attorneys if one does not exist.

Obtaining court and prosecution agreement to diversion is often not easy. The negotiations involved are a part of the core activity contributing to the justice system's dynamics, as the next section illustrates.

NEGOTIATIONS

Plea negotiation is the process by which the accused pleads guilty to a lesser offense than that for which he/she has been charged, and therefore receives a lower sentence. Plea bargaining is usually engaged in with the consent of the prosecutor and the defense attorney, and sometimes with the consent of the judge. While the whole process contributes to the efficiency of the criminal justice system, several significant questions arise, including: is justice served by this process? A related problem is: what does plea negotiation mean to the arresting officer? In a replay of their emotional response to diversion, arresting officers have gone to considerable lengths to identify the accused and to link him/her to the crime for which he/she stands accused; thus when the accused is able to negotiate a plea for a lesser sentence, the arresting officer's motivation is undercut. There is an unmistakable impression that the officer's time was wasted, even though there may be a greater purpose served in saving the client from harsher punishment.

The whole negotiation process (including the discomforting aspects for the arresting officers) has created controversy *and* suggestions of the need for a uniform plea negotiation system. Should there be policies and practices that guide the process, standardizing it from one person to the next and from one court to the next? Furthermore, it is often found that documentation of the entire process is slight; that representation by counsel is not thoroughly identified; that issues of time limits arise; and that the total circumstances in which the negotiation process takes place are vague and differ widely. Additionally, there is a need to know the effects of plea negotiations on ultimate disposition and sentencing. On the philosophical level, can the community accept a negotiated guilty plea that is significantly less serious than the first identified crime? The system in effect enables participants to adjust the punishment, which is usually set according to the seriousness of the crime, permitting the guilty to avoid the level of punishment that they actually are supposed to receive. The questions, in total, point to the need for examination of the nature and character of plea bargaining and its place in the court system.

In short, behavioral scientists could become involved in examinations of the very nature and relevance of plea bargaining in a philosophical sense; or they could examine operational problems, such as whether there is sufficient information collected to guarantee accountability with full due process. The following case indicates one type of involvement.

CASE FOUR: PLEA NEGOTIATION.   As noted in the above discussion, there is considerable negative reaction from police officers regarding plea negotiations. What is the extent of this reaction, and what would officers recommend? Neither reactions nor recommendations are known in many communities. This presents an opportunity for behavioral scientists.

Behavioral scientists in Middletown designed a personal interview study for the purpose of identifying police officers' concerns about and recommendations for the plea bargaining process.* One hundred fourteen officers in three counties were given structured personal interviews lasting approximately one hour each. The interview results were analyzed using the organizational systems model of Kast and Rosenzweig. This model divides organized systems (such as plea bargaining ones) into five subsystems: goals/values, technical, structural, psychosocial, and managerial. Questions for each subsystem were asked. The results indicated that police officers have the most concern about inadequate technical procedures that now do not guarantee fairness and which lead to wasted time. For example, there was no way for an officer to know which cases are bargained. They recommend that a simple information system be developed, as there was not any system in existence. They also suggested the need to further educate officers as to the purpose, process, and outcome of the plea negotiation part of the system.

Comments and Follow-up Work.   This case illustrates the use of behavioral scientists' interviewing techniques both to bring to the surface the specific problem and to create some recommendations for addressing the difficulties. The "process" aspects of being asked for their opinions helped the morale of the officers, and they generated real solution options.

What other work opportunities come to mind? Plea negotiation work

---

*Fictional case example.

could be greatly expanded, with the following only starting samples of topics:

1. Analyze the data on the nature and outcomes of plea negotiations in one court, or a set of courts in a given region, offering constructive advice on process development.
2. Assist attorneys in examining the interpersonal dynamics of plea negotiation, helping them to better serve their clients.
3. Provide consulting assistance to public defenders that would enable them to expand their negotiation expertise and the extent of negotiations in their particular client group.
4. Conduct educational seminars on negotiation and conflict resolution for judges, attorneys, and policemen.

Data analysis would lead to an identification of the status of plea negotiation, with the needs for research, education, and consultation identified as a result.

PRETRIAL PROCEEDINGS

Pretrial proceedings are the set of activities that involve the court as a whole, including the prosecution and the defense, in preparation for trial. There are many aspects to this part of the court system; some of the key ones are listed below:

- Arraignment, with presentation of the guilty or not guilty plea.
- Reduction of charges.
- Consideration of the sufficiency of the evidence.
- Pretrial release.
- Strategy and tactics preparation, including "judicial shopping," preparing witnesses, evidence, and exhibits, and final case preparation.
- Bail or release without bail.
- The issues of the right to a speedy trial and to extradition.

A quick and speedy diversion from the criminal justice system is less likely now than it was in earlier stages of judicial proceedings. The accused is now beginning the process that defines his/her formal connection to the system. It is not so much the first of the formal process, since the arrest is the originating point. Instead, pretrial hearings are more like substantive steps for taking the accused from arrest to trial, leading either to punishment or to clearance of the accusation.

As indicated above, there are many issues for concern at this point. Questions involving setting the amount of bail or deciding whether to place the accused in jail are often troublesome. The bail question has received significant attention from behavioral scientists in their field work. The next case illustrates the behavioral scientist function in research; the subject is decision making on questions related to the amount of bail.

CASE FIVE: THE BAIL PROBLEM.   A problem in all court systems is determining the criteria for deciding whether to set bail at all, followed by deciding the amount of the bail relative to the type of case. Behavioral scientists can provide useful assistance by scrutinizing how these decisions are made and by suggesting alternative processes. Criterion and process recommendations would help to make the decisions more accurate and more appropriate in individual cases.

Ebbesen and Konecni reported on a two-part project that was designed to determine how the amount of bail is set by court judges.[5] The bail-setting procedure was observed by the authors through the course of two studies. As one result of their study, they found five major types of information to be relevant, including: (1) the severity of the crime; (2) the prior criminal record; (3) the extent to which the accused has ties to the area; (4) the district attorney's recommendation on bail setting; (5) the defense attorney's recommendation. These appeared to be the variables critical for decision making.

The first study was designed to generate data relating to the differential use of the different types of information. Eighteen judges were given simulated versions of the information normally presented in actual courtrooms. The primary purpose of this first activity was to use observation to build an understanding of how the judges integrate the different types of information in order to arrive at a decision on bail. One finding was that the average recommendation was for higher bail when the accused was weakly tied to the geographic area than when he was strongly tied. The recommendation was also for a higher amount when the accused had a prior record. Finally, the bail increases as the district attorney's recommendation for higher bail also increases.

The second study was done with actual court hearings and had two initial purposes. The first was to determine whether the same factors that were important in the judges' *simulated* bail decisions would be important in their *actual* bail decisions. The second purpose was to determine whether the same information integration model used in the first study could be generalized to actual bail hearings. The intent was to find out whether their simulated bail decision making corresponded to the actual courtroom.

The procedure in this study used trained observers who sat in the courtroom to record the five types of information used in Study 1. The results indicated that judges seemed to rely mainly on the recommendations of the district attorney and the defense attorney in bail setting. Both prior record and localities played no additional role in the judges' decisions. The severity of the crime played a minor role, excluding those cases dealing with homicide. Overall, the study found that factors such as severity of the crime and local ties do indirectly affect the amount of bail set. They do so by directly influencing the district attorney's and defense attorney's recommendations, which then influence the judge's final decision.

Comments and Follow-up Work. This case is important because it indicates the kind of work that the behavioral scientist does in either a research or a consulting function. This study could be considered applied research that targets decision making in the pretrial process. However, it could also have been a consulting study requested by a judge who was concerned about the standardization of bail decision making among judges as a group. Behavioral scientists in the consulting function would be brought in to study the operational aspects of the decision-making process. They might suggest recommendations for standardizing the bail-setting decisions or, at the least, provide the judges with a more standardized set of criteria on which to make the decisions.

Although this is not specifically suggested by the authors, it is conceivable that behavioral scientists acting in a research or consulting function could also be asked to help the judges implement the new recommendations for changes in the decision-making process. In that work they could offer process consultation services, working with the judges to help them first understand how they *currently* make their decisions. They would next identify the information uncovered by the study, developing additional data as needed. Finally, they would use the new information to collaborate with the judges to establish new criteria for decision making that would then be integrated into the system using training and feedback techniques.

What other topics are possibilities in this area? Behavioral scientists could:

1. Analyze the relative effectiveness of different bail levels according to the type of offender.
2. Conduct a survey of attorneys to determine their views on improving the bail-setting procedure, including, for example, decision criteria.
3. Explore the design of innovative bail mechanisms that utilize non-dollar incentives such as peer responsibilities (a research effort).

Bail is only one of the elements of the process that leads eventually to the trial.

TRIALS AND COMPETENCY

Trial is the process by which the court sorts out the facts of the case in order to determine whether the accused is guilty or not guilty. Trials have been the focus of quite a lot of attention from behavioral scientists in nearly all of their functions, from assessment to research and consultation.

Behavioral scientists have been active in providing examinations and diagnoses for trials, for example, through the mechanism of expert testimony. Trials have been the subject of much research and increasing amounts of consultation. As noted in relation to other sections, a discussion of the structure and process of trials would require a book in itself, not a mere introductory page or two. However, several aspects of trial can be identified that enable us to review examples of behavioral scientists' work in this area.

A first key component of the trial is evidence. Since the topic is broad, classification produces several types of evidence, including: physical evidence; direct and indirect evidence; judicial knowledge; documentary evidence; and opinions. Evidence, once developed, is not just accepted; instead there are requirements for the admissibility of evidence, including such issues as competency, relevancy, and materiality. In screening the evidence to determine what will be used, there are opposing initiatives that can be taken by both the prosecution and the defense. Objections to evidence can be raised. These objections might include questions of whether or not the evidence meets the criteria mentioned above—competency, relevancy, and materiality—and whether or not it is heresay, for example. In short, the whole area of evidence is complex and can easily engage behavioral scientists in one or more of their functions.

Along with the subject of types of evidence, there is concern for the actual courtroom situation, involving such topics as police testimony, a review of the case, personal appearance by the accused, attendance at the trial by the accused and significant others, and the whole process of testifying. Within the courtroom, instructions to the jury play a key part in the trial process, including the role of the judge in providing the specific instructions and setting the tone. There is also the role of the defense, as well as the role of the court proceedings. In short, any and all aspects of the trial process become potential subjects for behavioral scientists' scrutiny.

At this time, it is more likely that this work will be research-oriented. Although there has been increasing interest on the part of trial lawyers in learning the behavioral aspects of trial work, this has not yet come to be widespread practice. Acceptance of such learning is not in doubt; just the timing and topics are. It will include a wide range of subjects from presentation style to mode of dress. The case chosen below addresses one of the more difficult subjects: competency to stand trial.

CASE SIX: COMPETENCY FOR TRIAL. A common dilemma for courts is deciding whether or not the accused is competent to stand trial. Various reasons are cited as to why the accused is not competent, including a wide range of mental disabilities and/or various physical conditions. This case example specifically concerns the problem of amnesia, of whether that condition can create a situation in which the accused can be judged not competent to stand trial. The case illustrates the behavioral scientist acting in a combined treatment and educational function.

In their report, Koson and Robey suggested the need for psychiatrists to examine several aspects of amnesia so that they can effectively assist the court in making the appropriate competency decision.[6] Their intention was to help to continue the education of the behavioral scientist with regard to amnesia and its effects on the competency decision. Questions that they found to be significant included: Is the inability to remember real or feigned? What is its cause? Is it temporary or permanent? If temporary, is it treatable? Is it crucial to the case that the defendant be able to remember? The authors also suggested that since the courts find the distinction between temporary and permanent amnesia relevant to their decisions, psychiatrists should keep abreast of current concepts regarding the diagnosis, course, and treatment of amnesia. That is, the courts through testimony must be continually educated on the various aspects of, and new developing knowledge about amnesia through testimony given by psychiatrists who have current knowledge on the latest scientific developments in this area.

In addition to discussion about the causes and types of amnesia, the authors also identified amnesia-related diagnostic problems that arise in the forensic setting. For example, many cases of amnesia are the result of alcoholic blackouts. In these cases the history of the extent of intoxication, the amount of alcohol used, the drugs involved, and the psychological profile are important.

Finally, the authors briefly discussed the evaluation and treatment of amnesia. They concluded that psychiatrists can significantly increase the value of their opinions to the courts if they have a complete understanding of the problem with which the court must deal. In this case the subject was amnesia, but the principle is obviously a general one.

Comments and Follow-up Work. Here the authors are involved in two behavioral scientist functions, assessment/diagnosis and education. Through their report they are attempting to inform the court and its agents (psychiatrists who could potentially be testifying in court as experts) about the criteria used for assessing and diagnosing the presence of "real" amnesia. These behavioral scientists are contributing an educational function by suggesting both to the courts and to the psychiatrists that they keep abreast of some of the new developments in this area. Presumably, they would be willing to present a one-day workshop. The workshop would cover amnesia and its involvement in the competency-to-stand-trial decision. The program would be directed toward a group of psychiatrists, judges, or prosecutors who might be interested in this aspect of trial work. Their report would extend the court participants' knowledge of this particular aspect of a trial, specifically relating what is a combined psychosocial/medical problem to the legal process.

For the court to address this problem successfully it needs both assessment/diagnostic help and continuing education on the topic. The latter can be provided directly through behavioral scientist–led workshops or indirectly through testifying experts who are up-to-date in their own learning.

Competency to stand trial has been and continues to be a key aspect of may well-known cases, particularly those involving great violence. Behavioral scientists could examine aspects of this linkage to high-violence cases, or they could engage in the following somewhat related activities:

1. Provide assessment services to the courts or to private attorneys regarding an accused's competency for trial.
2. Analyze the competency assessment procedures and methods of the court.
3. Offer educational sessions on new competency analysis methods to judges and attorneys.

In some competency cases, behavioral scientists would be called to testify about the status of the offender. The next section concerns this area of testimony.

TESTIMONY

Testimony is "a solemn declaration usually made orally by a witness under oath in response to interrogation by a lawyer or authorized public official." Testimony is one method by which the courts collect information about the question at hand. It is part of the "data set" that judges and juries use for their decisions. There are several topics related to the testimonial aspect of the court process that are appropriate for behavioral scientist involvement, including:

- The credibility and competency of witnesses
- The role of prosecutor and defense attorneys
- The rehearsal of witnesses
- Interpretation of the facts
- The admissibility of testimony

Within these larger topics are individual subjects of great range and depth. There are many legal and behavioral components in the court's use of testimony and in the procedures by which testimony is taken. Because testimony can be a turning point for the trial, attorneys have long scrutinized both the testimonial subject and the presentation process. The latter offers us a suitable case topic.

CASE SEVEN: TESTIMONY PRESENTATION. *What* testimony should be presented, and *how* should it be presented? These questions are ever present for both prosecution and defense. How can behavioral scientists help? Expanding the knowledge base through both the applied and the action research function is one way.

To illustrate the effects of testimony and particularly the management of the presentation process, Kaplan and Miller presented a report of research on certain aspects of memory and their relationship to testimony.[7] The researchers began with the belief that "any presentation factors which increase the likelihood that different sets of facts will be salient and memorable for different jurors should increase the variety of the information pool being shared during discussion and consequently should increase polarization." Their study then varied the order of presentation of facts to discover how it affected the "memorable sets of information" for each subject.

The subjects were 144 female undergraduates divided into twenty-four six-person juries. All subjects in each jury listened to a tape-recorded trial. Twelve juries heard an incriminating trial, and twelve heard an exonerating one. Six of the juries hearing each type heard the facts in the same order (homogeneous condition). Six of each set of twelve juries heard the facts in varied order (heterogeneous condition). After listening to the tape, each subject individually rated the guilt of the person. Each jury convened and deliberated, with the subjects again individually rating the defendant's guilt.

As a result of their research, the authors offered the following conclusions:

1. Deliberation did polarize judgments.
2. Polarization was greater for juries that received evidence in heterogeneous order than for those whose facts were given in homogeneous order.
3. Later presented information seems to be more likely to be recalled and discussed than earlier information.

In summary, they felt that "the polarizing influence of discussion was enhanced by evidential presentation factors which broadened the distribution of recalled facts which could be shared during discussion." They suggested that there was a need for further investigation of nonjudgmental variables such as memory in the study of group processes and judgments.

Comments and Follow-up Work. There are several findings from this research that an attorney (either prosecuting or defending) might like to consider from the behavioral perspective. First, if one can control the order of the presentation of facts during the trial process and would like the argument to establish a direction toward a certain outcome, the order of facts presented should be homogeneous. There is less likely to be polarization among the jurors as they attempt to decide the outcome if the facts are presented in a sequence. However, if polarization is the desired goal, facts should be presented in mixed order (i.e., to produce a divided jury). Second, the most important facts should be presented last. While this is a fairly well established point in learning and memory psychology, the introduction of its importance to the trial process could be noted and applied by participants in the process.

The function here is primarily research. Although it has some applied aspects, it does approach basic research in its concern for an understanding of memory and its relation to consensus formation. It is a very good example of the closely linked and overlapping boundaries of applied and basic research. The basic work would lead to fundamental research on group processes, while the applied aspects have relevance to how attorneys actually engage in trial work. Several other opportunities also reflect this division. Behavioral scientists could:

1. Analyze the interpersonal dynamics of the testimony presentation in one case.
2. Offer practice/feedback reviews for attorneys and their clients prior to and in preparation for trial.
3. Research the linkage of demographic factors such as age, sex, and race to testimony by types of trials, to determine trends and contributions.

Decision-making influences of testimony lead us directly to consideration of juries.

JURY: PURPOSE, PROCESS, AND OUTCOME

A jury is "a group of persons sworn to give a verdict on some matter submitted to them, especially a group legally selected and sworn to inquire into any matter of fact and to give their verdict according to the evidence."[8] The work on juries from the behavioral science point of view has been extensive. There is considerable research on the topic as a whole and on individual subtopics such as jury selection and jury instructions. It is not possible here to critique or even introduce each of the individual subparts of jury purpose, process, and outcome that have been studied to date. Instead, a brief listing is offered that highlights some of the issues, subjects actually researched, and adaptations that could be done. This is followed by a discussion and case examples of several subjects.

The following jury topics have been or could be the subjects of behavioral science consultation, research, and related activities:

- Historical background and amendments
- Jury function

- Trial jurors
- Jury as a constitutional issue
- Value of a jury
- Jurors' service
- Specific qualifications
- Jury as a decision maker
- Jury selection
- Group pressure toward conformity
- Juror challenge
- Jury system
- Jury size and composition
- Advantages/disadvantages of a jury trial
- Instructions to the jury
- Selection and impaneling
- Legal requirements
- Jury verdicts

The above list is extensive in both its range and depth, including topics specific to the criminal justice area and others that involve group behavior from a social psychological point of view. Future work could approach the subject from a single disciplinary direction, or it could involve several disciplines in one problem (e.g., the legal requirements for jury instructions in relation to alternatives for communicating them most effectively to different types of juries).

This area continues to be a fertile area for behavioral scientists' activity. The following case is but one example of the extensive reporting to date.

CASE EIGHT: THE JURY RESEARCH PROBLEM.   A problem that has confronted behavioral scientists for some time is that of how to conduct research on juries without being able to control the conditions under which the juries operate. One of the methods for solving this problem is the construction of mock juries. However, these are not "real" juries, in the sense that they are contrived by the researchers. As a result, the question of significance for behavioral scientists working with this method depends on whether the mock jury research is both valid and reliable. Is the mock jury sufficiently like a real jury to be considered truly representative? If it is not, the validity and usefulness of the considerable research that has already been done is threatened, and the mock jury method itself may be discarded by future researchers. This would leave them with a current and future methodological problem.

This question was raised by Gerbasi, Zuckerman, and Reis.[9] In their article, the authors review and critically evaluate the research of sociologists, psychologists, and lawyers that "documents the existence of various kinds of extra evidential influences on real juries' decisions." The article analyzes various areas of the research, including early jury research such as the mock jury experiments; the jury as a group (i.e., how they functioned as a group); the jurors as individuals (representatives of the population; personal and political interests; socioeconomic status); characteristics of the defendant and the victim (social class, sex, etc.); applications and ethics of the use of data; and research on legal issues (e.g., ability to follow judges' instructions; characteristics of evidence). The authors divided the research on the legal issues section into the ability of jurors to follow judges' instructions; number and severity of decision/alternatives; presentation of evidence; definitions of guilt; and the number of jurors in decision rules.

The authors cited specific studies in each of the areas and briefly discussed the strengths and weaknesses of the methodological procedures followed in those studies. The findings are discussed in terms of the current state of the work, with comparisons of the data identifying some of the problems related to each type of research. In conclusion, the authors noted that unless it can be further established that laboratory findings are generalizable to real juries, these studies have limited practical value. They also suggest that more research is necessary for "effective and beneficial implementation of the reforms these studies imply." There are now too many methodological deficiencies.

Comments and Follow-up Work. The broader issue addressed here is whether or not laboratory studies are an effective way to research "real" organizational systems problems. In the case here, can the development of laboratory situations for research be used as *the* method for providing information on how juries will respond in *actual* courtroom situations? Questions about the laboratory studies suggested here raise the methodological issue of whether we might realize greater gains from more naturalistic experiments that are along the line of anthropological field studies (in other words more qualitatively oriented evaluations). Rather than attempt to arrange or design parallel laboratory conditions that are hypothesized to match real conditions, we should encourage behavioral scientists to examine jury purpose, process, and outcome as it actually occurs in the courtroom setting. This is a new direction in research, as the emphasis has always been on control and experimental procedure that mirrors lab work. It is not a newly developed direction, but a renewal of increased support for the anthropological approach that has existed for a very long time.

In this example, behavioral scientists are functioning in a research role that is oriented toward "basic research" in its concern for methodology. Given the approaches and methods used in the existing jury research, is the outcome scientifically valid? If it is not, can these examples of jury research be used to raise basic research methodological questions, such as: which "research methods paradigm" is appropriate—the experimental/laboratory one or the nonexperimental/qualitative/field-based one? This is a fundamental question in social science research that ultimately has practical implications as well.[10] If the studies are not valid, there is no applied advice that could be given to participants of the jury process.

Validity questions are not the only topics. Although much research has been done, it could now be applied to local situations. Behavioral scientists could:

1. Analyze jury characteristics according to an identified geographical region.
2. Assist attorneys in identifying ideal juries according to the type of case and desired outcome.
3. Assist the court in creating jury recruitment processes and procedures that are truly representative of the local population.
4. Provide a training program for attorneys on the latest developments in jury selection techniques.
5. Relate the nonverbal behavior of a jury to the research literature on group dynamics that identifies "hidden meaning" in group work.

The way to research juries and their work continues to be problematic. The next case further outlines the troublesome elements.

CASE NINE: A SIMULATED JURY CASE. As a second case, we will take an example of jury composition research further illustrating the difficulties of some of the methodological and substantive detail involved.

This case report is one by Nemeth and Sosis, whose study purpose was to determine the effect that defendant attractiveness and race have on jury decisions.[11] Two sample groups were used. The first group was composed of twenty male and twenty female undergraduates from middle- and upper-middle-class backgrounds who were politically liberal and activist. The second group contained twenty male and twenty female undergraduates from working-class backgrounds who were largely Polish, Irish, or Slavic in ethnic origin. The subjects were divided into four groups of twenty. Each group was given a description of a defendant in a negligent homicide case. There were four different descriptions of the defendant: white and attractive; black and attractive; white and unattractive; black and unattractive.

The subjects were then given a questionnaire to measure attributes of guilt, severity of sentence to be given to the defendant, the defendant's assumed feelings about the accident, his moral responsibility for failing to take the advice the policeman had given him, and whether the subjects would have acted differently from the defendant. The results of the study showed:

- The unattractive defendant was sentenced more harshly than the attractive one.

- The working-class subjects tended to give harsher sentences than the middle-class subjects.
- The unattractive defendant seemed to be a more habitual drinker than the attractive one.
- The middle-class subjects saw the defendant, regardless of attractiveness, as a heavier drinker than did the other subjects.
- A white defendant was seen to be a heavier drinker than a black one.
- Both samples held that the attractive person felt more regret for his actions than the unattractive one.
- The race of the defendant was relatively insignificant.

The authors concluded that a major finding was that juror characteristics have "a marked effect" in sentencing a defendant (e.g., working-class subjects gave higher penalties). The authors suggested that this could be so because working-class children are more likely to come from "homes where parents are less permissive and more punitive for transgressions" than middle-class parents.

Comments and Follow-up Work.   The implications of this case for a defense attorney are quite clear. There are certain very direct interventions that could be made in preparing the defendant for trial, including presenting a good appearance and/or attempting to mediate the effects of perceived drinking (e.g., supportive testimony would be given regarding the moderate drinking levels of a defendant). These behavioral scientists have generated applied research of real value to a defense or a prosecution attorney. A sample implication: when jury selection options arise, prosecutors should choose working-class representatives if they are pushing for a harsh sentence in a highly visible public safety case (e.g., rape or child molesting).

What other topics are possible areas for work here? Behavioral scientists could:

1. Analyze the group composition factors of simulated jurys to inquire further into the validity question.
2. Construct a simulated jury for a private law firm to "model" the trial as it progresses, providing feedback on successful/unsuccessful points of presentation.
3. Survey various active practioners to determine their views about simulated jury work, and what they would recommend to improve the research (a good group would be trial attorneys).

The process next begins to consider possible outcomes of jury decisions. If not committed at the pretrial stage, offenders can be committed at some other point in the process.

COMMITMENT

To commit is to place in a prison or mental institution. While commitment is sometimes associated with incarceration in prison, it is most often linked to the mental institution.

Because commitment in the mental health system involves loss of liberty, often without the full civil liberties safeguards of the criminal justice system, it has received significant attention from clients rights advocates.[12] The general purposes of commitment were cited by Stone with particular reference to the mentally ill:

> Traditionally, civil commitment of the mentally ill has advanced four distinguishable social goals:
>
> (a) providing care and treatment to those who require it;
>
> (b) protecting allegedly irresponsible people from themselves;
>
> (c) protecting society from their anticipated dangerous acts; and
>
> (d) relieving society—or the family—of the trouble of accommodating persons who, although not dangerous, are bothersome.[13]

Behavioral scientists can become involved with this topic through several functions. As with many other topics, there are, for example: (1) criteria for commitment issues; (2) methodological questions; (3) error rates; (4) unwanted negative side-effects; and (5) the role of commitment in the system, particularly as it relates to the loss of liberty. The following case presents one sample problem.

CASE TEN: COMMITMENT PROTECTION. One problem that has been fairly widely recognized is concern for fairness in the commitment procedures for the mentally ill. Attorneys and other advocates have argued that too many persons are being committed too quickly, and often inappropriately. A question for behavioral scientists is: are the commitment procedures achieving the desired goal(s) of safety for the individual and the community without undue damages?

Hiday addressed this problem in research designed to determine whether mental commitment laws actually protect allegedly mentally ill individuals in commitment proceedings.[14] The then "new" North Carolina Civil Commitment Statute was intended to: reduce involuntary commitment; encourage voluntary commitment; grant due process to respondents subject to involuntary commitment procedures; ensure the right to treatment and basic human rights of both voluntary and involuntary mental patients; and assure discharge from mental hospitalization as soon as other means for treatment are possible. An analysis of the working effects of the statute suggested that a problem with the statute was that it failed to address two factors that tend to contribute toward commitment once court proceedings have begun: the propensity of psychiatrists to overpredict dangerousness and judges' and lawyers' inclination to defer to medical opinion.

The study examined court proceedings (records and procedures) in one county from September to December 1975. The sample used for the study involved 132 commitment hearings heard before three rotating judges. "The crucial question in the functioning of the court is whether judicial—rather than medical—decisions determine commitment."

The author discovered that when a psychiatrist recommended release or a psychiatrist and an individual agreed to voluntary treatment, the cause for commitment generally was seen to disappear, and the case was dismissed. The hypothesis of the author—that the judge would most often agree with the psychiatric recommendation to commit when allegations of violence were substantiated in court—proved true. Agreement between the court decision and the psychiatric recommendation was greatest when evidence of violence was substantiated in court. As one moved from evidence of violent acts to no evidence of danger, agreement declined.

Comments and Follow up Work. The question here concerns a fundamental issue of liberty for the mentally disabled. The question is whether the protection system that was designed to ensure that the mentally disabled are not inappropriately committed is fully and appropriately operational. The reviews found that the extreme case (with significant evidence of violence) could generate agreement. However, in the less obvious case where there is the most potential for error, there was less certainty.

Behavioral scientists have been working on this problem of appropriate commitment from a research perspective for some time. There is currently no consensus on certain aspects of it, such as the ability to predict dangerousness and its appropriateness as a criterion for commitment. In a consulting role, behavioral scientists might be asked to design processes/procedures that could be tested for efficacy.

Commitment is an area that is already open for behavioral scientists. Continued work could involve the following topics:

1. Analyze the reliability and validity of the assessment process and methods used for commitment decision-making in your area.
2. Examine the standardization of commitment process and method across communities, counties, or other jurisdictional areas.
3. Offer assistance to the public defender's office with regard to second-opinion assessment and diagnosis services that are typically unavailable to clients without financial resources.

4. Analyze commitment data for demographic trends (age, sex, race, etc.), evaluating whether they are representative of the normal distribution of citizens in the area.

Commitment can be a part of the sentence, but sentencing involves much beyond this single element, as discussed in the next section.

SENTENCING

A sentence is "the punishment ordered by a court to be inflicted upon a person convicted of a crime, usually either a noncustodial sentence such as probation and/or a fine, or a custodial sentence, such as a term of years of imprisonment, or a number of months in a county jail. Such an order usually identifies the authority which must carry out the sentence and authorizes and directs such authority to execute the order."[15] Two elements of the sentence are topics for behavioral science work, the process of sentencing and the type of sentence itself.

First, the process by which sentencing is done merits attention, as it must be comprehensive and equitable. Some of the sentencing process issues include the following:

- Establishing sentencing objectives
- The actual steps of the process
- Pre-sentence investigation and report procedures
- The court's role
- Educating judges regarding both standing and changing options
- Checks and balances in the sentencing process
- Steps for appellate review of sentences

The above elements in the process of making a sentencing decision are quite thoroughly interrelated with behavioral science issues. Behavioral scientists would naturally be interested in, for example, the dynamics of the group processes that occur during interdepartmental consultation. This would lend itself well to a process-consultation function whereby a behavioral scientist would observe and report back on strengths and weaknesses in it. The feedback would be used to improve the process.

What are the characteristics of the sentence that might be of interest to behavioral scientists? Some of the following issues are topics for initiating the research, consulting, or educational function. They are oriented toward the more static aspects of the nature of the sentence at a point or points in time.

- The rationale behind the sentence
- Sentence predictability

- Sentence equality
- Sentencing alternatives
- Minimum/maximum sentences
- Indeterminate sentences
- Consecutive and concurrent sentences
- Differential sentencing
- Sentence review

These constitute the elements of the design options given the court when it constructs sentences, both on an individual-offender basis and for groups of offenders whose crimes are similar in nature.

Behavioral scientists can be engaged in creating sentence design alternatives independently of the court in a research function, or in collaboration with court staff through consultation. In general there seems to be an ongoing need for educating court personnel (judges, attorneys) with regard to new sentence options and the effects of existing alternatives, as well as the new alternatives that are rapidly developing in various community programs. Last, the research possibilities are considerable, particularly those in applied research directed at solving a specific sentencing problem such as standardization. Action research is also useful when the court would like to "experiment" with certain innovative sentencing programs such as service in the community as opposed to incarceration in prison. Program model planning, development, and evaluation are activities that many behavioral scientists are interested in and experienced with.

The following case illustrates work in one of the problem areas, the sentencing equity issue.

CASE ELEVEN: THE SENTENCING DISCRIMINATION PROBLEM.
One question sometimes asked with regard to sentencing is: are the sentences for similar crimes similar for all inmates, or is there some discrimination in the process that leads to different sentences for different individuals and groups? The question could be addressed in a number of ways, either on a formal research function basis or through a consultation to management review of sentencing practices in one specific court. The following study indicates the kind of concerns that have been identified with the sentencing discrimination problem.

Hagan reviewed the research that targeted or was related to the charge of discrimination in sentencing.[16] He used as his data sample twenty studies done from a "sociological viewpoint." By this he meant that they were focused on race, sex, age, and socioeconomic status of the defendant. These characteristics are presumed to be legally irrelevant in sentencing. The "sociologically-oriented studies have attempted to detect their extralegal influence." The review was designed to address several questions: Are extralegal attributes of the defendant the basis of differential sentencing? If so, how much differential sentencing occurs, and in what particular setting, if any, does differential sentencing occur?

Hagan studied the relationship between these factors and the nature of judicial dispositions. He considered the statistical significance of the relationship, the strength and form of the association, the extent to which controls are introduced for the influence of legally relevant factors, and the type of sample used in each study. He found only a small relationship between the extralegal attributes of the offender and sentencing decisions. While there may be evidence of differential sentencing, knowledge of extralegal attributes apparently contributed little to the ability to predict judicial dispositions.

The author cited several implications of the review, offering suggestions for addressing them. First, in terms of methodology the information reviewed in these studies indicated that longitudinal data would be more adequate than fragmentary data for answering the questions. Factors related to the defendant's journey through the criminal justice system might "operate cumulatively to the disadvantage of minority group defendants." This possibility led to suggestions that researchers might use different approaches and different types of data to address the problem. Alternative variables that might be suitable for inspection include "the effects of organizational constraints such as caseloads and court referral rates; the role of community factors such as rescidivism rates; and the importance of the characteristics of those doing the judging."

Comments and Follow-up Work. This study offers an example of one method by which a court can address the question of the fairness of its sentencing process and its ultimate sentencing outcomes. The analysis provides a check on sentencing equality generally, and it can be aimed specifically at the individual organization under study. From a research perspective, a sufficiently complex or sophisticated research design would enable the behavioral scientist to generalize from an individual review of one court's sentencing process and outcome. It would also give that individual court some detailed information as to whether or not its sentencing is discriminatory; and in such a determination, behavioral scientists could be used as consultants, called in periodically to test the discrimination question in individual courts, perhaps as "evaluators" of this aspect of the system.

In summary, the sentencing question can be examined on two levels: (1) an individual organization-specific level and (2) a generalizable level that might include a number of courts. One could envision a rather rigorous study of the issue, using, for example, thirty state courts or thirty federal courts throughout the United States, or courts of the New England or mid-Atlantic region. Depending on the design, the study could offer information on the problem as a whole and on individual courts, providing data for both national and regional policy making and managerial action at the single court level.

What are additional topics? Behavioral scientists could:

1. Analyze the sentences given by type of offender to determine variability, use of new alternatives, and match of sentence with crime seriousness.
2. Provide a training program for judges and attorneys that identifies the new sentencing options and the types of inmates who benefit from community alternatives.
3. Provide process consultation to a court that has been identified as possibly discriminatory, helping the court to confront and address the issue.

Sentencing involves a consideration of the extent of the punishment to be handed out.

PUNISHMENT

Punishment is defined as the harm or penalty that must be given for the committing of a crime. Punishment, like sentencing, involves both a process and an outcome. Behavioral scientists can become involved through their functional options in analyzing the ways in which punishment decisions are made and punishment is delivered (process), or the effects that punishment has on individuals and groups (outcomes). There are both philosophical and operational questions.

Punishment implies a philosophy that is in direct contrast to a rehabilitation philosophy. Both are prevalent in criminal justice thinking. This difference in philosophy leads to the issue of the differential effectiveness of punishment in its different forms. What are the types, and how is it to be administered? Behavioral scientists can become involved in and contribute to a range of philosophical problems, including, for example, the relationship between punishment options such as the death penalty and human dignity. The broad question is: what types of punishment and what processes for its administration are acceptable in terms of the minimum requirements of human dignity? Is electrocution acceptable; is lethal injection?

With regard to the process of administration, the topics would include: what *types* of punishments are options; to be provided for what *reasons;* at what *times;* under what *conditions;* and by *whom?* Process can be analyzed from either a research perspective (e.g., applied or action research), or from a consulting one, in which the court administrator seeks knowledge about efficiency, alternative approaches, and other issues.

In addition to considering the ways in which punishment is provided and the available options, there is a second major area of the punishment topic. A most significant issue is: what is the outcome of punishment? Does punishment achieve one of its key objectives—becoming a deterrent for future crime? There is also the related question of whether the punishment handed out is appropriate for both the crime and the individual criminal. Is a punishment outcome of seven years in prison appropriate for the burglary of a table radio, particularly when a nineteen-year-old is the culprit? Will deterrence be the result, or criminal training? Behavioral scientists can become involved in evaluating the deterrent effect of punishment, analyzing the degree of achievement of one of the most appropriate outcomes of justice system activity. This topic might require an analysis of the correlation between individual criminal characteristics, the type and level of punishment administered, and future criminality. Essentially this would parallel the sentencing work reviewed earlier.

Questions for study and consultation will lead to difficult topics such as capital punishment, including both its appropriateness in terms of our modern view of humanity and its effectiveness in terms of achieving its objectives. In short, there is ample opportunity for behavioral scientists to become involved in highly philosophical and in day-to-day operations problems.

CASE TWELVE: PUNISHMENT/CRIME RATE RELATIONSHIPS. One frequent question is that of the relationship between crime rates and the punishments handed out by court systems. Do punishments affect crime rates? If so, why do they?

Tittle examined national statistics in an attempt to understand the relationship between crime rates and punishment.[17] According to Tittle, the research was intended to clarify the relationship between two characteristics of legal reaction: (1) certainty and severity of punishment and (2) the incidence of various kinds of crimes. The important question is: "Under what conditions are negative sanctions likely to be effective?"

The data base included every state in the country. Indexes of certainty of punishment, severity of punishment, and crime rates for all felonies for each of seven offense categories were calculated for each state. With these calculations and other analyses, the researchers developed four general observations. First, they found that certain punishment does have some relationship to the amount of crime that becomes known to the police. Second, official penalties alone cannot fully account for rates of deviance. Penalties must be considered as only one of many variables, not necessarily the most important. Third, the data suggested that the relationship between official negative sanctions and crime is complex, not simple and straightforward.

Finally, the author noted one important implication. Since according to the data greater certainty of punishment is associated with lower offense rates, proposals to reduce crime by improving law enforcement seem reasonable. Improvement of law enforcement would encompass greater police efficiency along with the usual response of more policemen.

Comments and Follow-up Work.   This case example illustrates how the behavioral scientist can analyze the relationship between crime rates and punishment, both at a national level and for an individual geographic area. For example, the punishment-distribution behavior of judges may be analyzed in terms of local crime rates to make a determination about whether changes in punishment patterns are having an effect on crime rates in a given area—although, in a research sense, it is very difficult to be sure of the reliability and validity of such data.

This kind of study could be conducted on a research basis, or on a consulting basis for an individual judge. A judge could request an examination of the results of a change in his/her individual punishment patterns in terms of the effect on the recidivism rates of his/her individual caseload. Alternatively, this same study could be developed for a group of judges in a given district or region.

Broading the approach could lead behavioral scientists to:

1. Analyze changes in punishments handed out by a local court, including the types and frequencies as matched to crimes.
2. Track crime rate changes over time in a region and make comparisons to neighboring regions, looking for reasons for change if change has occurred.
3. Provide a training program for judges and attorneys that identifies new punishment alternatives for certain offender groups (e.g., juveniles), including data on their relative effectiveness.
4. Provide consultation to one judge on his/her punishment decision-making process and outcomes.

What are other elements of the process, either immediately or following a sentence of imprisonment? Probation and parole are two possibilities.

PROBATION AND PAROLE

Behavioral science analysis can make a contribution to improved probation and parole procedures and outcomes. Probation is "a procedure whereby a defendant found guilty of a crime upon a verdict or plea of guilty is released by the court, under the supervision of a probation officer."[18] Probation is a procedure that allows the defendant to avoid imprisonment. Parole, a somewhat similar action, is defined as "a conditional release from imprisonment which entitles the person receiving the 'parole' to serve the remainder of his term outside the prison if he satisfactorily complies with all the terms and conditions connected therewith."[19] Both enable the offender to substitute monitored community control for institutonal time. Behavioral scientists have a wide range of parole and probation topics to choose from. One example would be a comparative analysis of different courts' rationale for either probation or parole. The whole probation/parole system could be studied, or only individual parts. *Who* makes the decision to parole, for example, and on the basis of *what* kind of evidence?

Behavioral scientists might be invited into the organization on a consulting basis to examine the parole and probation decision-making processes to determine whether they are achieving the intended objectives—even widely differing ones such as helping inmates with work opportunities versus reducing prison crowding. Alternatively, behavioral scientists might join with criminal justice staff in designing, developing, and presenting an education and training program for parole officers. This program might include information on decision-making criteria, the role of the lawyer and judge, methods and procedures for parole and probation supervision, and mechanisms for monitoring the progress of each individual within the parole and probation systems (i.e., a person-specific progress evaluation study).

Using such an evaluation method, behavioral scientists could also examine the "clinical impact" of probation or parole in terms of its contribution to crime reduction by an individual offender and/or an offender group (e.g., all war veterans). The way that probation and parole activities are integrated into the offender's treatment plan is certainly a suitable topic for analysis.

As with other aspects of the court system that already have been discussed, the process of probation/parole work and/or the outcomes can become the subject. Is the process working? Are the outcomes appropriate with minimal unintended negative side-effects?

CASE THIRTEEN: PROBATION AND PAROLE. What works and what does not work with regard to the clinical aspects of probation and parole? Behavioral scientists can examine this problem from a treatment-function perspective and have done so, as the following report indicates.

Newman begins by discussing a three-stage treatment process that field correction workers could use to help offenders adjust to their community.[20] The first stage is *investigation,* in which the worker tries to determine the internal and external factors that have shaped the offender. The second stage is *diagnosis,* or "codification of all that has been learned about the individual, organized . . . to provide a means for the establishment of future treatment goals." The third stage is *treatment supervision,* focused on increasing open communication to enable the individual more realistically to appraise his own behavior and its acceptance in relevant social systems. It may also involve providing material services to the offender, a need often overlooked in the rush to therapy.

The treatment begins with the first session. The purpose of the first session, including the investigation, is to see the offender's personality in action. An assumption of the program is that the only way to understand and then counsel an offender is to know the individual. After only a short time, the correctional worker must make an appraisal of the offender's ability to go back into the community. This appraisal is better done if it comes from "an understanding of the degree of discomfort which the individual feels in relation to his social or emotional problem."

Noting that continuous surveillance of the offender is not necessary, the author believes the correctional worker, whether in the institution or in field service, should be able to "recognize, understand and deal effectively with subtle as well as obvious shifts in the behavior and personality of the offender." This belief is part of the basis for a dual-purpose therapeutic relationship. In the therapeutic clinical management of the correctional worker and the parolee, crime prevention is incorporated in the treatment process. The parole officer is both an *enforcer* of certain restrictions and a *helper* for achieving social and psychological adjustment. When the offender realizes this dual contribution, one of the first major accomplishments of treatment has occurred.

Finally, Newman offers advice to correctional workers. First, it is important that the worker keep the relationship open, avoiding falling into rigid molds. Second, the worker must go into the field, investigating not only the offender but also his home, neighborhood and family, and whole social system. Third, if the parolee's behavior after release is still unsatisfactory, the worker must determine what is causing it, carefully working a method of change into the counseling. Sometimes the needed change can result simply from the correctional worker's listening to and feeding back what the parolee talks about. In other situations, it may require the counselor to create an interview environment filled with anxiety. Regardless of the method of treatment, the goal is to bring about self-acceptance in the parolee that in turn will aid his reentry to the community.

Comments and Follow-up Work. Here the behavioral scientist is reviewing the treatment component of probation and parole, outlining a total program model. The intent is to define one view of what contributes to the successful individual change and development of the offender in terms of a model that could be used in many settings. The analysis contributes to a refinement of thinking in this area, to the creation of models, and, if delivered in a training session, to the continuing education of the staff who want to know what makes them most effective.

In addition to this work, behavioral scientists could:

1. Provide assessment and diagnosis services directed toward identifying those offenders who would benefit from and do well in probation or parole.
2. Offer to provide treatment services to offenders on probation or parole, including both clinical and vocational services specifically linked to job acquisition and retention.
3. Research the existing information on probation and parole in the community, inquiring into who is eligible, who obtains probation and

parole, and what the effects are (e.g., using both demographic and follow-up data).

4. As a consultant, design a parole support group and help to implement it with offender leadership.

All sentencing and the decisions to grant probation or parole involve discretion. Its purpose and use are critical to the organization, as considered next.

DISCRETION

Discretion is present throughout the court system, a main theme in the story of how the system works. It is defined as "the reasonable exercise of a power or right to act in an official capacity; [it] involves the idea of choice, of an exercise of the will, so that abuse of discretion involves more than a difference in judicial opinion between the trial and appellate courts, and in order to constitute an 'abuse' of discretion the judgment must demonstrate a perversity of will, a defiance of good judgment, or bias."[21] At almost all decision points in the court system, discretion can be used. Behavioral scientists can focus their analytical skills on the use of discretion generally; on ways to enhance its use; and/or on its effects on individual aspects of court work (e.g., the decision to imprison or not).

Gifis further identified three types of discretion that are commonly found in the court process.[22] These three primary types are: *judicial discretion,* defined as "the reasonable use of judicial power (i.e., freedom to decide within the bounds of law and fact)"; *legal discretion,* defined as "the use of one of several equally satisfactory provisions of law"; and *prosecutorial discretion,* defined as "the wide range of alternatives available to a prosecutor in criminal cases, including the decision to prosecute, the particular charges to be brought, plus bargaining, mode of trial conduct, and recommendations for sentencing, parole, etc." As suggested by this differentiation, discretion is present as an option and is used at many points of the court process. Thus, it could be the subject of behavioral science interest from many functional directions.

For example, behavioral scientists could be called on to make an assessment of individual defendants to determine whether discretion would be clinically helpful in an individual case; behavioral scientists could be asked to research various aspects of the use of discretion in a given region (e.g., for younger offenders); or behavioral scientists could be engaged as consultants to examine the extent of the abuse of discretion in an area where it has been identified as questionable. That last consulting function engagement might be followed with a plan for change that would include a program to provide further education and training on the best use of discretion in the court process. The following example illustrates behavioral scientists at work in this area.

CASE FOURTEEN: DISCRETION CASE.   The issues involved with discretion are broad enough to enable behavioral scientists to employ all functions, depending only on the interest of the organization and/or its specific need.

Shaver, Gilbert, and Williams viewed discretion as one area that could be fertile ground for the participation of social psychologists in the criminal justice system.[23] They specifically cited as potential areas of work the social and psychological factors involved in arrest, investigation, selective enforcement, plea bargaining, criminal sentences, and prison operation. Related concerns involve such topics as personality and attitudes and resulting behavior.

Their specific purpose was to briefly review some of the ways in which social psychological issues have been raised in the system through litigation and through various other aspects of the system such as the police, prosecution, courts, and prisons. Their conclusion presented a list of areas not covered (which are of interest to behavior scientists generally) and a strong statement about reasons for working on the topic of discretion.

By confining the discussion to the discretionary power held, used, and too often abused by administrative officials in the criminal justice system, we have necessarily excluded a good deal of social psychological research that is of more general interest to the law. Problems of aggression, conformity and obedience, risk-taking, and bargaining; questions of perceived freedom and justice; the entire area of legal socialization (Tapp, 1971); public attitudes toward crime and victimization (Furstenberg, 1972; Stotland, 1974)—these are of obvious concern to legal professionals as well as to social psychologists interested in the law. But these broader questions do not specifically affect the exercise of discretion.

It is no longer even fashionable to assert that the sort of criminal justice practiced in the United States today is all too often *not* equal justice before the law. We can all think of numerous cases—from the local jails to the national government— in which the criminal sanctions applied to one defendant do not seem to apply with equal force to others similarly accused. To the extent that these inequalities are the product of individual decisions made by police, prosecutors, judges, and penal officials, they are the legitimate concern of social psychology.[24]

Shaver et al. followed this with a bibliography of 15 case citations and 132 references further exemplifying research work.

Comments and Follow-up Work.   Here the behavioral scientists reviewed examples of colleagues' work for the same purpose for which this book was written. They intended to inform their audience of some of the work to date, hoping to stimulate follow-up interest on the part of others. Taking a legal concept with extensive involvement throughout the system enabled them to demonstrate the equally extensive array of possibilities for further work, ranging from arrest by police to sentencing by the courts. The references cited offer the readers many actual examples of work done to date. Certainly those behavioral scientists with a social psychological interest should consult this list.

A sample of the work opportunities in this area includes the following:

1. Research the varied role of discretion in various decision points of the court system (e.g., probation, sentencing, parole).
2. Research a single case example of the use of discretion, outlining in detail the options available, the criteria for the decision, and its ultimate effects.
3. As a consultant, design a "discretion group" for judges and attorneys that would meet to discuss strengths, weaknesses, and criteria for discretion use (for purposes of mutual education and support).
4. Survey police officers to determine the criteria they use for *not* arresting a juvenile or youth when the crime is not serious or has not traditionally been regarded as serious (e.g., a fraternity member's drunk driving).
5. Conduct a training program for police officers on ways of avoiding physical conflict during arrest through the use of social psychological principles.

The high importance of discretion to the system means that this is an area in which work especially needs to be expanded.

SUMMARY

This chapter introduced the use of behavioral science in the various technical procedures and processes of the courts. The examples identified here are few in relation to the total work, and they are just briefly abstracted. The combining of court topics and behavioral scientist functions is by no means an exhaustive representation of the ways in which they could be involved in court work.

The area of usual interest for behavioral scientists in courts was reviewed. Thirteen technical procedures and processes of the court's organizational system were listed and cross-referenced with the five functions of behavioral scientists to create a work opportunity matrix.

The first court technical element discussed was intake and detention, which consists of arrest, processing, release or imprisonment, the magistrate appearance, and the plea. The case example used involves pretrial psychiatric examinations, particularly the guidelines determining who is to be tested. The case also addresses the guidelines for determining competency and possible commitment or follow-up plans for clients, consistent with the questions asked by the court. Opportunities exist in educating and training staff to recognize potential problems for clients, in updating the testing tools used, in researching problems that arise in using tests, and in consulting with the court organization to help analyze the intake procedure to improve its efficiency.

Processing often involves screening and diversion, which may take the client out of the criminal justice system to an alternative (e.g., parole or community service). The concerns here are in assuring that appropriate people are placed in alternative programs, and that these programs will be effective. The case example relates the desire of a family court system to channel cases to a community service. Using both research and consultation functions, behavioral scientists collected and analyzed data on client characteristics that would help identify those who could be placed with community services. It is easily conceivable that education and training functions could serve both corrections staff and staff in the community service programs. The treatment functions could involve the development of community programs and programs for individual clients.

Negotiation provides behavioral scientists with the opportunity to work in the controversial area of plea bargaining. Problems range from personal reactions to reduced charges to needed guidelines for the bargaining process. The case example involved a study of police officers' reactions to and recommendations for plea bargaining, a research function.

Pretrial proceedings consist of such elements as arraignment, charges, evidence, strategy for defense and prosecution, bail and/or release, and setting trial dates. One case example examined bail-setting practices as studied by Ebbesen and Konecni. The study illustrated how applied research can help the court recognize its own behavior and monitor individual decisions concerning a specific practice.

Trials have been the focus of attention for behavioral scientists in nearly all their functions. The complex questions of competency, relevancy, and materiality in evidence provide areas for contributions in all five behavioral science functions. The actual presenting of the evidence and other courtroom behaviors are potential subjects for scrutiny. The case example of competency to stand trial shows a combination of treatment and education functions, both a concern for individual clinical needs and the need to educate and inform. By combining functions, behavioral scientists can present workshops that address various treatment-oriented problems in the courts and corrections systems.

The what and how of testimony are crucial aspects of any trial. Behavioral scientists have been involved here with the human issues of reactions to, memory for, and interpretation of facts as presented in testimony. The function used most is research. The work by behavioral scientists in the jury aspect of trial proceedings has been extensive, though hardly exhaustive at this point. A list of areas addressed is provided in the section on "Jury: Purpose, Process, and Outcome." The first case on this topic questioned the work done by behavioral scientists using mock juries. It was suggested that naturalistic experiments may be needed. The second case involved jury composition and its "marked effect" on sentencing. Both defense and prosecution can use jury composition information to achieve their respectively desired results.

Commitment procedures are an aspect of the court's procedures that have been the subject of questions regarding the civil liberty safeguards of the criminal justice system. Behavioral scientists can become involved with criteria for commitment, methodological issues, error rates, negative side-effects, and the role of the community in the system. The case example, concerning individual protection during the procedures for commitment, was an examination of the North Carolina commitment statute. It found that agreement between psychiatrists and the court was greatest in cases involving violence. The functions of behavioral scientists fit well with this entire commitment area. Research opportunities are abundant. Results of studies can be used for treatment, for education and training, and for consultation to secure change. Appropriate commitments are obviously the most important area of study, but here again subtopics and spinoffs that can be used by courts and corrections are almost limitless.

Sentencing covers both custodial and noncustodial types, with the issues ranging from objectives to the appellate review of sentences. The research, consultation, and education functions were related to the design options given the court in sentencing. The case example deals with equity in sent-

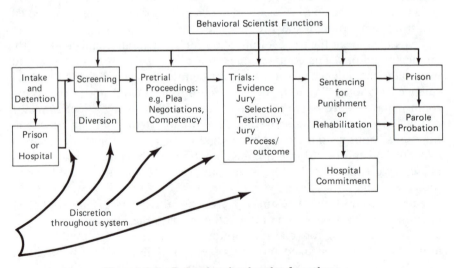

Figure 2-2. Behavioral scientist functions.

encing for similar crimes, analyzing legal versus extralegal issues in determining sentences. Behavioral scientists can work on two levels: the single organization level or generalizable, across-court studies.

Punishment involves sentencing for retribution rather than for rehabilitation. It must address fairness in application and effectiveness as a deterrent. The case example was a national study showing that greater certainty of punishment was associated with lower offense rates. The questions of appropriateness, effectiveness, and factors affecting punishment decisions are filled with opportunities for behavioral scientists.

Probation and parole are both forms of supervised alternatives to imprisonment. Probation is in lieu of imprisonment, whereas parole is a supervised release from imprisonment. This is a sentencing decision and is therefore closely allied to the sentencing issues already presented. The contributions of behavioral scientists to improving the quality of the decision-making process and specific probation and parole programs are needed. The case example considered the clinical aspects of the problem from a treatment function perspective. Specifically, it addressed the need to help offenders adjust to their community after an absence due to imprisonment. Behavioral scientists can help corrections workers define their roles and refine the programs used to aid reentry, also offering direct clinical services.

Judicial, legal, and prosecutorial discretion provides flexibility in the court organization systems. Discretion is used to accommodate the endless variations of human behavior in criminal situations. Studying these variations, providing input about when discretion is effective, as well as the types of discretion that are effective, is a primary contribution for behavioral scientists.

Figure 2-2 summarizes these points, indicating the potential involvement of behavioral scientists in all parts of the technical work of the courts. Discretion is shown as a process cutting through all of this work. Chapter 3 will address the other subsystems of the courts, including their goals and values, structural, psychosocial, and managerial elements. It will be clear that behavioral scientists have many opportunities in these areas as well.

REFERENCES

1. Kast, F. E., and Rosenzweig, J. E. (1979). *Organization and Management*. New York: McGraw-Hill.
2. Geller, J. L., and Lister, E. D. (1978). The Process of Criminal Commitment for Pretrial Psychiatric Examination; An Evaluation. *American Journal of Psychiatry,* 135, 53–60.
3. Ibid., p. 53.
4. Kohn, M., and Sugarman, N. (1978). Characteristics of Families Coming to the Family Court on PINS Petitions. *Psychiatric Quarterly,* 50 (1), 37–43.

5. Ebbesen, E. B., and Konecni, V. J. (1975). Decision-Making and Information Integration in the Court: The Setting of Bail. *Journal of Personality and Social Psychology, 32,* 805–21.
6. Koson, D., and Robey, A. (1973). Amnesia and Competency to Stand Trial. *American Journal of Psychiatry,* 130, 588–92.
7. Kaplan, M., and Miller, C. (1977). Judgments and Group Discussion. Effect of Presentation and Memory Factors on Polarization. *Sociometry,* 40, 337–43.
8. Gifis, S. H. (1975). *Law Dictionary.* Woodbury, New York: Barron's.
9. Gerbasi, K., Zuckerman, M., and Reis, H. T. (1977). Justice Needs a New Blindfold: A Review of Mock Jury Research. *Psychological Bulletin,* 84 (2), 323–45.
10. Posavac, E. J., and Carey, R. G. (1980). *Program Evaluation: Methods and Case Studies.* Englewood Cliffs, New Jersey: Prentice-Hall.
11. Nemeth, C., and Sosis, R. (1973). A Simulated Jury Study: Characteristics of the Defendant and the Jurors. *Journal of Social Psychology,* 90, 221–29.
12. Ziegenfuss, J. T. (1983). *Patients Rights and Professional Practice.* New York: Van Nostrand Reinhold.
13. Stone, A. A. *Mental Health and Law: A System in Transition.* Washington, D.C.: Health and Human Services, NIMH, 1975.
14. Hiday, V. A. (1977). Reformed Commitment Procedures: An Empirical Study in the Courtroom. *Law and Society Review,* pp. 651–62.
15. Gifis. Op. cit.
16. Hagan, J. (1974). Extra-legal Attributes and Criminal Sentencing: An Assessment of a Sociological Viewpoint. *Law and Society Review,* 1, 357–83.
17. Tittle, C. R. (1969). Crime Rates and Legal Sanctions. *Social Problems,* 16 pp 409–423.
18. Gifis. Op. cit., p. 163.
19. Ibid.
20. Newman, C. L. (1961). Concepts of Treatment in Probation and Parole Supervision. *Federal Probation,* 24 (1), 11–19.
21. Gifis. Op. cit., p. 61.
22. Ibid., p. 61.
23. Shaver, K., Gilbert, M., and Williams, M. (1975). Social Psychology, Criminal Justice, and the Practice of Discretion: A Selective Review. *Personality and Social Psychology Bulletin,* 1(3), 471.
24. Ibid., p. 478.

3
BEHAVIORAL SCIENTISTS AND COURT VALUES, STRUCTURE, AND MANAGEMENT

This chapter relates the functional options of behavioral scientists to various aspects of court organization and management. The analysis in Chapter 2 reviewed the opportunities for behavioral scientists in the technical system, one of the five subsystems identified in the opening chapter. Chapter 3 will focus on behavioral scientists' functions as they are used in the four other systems of the court organization. These systems are identified in Figure 3-1 as the goals/values subsystem, the structural subsystem, the psychosocial subsystem, and the managerial subsystem. A brief review of definitions is useful, as they are critical to the presentation of this material.

The goals and values subsystem concerns "the ends or desirable future of the organization with high relative worth or importance."[1] This subsystem involves the concept of the organizational culture as a whole, including the philosophy of the organization and the core goals and values that the court system uses to define itself, both in theory and in practice. This is the organizational mission and purposes subsystem.

The structural subsystem is defined as "the ways in which the tasks of the organization are divided (differentiation) and coordinated (integration). In the formal sense, structure is set forth by organization charts, by position and job description, and by rules and procedures."[2] The structural subsystem includes the formal structure on a macro level and the structural details of such components as the personnel policies, compensation system, management information system, and others. This is the "organization chart" subsystem.

The third of the subsystems covered in this chapter is the psychosocial subsystem. This is defined as "the individuals and groups in interaction. It consists of individual behavior and motivation, status and role relationships, group dynamics and influence systems. It is also affected by sentiments, values, attitudes, expectations and aspirations of the people in the organization."[3] With reference to court organization subjects, this subsystem concerns, for example, the attitudes of judges, prosecutors, and defenders as they each fulfill their respective roles in the system. This is the human relations subsystem.

The last of the subsystems making up the court organization as a whole

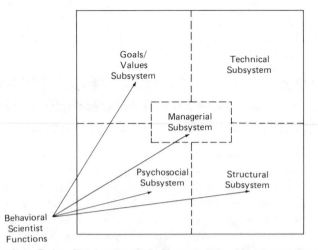

Figure 3-1. Behavioral scientists functions in court goals/values, structural, psychosocial, and managerial subsystems.

is the managerial subsystem. The managerial subsystem "spans the entire organization by relating the organization to its environment, setting the goals, developing comprehensive, strategic and operational plans, designing the structure, and establishing control processes."[4] The managerial subsystem involves planning, organizing, directing, and controlling as the four traditional activities of its sphere. This is the work of the managers and administrators at all levels.

The ways in which behavioral scientists could become involved in these areas of the court organization are virtually unlimited. This chapter presents some selected examples of behavioral scientists' activities in these four subsystems to illustrate the range of involvement that has already occurred. Two additional points must be noted.

First, as the reader will notice, there is not an equal distribution of work examples in the four subsystems. In the "pool" of case reports there was considerably more work in the management system than in the others. This should not be taken to be a stronger endorsement of behavioral science efforts in court management work. If any implications have surfaced, they are more in the direction of the need for behavioral scientists to *extend* their work in court goals/values and structural subsystems. Psychosocial subsystem activities could be expanded as well, although the recent surge in journals in this area (e.g., see *Behavioral Sciences and Law, Law and Human Behavior*) is already generating greater interest.

Second, the topics under the various sections are not meant to be an exhaustive presentation of all aspects of these organizational areas. Instead, several key elements in each of the subsystems are defined in enough detail to permit an understanding of the behavioral scientist's intervention. For fuller treatment of each of the subsystems, readers should consult texts in organization and management that have the courts as their subject industry.

The first subsystem for review involves goals/values and mission, a most difficult and often conflict-laden area in court organization.

THE GOALS AND VALUES SUBSYSTEM

The definition of this system that was just presented is a somewhat general one. A key to understanding the subsystem involves consideration of it as the philosophy behind the action of the various technical areas of court operation. For example, what are the court's goals and values with regard to such technical service issues as sentencing or probation and parole? The behavioral scientist can investigate this subject in several different ways in an effort to address these philosophical questions. A fundamental and well-known conflict for sentencing is the punishment-versus-rehabilitation dispute. Is the court interested in punishing the offender, or does the court have a more rehabilitation-oriented philosophy? Prime questions for analysis are: what is the court's core mission, or if there are several missions, how does it assign relative values to the competitive missions?[5]

A brief elaboration of the definition of goals and values will extend the potential base for behavioral scientists' work:

> Organizational system goals pertain to the purposes and desired conditions that the organization seeks as a distinct entity. Self-perpetuation, stability of operations, a high rate of return, growth, satisfaction of participants, enhancement of position in field, technological leadership, and innovation are examples of system goals.

> Organizations have multiple goals rather than a single goal, and this goal set is determined in response to both external and internal forces. Organizations, like other open systems, display the characteristic of equifinality—they generally have alternative means for the accomplishment of system objectives. The organization has substantial discretion concerning the goals it attempts to satisfy and also alternatives within its transformation functions as to the means for their accomplishment. However, it must operate within the constraints imposed by environmental forces and the need to maintain the contribution of internal participants.[6]

Behavioral scientists have, in the topic of organizational goals, a rich field for review, with most enticing comparisons possible (e.g., court achievements, satisfaction of members, leadership, and willingness to innovate). What are the values that define the court?

The goals the court establishes for itself are associated with and intimately linked to its values.

> Organizations appear to hold certain values, but defining them precisely and showing how they influence decision making is difficult. However, there are several broad generalizations. Organizations depend on a minimum level of shared values among internal participants and the external society for their very existence. Deeply ingrained cultural values provide a measure of cohesiveness. Values such as "individual human dignity," "individual property rights," "everyone should work for a living," and "acceptance of legitimate authority" provide a foundation without which organizations could not exist. Every human participant brings a certain set of values to the organization. Value inputs also come from a wide variety of external sources—customers, competitors, suppliers, and other elements of the organization's task environment.[7]

How do the organization's values or value set affect individual and organizational behaviors such as sentencing or parole decision? At the basic level, we could ask whether there is value consistency within the organization. This questions whether there is a formal or an informal educational mechanism for transmitting and monitoring adherence to the value set. For example, would this mechanism produce, for similar crimes, similarity of sentences by a diverse group of judges within the same court system?

Behavioral scientists potentially have a wide range of functional roles within the court's goals and values system. For example, behavioral scientists may be asked to educate and train staff or administrators; may be brought in as consultants to examine the consistency of philosophy with operations; and/or may conduct research regarding the protection of the offender from arbitrary state action. The following examples illustrate these roles.

CASE FIFTEEN: THERAPEUTIC OR PUNISHMENT ORIENTATION OF THE COURT. Behavioral scientists may be asked to determine whether a given program is consistent with the organizational philosophy of the court; in particular, whether the programs established by the court have a therapeutic versus a punishment orientation. Alternatively, behavioral scientists may be asked to help design and develop such programs with one philosophy or the other. One example demonstrates the linkage of program design and philosophy.

Nir and Cutler presented an analysis of how the juvenile court can be used as part of a therapeutic regimen.[8] Their article describes the court clinic of the Jewish Board of Guardians in New York City, a collaborative effort between an adolescent clinic and a juvenile court. The goal of the clinic was to provide psychiatric evaluation and treatment to adolescents and their families who were in court as a result of a psychiatric condition.

The clinic places special emphasis on handling the family's reluctance to accept treatment, which is a common occurrence, and the adolescent's tendency to act out (i.e., to commit delinquent behavior). To manage both of these problems the clinic begins with a very detailed diagnostic study. There was a general tendency in the past to deal primarily with the presenting symptoms of the delinquent rather than to study him or her in the depth necessary to create real understanding of the derivation and scope of the problems.

According to the authors, this program (jointly developed by the clinic and the juvenile court) had "successfully handled otherwise untreatable court-referred adolescents. The clinic has used the authority of the court to handle the general resistance to treatment. Since therapy is court ordered, the therapist can avoid being seen as condemning the youth's behavior, while the adolescent's self-esteem is preserved, because he or she did not ask for help. It is as if the youth and the therapist were saying: 'The court forces us to meet; what do we do now?' The therapeutic interaction takes place then in a 'demilitarized zone' of the adolescent's warfare with society and parental authority." With the introduction of court authority, acting-out is blocked because of the new situation. The cycle of troublesome events perpetuated by the acting-out is interrupted. Simultaneously the crisis is intensified, making the patient more open to help.

The authors summarized their program description, stating that they "believed the combination of authority and psychotherapy (or even the judicious use of authority alone) as 'treatment' is particularly justified with adolescents because it can deal effectively with the tendency to act out and is appropriate to the current developmental stage of the patient." The court's authority both supports treatment and *is* treatment to some significant extent.

Comments and Follow-up Work. Here we have an example of behavioral scientists in two different functions. First, behavioral scientists were able to help to establish a program design by which the court's therapeutic interest and philosophy were utilized to assist juveniles in coming to grips with their personal needs and problems. In this sense, behavioral scientists were using their treatment function as a linkage to one of the court's basic missions and philosophical directions; that is, to achieve rehabilitation and ultimate diversion of young juveniles from the criminal justice system.

Secondarily, the example also illustrates the use of behavioral scientists in a research and development task. They helped to design a therapeutic program that assisted the court in meeting its objectives. Behavioral scientists were used to help create a program that matched the criminal justice system's requirements with the therapeutic development needs of young offenders. The juveniles were in danger of becoming absolute captives of the criminal justice system, a situation that would decrease the likelihood of their being treated. The linkage of justice with treatment requires that both court and therapeutic personnel be jointly involved in order to achieve successful program development. The behavioral scientist through this function acts as a bridge between the criminal justice mission and the psychological/psychiatric treatment mission. A complex interdisciplinary problem is dealt with in the manner required to solve it—a combination of law/justice and treatment initiatives.

There are other work topics. Behavioral scientists could:

1. Analyze the sentences given by a local court to determine whether they are exclusively punishment-oriented or whether they allow for some discretion with certain offender groups (e.g., juveniles).
2. Survey the staff of the court to determine the extent of their knowledge of and support for the dual mission of therapeutics and punishment.
3. Consult with a judges group to assist them in determining the court systems impact of the national pressure for tougher sentencing (e.g., higher caseloads, less willingness to negotiate pleas)

These suggestions lead to the question of integrating philosophy with action, the subject of our second case.

CASE SIXTEEN: MATCHING PHILOSOPHY WITH PRACTICE. A second problem common to all organizations including criminal justice ones is ensuring that organizational philosophy is consistent with the supposedly resulting policy and the actual day-to-day operations of the organization. The following example typifies the philosophy–policy–practice problems, illustrating how behavioral scientists might become involved in addressing the issue.

Gottfredson, Hoffman, Sigler, and Wilkins presented a paper in which they discussed the need for more explicit definition of the elements governing parole selection, in particular determinations of the weights that should be given to each element.[9] The study presents a method for conducting an analysis of parole board decisions that will help to make existing paroling policies more explicit.

The National Council on Crime and Delinquency conducted a study to identify the weights given to various parole determination criteria (e.g., prisoner's offense, prior record, educational employment history, drug and alcohol problems, etc.). The study sought to identify the criteria used by parole boards to determine whether a prisoner should be granted parole or should be subjected to further incarceration. To begin the analysis, a chart was constructed with one axis representing the offender's severity, the other reflecting parole prognosis (the "risk" of parole failure). The intersection of the axes would identify the expected decision. To create this decision matrix, eleven questions were used to determine the prognosis score, with six severity levels used in the severity scale. A chart was then created that listed the number of months that must be served before parole would be granted based on the prognosis and severity levels.

The authors believe their system to be in the early developmental stages. Even without complete refinement, it is useful in attempting to identify empirically the practical or operational results of parole policy. In effect it enables the organization to evaluate policy outcomes.

Comments and Follow-up Work.   In this case, behavioral scientists report the results of a developmental study designed to collect empirical evidence of the effects of paroling policy. This evidence could then be used to determine whether the operations of one court organization (and/or the criminal justice system as a whole) are consistent with a mission of helping the offender to make a swift and successful adjustment to community life. For example, are the parole decisions more severe than what was or is intended by the organization's mission? According to their *intended mission,* is the court willing to take more risk with offenders than is indicated by the empirical data developed by the behavioral science study? The risk issue raises the philosophy question in terms of risk-taking intent. The philosophy of the court may be to take a "calculated risk" in order to maximize offender opportunity for positive change and development. This may be reflected in a *policy* of some leniency but a *practice* of slow decision-making and quick revocation of parole. Here behavioral scientists contribute data to and help with an examination of that match: philosophy with policy with practice.

These are related subjects. Behavioral scientists could:

1. Research the court's sentences for first-offense juveniles, comparing them with a neighboring court in terms of their consistency with a therapeutic or a punishment philosophy.
2. Research the behavior of police officers at the arrest point with regard to their philosophical position and its match with their actions (e.g., tough enforcement orientation vs. service security orientation).
3. Conduct a training program for police officers informing them of how certain behaviors are perceived by the accused and how they increase the likelihood of a violent confrontation.

The two cases just presented are direct demonstrations of the goals/values issues that confront the courts. Behavioral scientists can inject themselves into the middle of these debates by providing both data and consultative assistance for problem solving. Once goals and values are established (both overtly and covertly), an organizational structure is developed to ensure their achievement. That is the next subject for potential behavioral scientist work—the structural subsystem.

STRUCTURAL SUBSYSTEM

This section concerns the organizational structure of the court system. As noted by Holten and Jones, there is now a commonly accepted view of the criminal justice system as a multilevel system "incorporating four major components: law enforcement, prosecution, courts, and corrections."[10] This section will briefly discuss the structure of the courts on both a macro and a micro level. It is useful to outline for the uninitiated reader and as a common starting base the types of courts that are found in the American system. Holten and Jones explain most clearly:

> There are two broad types of courts: trial and appellate. Trial courts are those that dispose of cases by verdicts reached after the facts are examined and the relevant law is applied. Appellate courts decide cases involving disputes over law or procedures that rise out of actions of trial courts.
>
> Trial courts—called courts of original jurisdiction because they are the first to deal with the case—are divided into at least two types:
>
> 1) Courts of general jurisdiction—sometimes superior courts—process cases in both civil and criminal law without special limitations as to the parties who may come before them or the subject matters with which they deal.
>
> 2) Courts of limited or special jurisdiction—sometimes referred to as inferior courts—process cases that fall within narrow limits as to parties or subject matter. Examples of these latter courts are small claims, probate, family, magistrate, and, in a few states, juvenile courts. (The latter, incidentally, usually handle all sorts of matters in which juveniles are the focus of the activity, thus combining civil with criminal functions.) Among the inferior courts, many keep no transcript of their proceedings and are thus called courts of non record.
>
> Appellate courts also fall into two broad types: intermediate courts of appeal and courts of last resort. Intermediate courts of appeal hear cases from trial courts. whereas courts of last resort (usually called supreme courts) are the ultimate level of appeal in each state.[11]

At every level of the court system (general, appellate, etc.) the issues to be addressed may relate to one or more of the following structural elements, identified by Daft:[12]

- Formalization
- Specialization
- Standardization
- Hierarchy of authority
- Decentralization
- Complexity
- Professionalism
- Personnel configuration

It is apparent from this short list that the court systems involve a wide range of organization and management issues within the general category of "structure." The task here is not to outline the structure of the full court system with all of its alternative organizational designs. For additional information on court organizational structure, there are many texts written on the system of criminal justice as a whole. These have specific references to court structural design that provide the interested reader with a detailed understanding (see, e.g., Kalmanoff,[13] Holten and Jones,[14] and others).

Instead the purpose here is to review what behavioral scientists can do. Behavioral scientists' functions in the area of court organizational structure include a wide range of possibilities, especially education and training, consultation, and research and development. The following examples illustrate some specific activities. In this model, the organizational structure elements are mostly the formal ones, not the informal. The latter topics concern work-group behaviors, attitudes, status, and influence systems and are discussed as a part of the psychosocial subsystem.

The structural subsystem was defined earlier as "the ways in which the tasks of the organization are divided (differentiation) and coordinated (integration). In the formal sense, structure is set forth by organization charts, by position and job descriptions, and by rules and procedures."[15] The question of the structure of the court system can be considered in several ways. We can describe how the system is structured on the state and federal level, and/or the individual organizational structure of each court system. There is obviously potential for a wide range of behavioral scientists' functions within the list of organization structure topics introduced above.

Structure could be examined from several different perspectives. First, structure is part of the organizing elements of the court as a whole. How does it contribute exactly? Second, structure involves the size of the court organization, whether it is large enough to be decentralized or small enough to be fully integrated. Could several courts be merged? Third, structure involves the nature of the technology. How are the individual court system's components arranged? Are there more productive arrangements? And last, structure concerns some relationship to the organization's environment, for example; the influences beyond the court system that affect its design and operation. How do these influences change, and how do they change the structure? The case example addresses structural boundaries.

CASE SEVENTEEN: PROBLEMS OF COURT BOUNDARIES. Courts have traditionally defined the boundaries of their system as *excluding* work *inside* prisons, which has been considered the work of the correctional system. But with regard to certain topics (e.g., prisoners rights) the court involves itself on a case-by-case basis—simply a judicial "interest." No boundaries are impenetrable, but on a larger scale this is an extension of the structure of the court's role. What is the role, and what structural effects does this incursion have? A case summary will make the point.

Kutak analyzed the nature of the increasing interest of judges in the activities of the correctional system, summarizing the changes as follows:

> Courts are assuming a new activism in their approach to corrections. Perhaps this is attributable to a growing impatience with American penology which uses, as Norval Morris observes, eighteenth and nineteenth century methods in the middle of the twentieth century. Four decisions this year suggest that the courts may take the lead in protecting the rights of prisoners with the same intensity and thoroughness that they have exercised for many years in the fields of race relations, rights of accused, and reapportionment. These cases signal a changing judicial attitude that must be recognized by those involved in the correctional process.[16]

Four cases were used to illustrate this development interest, in Arkansas,[17] Louisiana,[18] Rhode Island,[19] and New York.[20] Changes to each state's correctional systems were identified that were thought to result from the litigation. For example, in Rhode Island the structure of the classification and disciplinary system was altered to include five steps: written changes, investigation and review, hearing, administrative review, and maintenance of a record. The court's intervention produced a new structure within the correctional disciplinary system.

Comments and Follow-up Work. This illustrates structural change for the prison that was the result of court action. Would prison personnel have liked to know the potential effects? A behavioral scientist could provide some advance impact-planning by analyzing the litigation's likely effects on the correctional organization prior to the culmination of the case.[21] This would add a "change impact analysis function" to the structure of the courts. Behavioral scientists could be used as expert consultants engaged in a case-by-case impact analysis. They could become an ongoing activity—an applied research and evaluation function.

Does the new interest of the judges create a need for an expanded management structure to monitor and report on the correctional organization's response? If the court's role is expanding, the structure of its own organizational system must be expanded to incorporate that new technical activity. An appropriate alteration in its management structure may have to be made. Behavioral scientists could be engaged as *expert* management *consultants* to analyze the policy and procedural impact of the court's new activities, making recommendations for their integration into the system.

These two examples are not the sole opportunity here. Behavioral scientists could:

1. Research the impact of civil rights–oriented litigation on one area of the court (e.g., police holding practices) as to the nature of the changes that have occurred.
2. Research the impact of conflicting decisions by higher courts on the plaintiff's personal status (e.g., ability to pursue the case; total burden of the continuance without a problem solution).
3. Consult with the court, mediating a conflict between a judicial activist interested in improving prison conditions (e.g., medical services) and a resistant prison administration, helping them to negotiate a joint agreement without the use of litigation by an outside advocate.
4. As a consultant to corrections management, conduct a survey that collects and analyzes judges' perceptions of the need for change within corrections, using the data to develop new program ideas.

Perceptions of needs for structural change provide input to the discussion on structure and suggest the next subsystem—psychosocial—where individual attitudes and perceptions are particularly considered.

THE PSYCHOSOCIAL SUBSYSTEM SYSTEM

Every court has a psychosocial system, one of the five primary subsystems in the Kast and Rosenzweig model. The psychosocial subsystem was defined as follows:

A psychosocial subsystem . . . is composed of individuals and groups in interaction. It consists of individual behavior and motivation, status and role relationships, group dynamics, and influence systems. It is also affected by sentiments, values, attitudes, expectations, and aspirations of the people in the organization. Obviously this psychosocial subsystem is affected by external and environmental forces as well as by the tasks, technology, and structure of the internal organization.

These forces set the "organizational climate" within which the human participants perform their roles and activities.[22]

This subsystem includes both formal group dynamics and what has been called the "informal organization." It involves, along with attitudes and values, the interpersonal and group relations that supplement the formal patterns of communication, control, and structure within the organization.

To elaborate briefly, there is attention paid in this area to the values and norms of the informal groups, the group associations, the status hierarchies among the members of various informal groups, and the customs and usages of activities and behaviors that establish the "pecking order of the informal system." The skills of behavioral scientists are particularly useful for examining various aspects of this subsystem. For example, there is a long and vigorous history of social psychological work on the comparative analysis of formal and informal behaviors of persons within organizations.

What are some court-related subjects? Behavioral scientists might be called on to examine such group dynamics issues as cohesiveness among prosecutors, the effect of punishment severity and the expression of hostility among public defenders, group pressures and group standards of judges, the use of conflict to enhance development of young prosecutors, the detrimental effects of conflict and conflict resolution strategies in plea negotiations, methods for overcoming resistance to change in court philosophy, and considerations of informal social communications in court discretionary justice. Psychologists and other behavioral scientists have long been involved in examining individual motives and group goals, including the congruence of individual and group goals and the effects of cooperation and competition upon group process and group achievement of individual tasks. Other areas of interest in court systems would include leadership activities of court administrators and their comparative group performance. A key assumption behind this work is that there should be a firm understanding in the court system of the group dynamics within its informal structure.

An example cited in Chapter 2 is also applicable for discussion in this subsystem. What are the informal reactions of police to pretrial negotiations? Formally, the reaction will probably be consistent with formal departmental policy and public positions taken on the individual case. But policemen who have devoted considerable time to the investigation and arrest process might hold (and sometimes express) considerable hostility. Resentment of pretrial negotiations that involve plea bargaining may be expressed only when an informal group of officers is meeting over coffee or at the gym. How the court system and the greater criminal justice system may constructively utilize this conflict to yield issues of value to the court is a problem that behavioral scientists could help to address. They could begin the process, for example, by obtaining informal views of system participants through survey research.

Other points of conflict center on such issues as the selection of some personnel and the discipline and removal of others. Since personnel actions are a particularly sensitive topic, conflict of a highly emotional nature is generated, even at the opening of the issue. When certain groups such as judges become the subject, the stakes and the sensitivities are even higher because of those individuals' visible role in the system and the recognition that they are value transmitters through punishments and sentences. What methods would best be used to manage this kind of conflict? Behavioral scientists could be used in several functional roles, including those of con-sultant/mediator of the conflict or educator/trainer with regard to new methods of conflict resolution. Possibilities for the research function appear to be almost limitless.

This psychosocial subsystem is in one view the *implied* and *intuitive* aspects of the court's activities and the interactions of its individual par-ticipants. The first case illustrates the issue of the psychology of defendant–judge interaction.

CASE EIGHTEEN: PERCEPTIONS OF DELINQUENTS.   As a dem-onstration of these aspects of the psychosocial subsystem, one question that has surfaced concerns the "presentation style" of judges in the court-room. Commentators have asked, how are the judge's demeanor and be-havior experienced by young delinquents, and what effects do different styles have? Does style have an effect on the proceedings, either positively or negatively? Simultaneously, there is related interest in the projection of the young delinquent's own difficulties into the courtroom situation, thereby eliciting reciprocal actions and feelings from the judges. Behavioral scientists can provide information about this interaction process, as one case example illustrates.

Lipsitt conducted a study designed to focus on the juvenile offender's perceptions of and attitude toward his experience in court.[23] "If the judge is able to 'reach him' and respond to him in a meaningful manner, it may be possible to achieve participation by the offender in the court process." A positive and constructive interaction between judge and defendant could enhance the court's processes, could provide benefits to the individual defendant in terms of understanding and options, and could affect the ultimate judicial outcome. To develop data for anal-ysis, Lippsitt examined 265 boys appearing in juvenile court on a delinquency petition before two referees and four judges in three metropolitan centers in the Midwest. The boys were given twelve semantic differential scales. They rated themselves and the judges using pairs of words on a seven-point scale.

The findings of the study indicated that judges can be differentiated by the boys. Delinquents' reactions to the judges and the whole justice process are related to both their own predispositions and their experience in the courtroom. The author suggests that the study showed that the court can act as a "laboratory" that both enables and is a forum for the projection of dynamic processes in the youngster's personality. These projections and the overall court behavior pattern of the youth (in this "laboratory") may provide clues for future treatment and may suggest channels for rehabilitation.

Comments and Follow-up Work.   This study focused on the projection of the attitudes and values of the individual delinquent, but it is apparent that the judge's attitudes and values were involved as well. Here the behavioral scientist is shown in an activity that combines treatment and consulting functions through an applied research effort. He was brought in to examine an interactive psychosocial subsystem question. As a result of the engagement, the behavioral scientist discovered that the findings and observations of the interactive social and psychological processes in the court can be used to help to determine appropriate treatment directions for the delinquent. This is not a part of the formal agenda in the courtroom as it is traditionally defined. Instead a behavioral scientist has taken the informal system as it exists and developed a "treatment use" of it. Through the work, a method for treatment and an innovative use of behavioral science are demonstrated.

The psychosocial subsystem of the organization is a familiar one for behavioral scientists, allowing for easy identification of other topics. Behavioral scientists could:

1. Conduct a program for judges that uses role modeling and other behavioral demonstrations to educate them about alternative ways of interacting with juveniles, ways that would enhance the positive aspects of the experience.
2. Research prosecutor and public defender attitudes toward the pressure for increased toughness in sentencing, using the results as feedback for the judges relative to their sentence decision-making.
3. Consult with the court organization on ways to address the burnout of public defenders and public prosecutors (e.g., conducting a job redesign effort that would reduce troublesome job characteristics based on *their* identification of what those are).
4. Consult with the court on the design and development of a citizen's advisory board, helping the court to see its psychological benefits for certain groups (e.g., minorities) and the resultant increased sensitivities on the part of court personnel to these psychological issues.

The next case continues this interest in the psychological aspects of the court by examining the dynamics of the jury's group process. Since there are constant interactions of all participants in the court system, should we not consider the mutually interactive effects of jurors on each other? Furthermore how do these interactions affect the court's process of deciding guilt or innocence?

CASE NINETEEN: JURY PERSONALITY COMPOSITION. A task of prosecutors and defense attorneys is identifying and dismissing those potential jurors who are biased against their client's case. This has been done for the most part through experienced attorney "intuition." Behavioral science researchers are now getting involved in an effort to improve the accuracy of this intuition. One question is: does individual personality makeup affect jury outcome?

Buckout and associates investigated this problem by examining whether authoritarianism would affect a jury's decision making.[24] Specifically they were following up previous research that reported that "These findings suggest that a measure of authoritarianism . . . may be more useful in predicting behavior in group deliberations than in ascertaining gut reactions to a criminal case, the evidence, or the defendant." They constructed a simulated murder trial with authoritarians and equalitarians facing a guilty, not guilty pre-verdict. They summarized their findings as follows:

In a previous study we concluded that the authoritarian juror is "rigid" or resistant to change as a function of deliberation, and when he does change his verdict, he is more prone to change from not guilty to guilty. On the other hand, the equalitarian juror was labeled as more "flexible" or prone to change in the face of persuasive arguments during deliberations, and that change was more likely to go from guilty to not guilty. While the results of this study confirm our previous results, they indicate that interpersonal dynamics owing to the makeup of the jury may well be as important as, if not more important than, the mere personality label. Obviously, the pure authoritarian or pure equalitarian jury represents an ideal jury in the eyes of the prosecutor or the defense attorney, respectively. Such ideal situations, in an adversary system where both sides have a chance to select members of the jury, occur rarely. True to form, the pure juries lived up to the ideal expectations of them. That is, the pure authoritarian juries convicted more often than the equalitarian juries. Further, individual authoritarians convicted more often than equalitarians.[25]

The study suggests that there is an advantage to selecting jurors based on a personality characteristic (authoritarianism); that is, it has an effect on court process that can be predicted.

Comments and Follow-up Work. This case shows the behavioral scientist in an applied research role, but one that is very close to and associated with the assessment role. The research uses clinical assessment techniques to evaluate personality. Once the research demonstrates the utility of doing so, the behavioral scientist/clinician findings can be used for the actual work of attorneys and other court participants.

Other work in this area is possible. Behavioral scientists could:

1. Extend the research work on the impact of personality on jury behavior, incorporating the latest thinking about both intuition- and data-based thinking.
2. Research the impact of judge–jury interactions with regard to nonverbal as well as verbal cues, investigating effects on jury decision-making.
3. Survey local citizens' views of serving on juries, identifying both their perceived interests and resistances.

The survey data, for example, could be used to assist in such activities as jury recruitment.

THE MANAGERIAL SUBSYSTEM

One final subsystem completes our model of the court organization as a whole: the managerial subsystem. Kast and Rosenzweig have defined this subsystem:

> The managerial system spans the entire organization by directing the technology, organizing people in other resources, and relating organization to its environment. . . . One approach to the study of management focuses attention on fundamental administrative processes—planning, organizing, and controlling—that are essential if an organization is to meet its primary goals. These basic managerial processes are required for any type of organization—business, government, education—where human and physical resources are combined to achieve certain objectives. Furthermore, these processes are necessary regardless of the specialized area of management—production, distribution, finance, or facilitating activities.[26]

In the court organization, the managerial component involves particularly the coordinating of activities, the management of personnel, and the development and operation of performance and control systems. While these activities take a great deal of time, it must be remembered that "the managerial subsystem spans the entire organization by relating the organization to its environment, setting the goals, developing comprehensive, strategic and operational plans, designing the structure, and establishing control processes."[27] The court organization, like all other large organizational systems, requires a formal and effective management subsystem. There is a need for strong management that demonstrates leadership in designing the internal aspects of the legal system as well as relating the court to the sources of its environmental pressures, such as politics, environment, economics, law, and culture. The court's philosophy and its actions influence, and are influenced by, its management team's relations with its organizational environment.

At what points can behavioral scientists become involved in the managerial system of the courts? Clearly, as wide a range of possibilities exists here as in the other subsystems. Behavioral scientists can provide assistance in the traditional areas of planning, organizing, and controlling, for the court as a whole and/or its subparts (e.g., case scheduling). Behavioral scientists could be asked to develop performance systems for various personnel within the judicial system. As one or two of the case examples will illustrate, the evaluation of judicial performance is particularly troublesome and in need of outside assistance in terms of approaches, methods, and manpower. Involving behavioral scientists (e.g., industrial psychologists) with their knowledge of personnel performance systems and personnel assessment methodologies can be particularly productive and much more economical than do-it-yourself attempts. As a group, behavioral scientists represent a diverse pool of expertise from which the court can draw information relating to problems solved and methods used (e.g., information on personnel performance systems in other kinds of organizations).

What are the specific areas of the courts that are now especially confronted by management difficulties? Holten and Jones note that "there are several specific matters over which court administrators may exercise responsibility and in which innovative techniques are being employed. These include case flow or calendar management, witness and juror management, planning new courthouses, and managing existing courthouse space."[28] It is apparent that there is an executive/administrative group (court administrators) that is now beginning to exercise increasing leadership in this area of the court's system. Who is in the group who would need the contributions of behavioral science? The "court manager" was defined by Ruben, as Holten and Jones noted:[29]

He is known by different titles, but most typically he is called the court administrator. In different state or local court systems, he may also be referred to as a judicial administrator, a court executive officer, a court coordinator, administrative director, or executive secretary to the courts. He may be a state court administrator, with either administrative or coordinating responsibility for all courts in the state. He may be a trial court administrator with management responsibility for his local court. He may be a criminal court coordinator, managing the criminal division of a general trial court under the supervision of the trial court administrator. He may be a juvenile court administrator.[30]

The attention paid by Holten and Jones in their strong text underscores the court administrator's increasing tendency to be involved in a wide range of activities traditionally handled by other court participants, such as judges and attorneys from both the prosecution and the defense. The management work is increasing in quantity and complexity across a wide range of subjects. Courts are now setting up witness management programs. Case scheduling is critical and difficult, with overload volume. There are many new efforts under way to develop and design new facilities. Until this expansion is complete, managing existing space with increasingly large caseloads will be a significant managerial problem/challenge.

The range of potential applications of behavioral science in the managerial subsystem narrows somewhat in functional terms. It is fairly unlikely that either assessment and diagnosis or treatment functions would be much used. While it is possible that some court managers may need assessment, diagnosis, and treatment for work-related or personal problems, behavioral scientists are unlikely to be utilized very often. This is a limitation defined by the nature of the subject—management. The following examples tend to concentrate on the education and training, research, and consultation functions.

To match the functions with management work opportunity we need to ask: what elements constitute the managerial system? An answer to this question provides at least an introduction to topical areas of potential work for behavioral scientists in this subsystem. There are many views of what management is. A common one is that management is composed of four major elements:

- Planning
- Organizing
- Directing/leading
- Controlling

These four main topics will serve as organizers for our description of actual and potential behavioral science activities in this area of the organization.

Planning

Planning is "the selecting of missions and objectives—and the strategies, policies, programs and procedures for achieving them; decision making; the selection of a course of action from among alternatives."[31] Planning in the court organization in practical terms requires such activities as: establishing a calendar for receiving cases, determining which judges will preside over which trials, establishing priorities for cases, managing the backlog and delays of cases, dividing the work among court staff and affiliated groups, establishing case specializations for personnel, matching appropriate assignments with individuals, and in general ensuring that the coming work is expected and "planned for" in its total sense. Behavioral scientists can make useful contributions to planning activities, notably through their consultation, education and training, and research and development functions. It is possible that they may offer some assessment, diagnosis, and treatment services, but these are far less frequently required.

For example, behavioral scientists can become consultants to management helping to develop the court's strategic or long-range planning activities. This would involve process guidance in organizing the whole and subgroups for planning work, and mediating the conflicts that will arise over both the process and the substance. This was done by two behavioral scientists for a church-affiliated nonprofit nursing and community services organization.[32] One served as the internal consultant/coordinator while the other was the external consultant. The majority of the work was process-oriented during the one year needed to develop the plan. The consultants educated the group about planning and staffed the task forces. The five-year plan is in place and being used.

In other cases, behavioral scientists could become involved in the more technical aspects of planning, projections of future growth, and general data analysis work. For example, they could analyze census data, client load projections, and budgeting figures to help to determine the possibility of service expansion in the future. The identification and analysis of technical options is one planning activity that has already involved behavioral scientists, as the next case illustrates.

CASE TWENTY: A PLANNING/DECISION-MAKING PROBLEM. One problem that continually plagues the court system and one that creates quite a management problem is the overcrowding of jails. This in turn affects bail practices and the sentencing decisions that the courts must make. Behavioral scientists could be brought in on a consulting basis to develop a methodology for examining the problem and assisting the court in planning and organizing a response to this problem.

Roesch presented a method by which the short- and long-term effects of three traditional bail practices (release on recognizance, pretrial diversion, and expediting criminal case disposition) on the jail population can be predicted.[33] Only the predictable and measurable effects that implementation of the three alternatives could have on pretrial jail populations were addressed in the study.

The subjects for the research were unsentenced defendants in two county jail systems, located in Harris County, Texas and in Clark County, Nevada. The total number of subjects in Clark County was 73, representing approximately 25 percent of the total unsentenced population. The total sample in Harris County was 400, which represented approximately 50 percent of the total unsentenced population. A sixty-nine-item questionnaire was given to the presentenced defendant. The criteria developed by the Manhattan Bail Project were used to determine release on recognizance eligibility. Pretrial diversion eligibility was determined by whether or not the defendant was charged with a misdemeanor or a nonviolent felony. A ninety-day average length of incarceration prior to sentencing was used as the standard for estimating the effects of reducing the delay between arrest and disposition.

The author found that using release on recognizance in Clark County would have a minimal effect on the unsentenced population. In Harris County, on the other hand, release on recognizance could potentially reduce this population by about one third. Pretrial diversion was found to have a large impact on both jail populations. Finally, reducing the length of time between arrest and final disposition obviously has an effect on the unsentenced population.

Comments and Follow-up Work. This study illustrates a very practical outcome of an empirical test of several strategies for reducing the jail population. The information could have been developed by behavioral scientists in a consulting or an applied research role. The critical point is that a problem of significance to a particular court was addressed, with results that suggested recommendations for solution. Importantly, this problem solution was useful to both the individual court and the wider set of local, state, and federal courts; the findings had planning and management systems implications for the field as a whole.

Opportunities for engagement in the management planning aspects of the organization are expanding rapidly as more behavioral issues surface. Behavioral scientists could:

1. Survey the extent and nature of management planning now under way in court management, identifying who is doing the planning, what is being planned for, the planning methods used, and the costs and impact of the work.
2. Research the types of data used as the basis for the court management's planning work.
3. Educate court management about the types of organization planning techniques in use by or most suited for court management.

4. Consult with court management to help them establish a planning process, contributing ideas on design and acting as a facilitator to the initiation of the process.

Certainly planning leads up to and is a part of the organizing activity.

Organizing

Organizing is that aspect of the court organization which involves "establishing an intentional structure of roles in a formally organized enterprise."[34] The court administration is responsible for developing the structure of the system; for establishing the respective roles of judges, prosecutors, and attorneys; and for developing the information and management system that will support the total functioning of the court organization. This organizing can produce a structure as described earlier, but it is an activity or process as noted below:

In looking at organizing as a process, it is apparent that several fundamental inputs must be considered. In the first place, the structure must reflect objectives and plans because enterprise activities derive from these. In the second place, the structure must reflect the authority available to enterprise managers; this depends upon such social institutions as private property, representative government, and the host of customs, codes, and laws that both restrict and sanction individuals in operating a business, a church, a university, or any group venture. Authority in a given organization is, then, a socially determined right to exercise discretion; as such, it is subject to change.

In the third place, organization structure, like any plan, must reflect its environment. Just as the premises of a plan may be economic, technological, political, social, or ethical, so may be those of an organization structure. The structure must be designed to work, to permit contributions by members of a group, and to help people gain objectives efficiently in a changing future. In this sense, a workable organization structure can never be either mechanistic or static.

Fourth, the organization must be staffed with people. Obviously, the activity groupings and authority provisions of an organization structure must take into account people's limitations and customs. This is not to say that the structure must be designed around individuals instead of around goals and accompanying activities. But an important consideration—often a constraining factor for the organization architect—is the kind of people who are to be employed. Just as engineers consider the performance strength and weaknesses of materials going into their projects, so must organizers consider their materials—people.[35]

Behavioral scientists can surely contribute to analyses of, change in, research on, and development of various aspects of this organizing process. Two examples of work with special offenders demonstrate this point.

CASE TWENTY-ONE: ORGANIZING. The court constantly has the problem of what to do with offenders in need of clinical assessment and treatment. How does the court organize and deliver clinical services either directly or through referral? Can behavioral scientists contribute at the organizing level as well as the clinical service delivery level?

In a review of the psychologist's role in the courts, Kaslow noted the following descriptions of assessment and treatment activities:[36]

> In many court clinics, psychologists conduct presentence evaluations on the basis of which they can make appropriate recommendations to the court regarding case disposition. The use of psychiatric (and psychological) consultation at the point of sentencing is rare. However, signs of change are on the horizon. The Forensic Clinic at UCLA offers consultation to the court at the sentencing phase, and Suarez suggests that this program can serve as a model.[37] The clinic's agreement with the court is that the clinic will restrict exploration to issues pertinent to sentencing and disposition. Evaluation concentrates on "what is happening in the individual, how the offense fits in this context, (and) what the individual needs in terms of therapy and rehabilitation (including) specific discussion of these needs and the agencies that might need them."[38] In shifting the emphasis away from the verdict and toward the disposition, resistance has been encountered from judges and lawyers; therefore the clinic staff embarked on an extensive educational program with courtroom personnel. Suarez considers these collaborative efforts to have been fruitful.

Behavioral scientists can deliver these services directly or they can help to develop designs and structures that enable others to provide the services. Both assessment and educational functions are noted, the latter regarding the purpose of the newly organized unit.

The treatment function must also be established and a system of delivery organized. As Kaslow wrote:[39]

> Many juvenile and family courts now have their own clinics, either in court facilities or as nearby satellite centers, offering individual, family and group therapy to justice clients. Sometimes becoming involved in therapy is made a condition of probation; sometimes it is used as an alternative to probation or detention. Where no court clinic exists, or where additional services are needed, judges send court-mandated referrals to community mental health centers. Increasingly more courts are establishing their own clinics, since they are assured more rapid service, easy communication and no refusal of their referrals.

Last, she noted that the clinical psychologist can serve "as a consultant and staff trainer to clinic staff."

Comments and Follow-up Work. Here we see an example of the wide range of functions potentially provided in one part of the court's total organizing responsibilities. It is not difficult to see analogous opportunities for behavioral scientists in other units or service areas. Again the critical point is that there is a dual responsibility potential, both organizing and delivering the services, which requires a range of functions from consultation to research and development to treatment.

Other possibilities are open. Behavioral scientists could:

1. Research the new developments in organizational structures at the national levels (e.g., the new models tested) and consider how they might be adapted to fit local court needs (e.g., a matrix design).
2. Conduct an in-depth personal interview of judges and attorneys to determine what organizational problems exist; without predefining a set of possibilities, allow the problems to "emerge" from the interviews.
3. Analyze the changing values in the culture for their effects on court structure (e.g., increasing concern for punishment and a general fear of environment safety limit the options for community alternative to prison program sentences *and* simultaneously increase the "level of security" requirements in community facilities).
4. Consult with the court to help to solve the diminishing public resources versus increasing court costs problem; offer to design/redesign the organization to increase the efficiency.

In addition to the broader concerns of "whole system" organizing, there are specific subareas that must be addressed, as the following case illustrates.

CASE TWENTY-TWO: SPECIAL SERVICES ORGANIZATIONAL PROBLEM. A most troublesome problem for the courts is how to design, develop, and operate special services. One kind of special service is labeled "forensic services." It can be further delimited to include provision of mental health services to clients in first contact with or already in the criminal justice system. An organizational debate current in the field is about whether to centralize or decentralize these services. Which is more *cost-effective?* Which is more *clinically effective* for the individual, in terms of providing both criminal justice and treatment services?

Two professors demonstrated how behavioral scientists could provide some research and consultation consideration of these issues. In a study published in 1976, Laben and Spencer presented a discussion of the issue of whether to decentralize forensic services. They noted that "a major reform in these units can be effected by the administrative decision to decentralize the facilities. From decentralization can come the additional necessary reforms and therapies and services. Without it, such reforms can be impeded until the opportunity for them no longer exists."[40] In their analysis, the authors summarize the problem, including some of its historical aspects. They identify the pressures for change, particularly "the isolation and security of the facility (which has) allowed communities, agencies, and other institutions to indulge in preventive detention and to maintain the residents at a distance for their alleged 'dangerousness'."[41] They examined the cost and the legal and service issues. In terms of cost, it first appeared that centralized services could save money. But, with waiting times and the difficulties of admission, many of the service facilities continued to bear much of the cost in spite of the fact that centralized facilities existed.

In summary, they identified the following as results of the decentralization of services to mentally ill citizens in the criminal justice system:

1. Because of the reduction in census, the staff social workers had time to contact patients' families and other significant and community contacts.
2. Because of the reduced census and increased linkages with the patients' origin communities, shorter hospitalizations were evidenced.
3. The decentralization of forensic hospitalization enables mental health professionals to work with forensic patients on a part-time basis.
4. As more mental health professionals throughout the state system came in contact with forensic patients, a differentiation in their minds began to take form. The link between the development of forensic programs and the need for greater maximum security in hospitalization became undone.
5. As hospital staffs in Tennessee became adjusted to receiving forensic patients those who became dangerous in some way seemed to be treated in a different light. Although initial requests for maximum security hospitalization for "security risks" did not decline at first, the number of times a central office consultant could successfully intervene to prevent unnecessary maximum security hospitalization increased.
6. All of the intervention to decentralize forensic services resulted in reduction in security surrounding forensic services.[42]

Comments and Follow-up Work. This study illustrates an example of a behavioral science intervention in two significant problems for the court. How are the facilities for the services required by mentally ill offenders organized? And, how are patients assigned to various facilities? While the issue here is closely related to the intersection of various service systems—the community mental health system, the court system, and the corrections system—someone must have overall responsibility. The courts can allow this to become a responsibility of either mental health or corrections. But they will nevertheless retain some responsibility for making a determination at the time of judicial disposition. With a decentralized forensic system, courts can aid in ensuring that the offenders are placed in service facilities close to their home.

While this particular study was essentially a case analysis of the decentralization problem, it did present excellent data with which to consider the issue. That is, the common and all-too-frequent mind-set that "centralization of services is better" was undercut by this case example.

In addition, behavioral scientists could:

1. Research the numbers and types of special services units that have been created and must be managed by the courts (e.g., forensic psychiatry units) with an analysis of their individual problems.
2. Provide educational sessions on the new special services available and how they fit the existing organizational structure, including referral linkages, management responsibility, and authority distribution.
3. As consultants help the court to determine the need for a special services unit and its financial feasibility.

One aspect of special units' needs analysis is personnel, which is an individual topic with its own set of work opportunities.

Personnel. A major area of the management subsystem involves the organizing or personnel, including recruitment, supervision, and performance appraisal. This aspect of the court system offers many opportunities for the involvement of behavioral scientists. Some behavioral scientists (e.g., industrial and personnel psychologists) have been concerned as a part of their core professional interest with the personnel function. Three key areas that have received close attention are recruitment, selection, and personnel performance.

Recruitment is "the process of attracting candidates from either inside or outside the organization who are qualified for and interested in the position."[43] The courts, like other organizations, are responsible for recruiting their personnel. A problem for managers of the court system is identifying the best processes and procedures for doing so. This may require an assessment of external and internal recruitment requirements, the former involving the use of such media as newspapers, agencies, colleges, personal contacts, and associations. Internal recruitment issues would concern promotions, transfers, career planning, and transition management. Behavioral scientists might be asked to examine current processes; or to relate the organization's current procedures to what is now the state of the art. Closely related is development of a system for forecasting human resource needs including specific knowledge and skill requirements.

A second aspect of personnel work involves selection, "the process of choosing the most qualified person from the available pool of candidates."[44] Selection involves such steps as résumé review, application screening, personal interviews, reference checks, physical examinations, and sometimes psychological testing. Behavioral scientists can contribute to designing, developing, and operating systems for aiding the selection process at any one of these points. The organizing challenge is significant, as there is a wide range of personnel within the court system, including judges, prosecutors, court managers, and other staff. As in non-justice-related organizations, the court can use both education and training with regard to new selection processes and procedures, and consulting advice directed at specific problems that are encountered as a result of the uniqueness of the court.

A third aspect of personnel activity is performance appraisal, "a formal written process for periodically evaluating managers' performance." Organizing a performance appraisal system is a necessary part of every organization's functioning, with the court system certainly no exception. Huse notes the following key elements of organizing a performance appraisal system:

1. *Work Improvement.*   A subordinate may need to obtain information about the improvement of personal performance.
2. *Salary Administration.*   The manager may need to review carefully the performance of subordinates in order to determine appropriate salary action.
3. *Information Storage for Administrative Action.*   Most organizations need data about employees to be used in future administrative actions, such as promotion, demotion, or transfer.
4. *Isolation of Training Needs.*   Clear, current information about the strengths and weakness of the organization's members is needed if the organization is to create appropriate and timely development and training programs.
5. *Selection of New Employees.*   Prediction of future performance is based largely on the understanding of past performance. Thus, employers used appraisals of current employees to validate tests that will be applied to new employees.[45]

These elements can be related to specific personnel and personnel groups within the court. For example, how would behavioral scientists be used to address the performance concerns of judges, including: tenure, competence, removal, assignment, qualifications, training, discipline, promotion, and development? The cases to follow offer examples of behavioral scientists' involvement in performance appraisal. The issues and problems in this area will most likely be addressed by behavioral scientists functioning as educators, trainers, and consultants. Basic research in this area is quite active, but it has little direct application to the court in an operational sense.

A second court personnel group that further illustrates the issues are the prosecutors. What are the major conceptions of the prosecutorial role? What are the aspects of the job that involve plea bargaining and jury selection, and how are they evaluated? Where are the best candidates drawn from? What kinds of supporting staff and facilities are needed? Can we develop good descriptions of preparatory education for prosecutors and for continuing education programs once they are on the job? Behavioral scientists could design and/or deliver parts of this education and training. They could also be invited by prosecutors to analyze aspects of their job system. In the latter case they would be acting in the expert consultation role.

The following two examples illustrate the nature of behavioral scientists' involvement in personnel work. The first concerns organizing a performance review system for police; the second deals with manpower distribution.

CASE TWENTY-THREE: POLICE PERFORMANCE. How do we monitor and control the performance of certain of the court organization's components? On an individual level, the issue is job performance. On the organizational level, it is unit performance. The problem addressed here is the police unit's rating measures: what are the options, and which are best?

Marx examined alternative measures of police performance in order to identify those measures that would aid in and support evaluation and accountability and contribute to reforms of the system. He identified the following list:[46]

internal (sergeants, self-reported rates, inspections)

supervisors–peers–self–citizens—single or multiple indirect (internal bureaucratic regulations such as those about appearance)

subjective–objective production rates; goals (how much—number of arrests, tickets, field interrogations)

general qualities (integrity, appearance; this is often part of a citywide form)

law enforcement–community service—conflict management punishment for failure (penalties for failure to live up to bureaucratic regulations or achieve expected production rates) individual (number of field interrogation reports one man writes)

what others do—comparing one man with an average for the department or all departments nationally

an absolute ideal standard, e.g., having every citizen report he feels safe or a rule about never shooting into a crowd

These were considered as a set of options with the concluding comments providing an excellent linkage to the organizational control aspects of managerial work:

> Performance measures, of both an individual and organizational nature, are crucial for understanding the workings of a police department and for administration.
> Such measures can indicate the extent of compatibility and trade-offs among various goals. They can indicate the extent to which various segments of the community (either geographical or social such as race, age, class, etc.) receive equivalent police service, or have equivalent needs for police services. They can help assess the consequences of particular programs and experiments.
> They can identify areas where performance is particularly weak or strong. They can permit a more rational allocation of resources, and selection, training, placement and promotion procedures linked to actual needs. They can help establish equitable workloads among personnel. They can be important factors in developing a reward system more closely geared to the kinds of performance valued by police administrators and citizens. They can be factors in helping clarify what is expected of a police officer and the nature of the police role.[47]

The final summary includes a recommendation for further emphasis on the "microlevel work" of selection, training, evaluation, promotion, etc.—traditional areas of personnel activity.

Comments and Follow-up Work. This case is an example of behavioral scientists' involvement in organizational control aspects of police work. The function represented is a combined one of applied research and education—research on the indicators reported to "educate" the police management community. It is fairly evident that Marx could also be brought into the system as an expert consultant to provide expert knowledge of the performance indicators options.

Behavioral scientists working in this area could:

1. Research the range of performance systems used by courts in different regions and at different levels.
2. Provide an educational seminar on new performance techniques.
3. Provide an educational seminar on methods used by court personnel to avoid burn-out.

These are personnel problems that involve the employees already on the job. There is the problem of an inadequate number, as the next case indicates.

CASE TWENTY-FOUR: MANPOWER PROBLEM—PROBATION AND PAROLE.   One area in which behavioral scientists can become involved is that of manpower planning, including manpower distribution. While the subject area involves all personnel, the problem is especially acute in probation and parole. The hard question often confronting administrators of court organizations is that of how to meet the caseload requirements in their parole and probation departments. One mechanism frequently suggested as a way to add personnel resources is the use of volunteers. Behavioral scientists could be involved in several different ways with regard to volunteer use. For example they could design and develop a model volunteer program, or they could evaluate the usefulness of a model developed by others. The following case example illustrates one attempt to examine the idea of volunteer efforts.

Andrews, Young, and Wermeth conducted a study to determine the feasibility of using community volunteers in counseling.[48] The study was part of a demonstration project on the effects of short-term structured group counseling in prisons. A theoretical framework for using volunteers in group work with criminals was cited: the differential association theory. According to this theory, attitudes and beliefs favorable to lawbreaking are learned through association with criminal patterns and isolation from anticriminal patterns. Reversal of these attitudes and beliefs would result from association with the anticriminal patterns of volunteers.

The program was described with start-up activities requiring weekly meetings of offenders and volunteers. Personal, social, and moral aspects of the law were discussed, and attitude measures toward law and law violation were taken. For the main part of the study, twenty residents of two minimum security institutions and eleven female undergraduate volunteers were used. Each volunteer participated in an orientation meeting before the community group sessions began. Offenders were recruited through announcements over the public address system and notices on bulletin boards. The community groups met for eight weeks, one day per week. Each session lasted ninety minutes, with thirty-minute unstructured coffee-break sessions. The discussions during the sessions were guided by volunteers with predetermined topics they were to try to discuss.

The researchers examined the results of the program, including: comparison of volunteer and offender attitude measures concerning tolerance for violation of the law, awareness of limited opportunity, law and judicial process, value of employment, and value of education. Pre- and post-session attitude measurements were taken for the volunteers and offenders. Measures were also taken for a controlled group of incarcerated offenders and a controlled group of volunteers. They found significant pre-treatment differences between offenders and volunteers concerning identification with criminal others (friends, associates), tolerance of law violation, respect for the law, and awareness of limited opportunity. Control group offenders showed increased identification with criminals and increased tolerance for law violations, while the offenders' treatment group showed decreased identification and no difference on tolerance. The control group offenders devalued education and employment, while the treated offenders did not do so. The treatment had minimal effects on the volunteers.

Comments and Follow-up Work.   This program illustrates one way volunteers can make a contribution toward reducing probation and parole personnel shortages. The study indicated that volunteer counselors could be used to supplement probation and parole counseling efforts. This innovative use of personnel had positive effects for the offenders and no negative side-effects for the volunteers, at least in terms of value and attitude change.

Here the behavioral science function is an applied research one, with some theoretical elements. Essentially the study design was a summative evaluation of the volunteer counseling in the probation/parole program. The evaluation had very specific implications for the court's probation/parole personnel problem and could have been conducted for just that purpose. Since the program was found to be successful, there could be further follow-up studies examining the design options available and an implementation plan for expansion of the program.

Other topics in the personnel field involve the full range of human and industrial relations issues. Behavioral scientists could:

1. Research the types of productivity programs available for increasing the use of existing personnel.
2. Conduct an educational seminar on productivity and quality of working life for court supervisors.
3. Consult with management as process consultants, helping the organization to design and implement its own productivity improvement program.

These kinds of activities require an invigorated management with real leadership. These issues too can be the subject of behavioral science work.

Directing and Leading

This aspect of the management subsystem involves "clarifying, guiding, teaching, and encouraging participants in an enterprise to perform effectively and with zeal and confidence."[49] In this part of management, the manager or chief executive of the court organization is responsible for establishing leadership. Leadership is obviously necessary for realizing the organization's purposes as defined in the goals and values subsystem, using the structure that was designed to support both technical activities and people needs (the psychosocial subsystem). This directing/leading is the pattern of behavior of the management team that produces or collaboratively results in an employee group that willingly and enthusiastically acts to achieve the mission and goals of the organization.

Some of the directing/leading issues that could become the subjects of behavioral scientists' work in the court organization would include:

- The question of who the leaders are—judges or executives
- Formal versus informal leadership
- Authoritarian versus democratic leadership
- Listening as a leadership tool
- Development of subordinates
- Protection of organizational values
- The group's expectancies

The number of studies in all fields of leadership and organizational directing is voluminous. Obviously many of these studies have some relevance to the management of the court organization, while others are more industry-specific and would be less easily transferable (e.g., those that address issues of technological obsolescence, as in the steel industry). With some parallels to the medical area, the court organization's management team must confront the fact that they must direct and lead professionals who know themselves to be a key but *autonomous* aspect of the organization (i.e., judges, defenders, prosecutors). This situation requires more persuasion and negotiation than would be used in the management of other organizations, where the leadership can be more directive. Since the authority relations are unclear and the presence of professional managers is relatively new, behavioral scientists have many opportunities for research on leadership and the related activities involved in directing the court. The following case reports on only one aspect of this wide territory.

CASE TWENTY-FIVE: JUDICIAL LEADERSHIP. Who leads in the courtroom? What are the basic nature and characteristics of the leader? How can these characteristics be developed, refined, or reinforced? These are subjects for scrutiny by behavioral scientists, as the following case indicates.

Saks and Hastie examined the judge's role in the courtroom in an effort to define what role exists and to identify some possible recommendations or suggestions. They noted that: "In the public eye, the judge is the central actor in the courtroom. Of all the participants in the legal process, he or she is the most prominent symbolically, the most prestigious, and the most powerful during the trial itself." This view leads the authors to an analysis of judicial background, arraignment and bail, plea bargaining, instructions to the jury, and sentencing with regard to their contributions to the judge's role set. For example, in the decision on sentencing, they note that the courtroom "leader" is freed of the laws, court rules, and roles of the other participants, allowing full freedom in decision making. This unbounded discretion has in turn contributed to a great range of sentences for the same or similar crimes.

They conclude their analyses with the following summary of the psychology and technical activities of the judge:

> This chapter on the psychology of the trial judge began with a review of the tasks performed by the judge in the courtroom. There followed a short section on the nature of individual differences between judges, emphasizing the diversity of personal characteristics to be found on the bench. Next the bail-setting process was explored in an extensive analysis of two studies by Ebbesen and Konecni. Experimental and correlational methods were compared, and a mathematical averaging model of the trial judge's decision-making policy was examined. A short review of research on the judge's communications with the trial jury, instructions during the trial, was presented. The general conclusion that the trial judge's instructions could be improved in comprehensibility and effectiveness was advanced. Finally, the chapter concluded with a summary of research on sentencing policies.[50]

The work examines the judge as court leader in certain technical areas including the communications aspects that cut across all activities. Areas of and methods for improvement were also presented as one outcome of the work.

Comments and Follow-up Work.   Here the behavioral scientist is operating in an applied research and educational role. Judicial leadership is analyzed with suggestions for alternative means of behaving, and some possible uses of new methods are given. Conceivably, the authors could be engaged by a judge to examine these aspects in his or her courtroom. In a consulting role the authors could provide valuable suggestions for system improvement on a collaborative, interactive basis. These are just two examples. Behavioral scientists also could:

1. Research the potential/actual role conflict between court administrators (the new managers) and judges (the traditional managers), identifying ways to avoid and/or resolve the conflict.
2. Research the male/female ratio among judges, including regional differences and the development of a set of strategies for increasing the number of women judges.
3. Consult with a judges group regarding the use of mandatory retirement versus a performance review system, working on such issues

as criteria for the reviews and a process that is characterized by fairness to all parties.

Organizational Development. One directing/leading topic that deserves special attention is the behavioral scientist's involvement with management in organizational development initiatives. While this may be considered a part of the consultation function, the increasing interest in organization development efforts deserves special notice. This activity is defined by Gray and Starke:

> Organization development is a long-range effort to improve an organization's problem solving and renewal processes, particularly through a more effective and collaborative management of organization culture— with special emphasis on the culture of formal work teams—with the assistance of a change agent or catalyst and the use of the theory and technology of applied behavioral science, including action research.[51]

Using this definition as a guide, the court could involve the behavioral scientist in a long-range effort to improve the organization as a whole, or specific parts of it. If a behavioral scientist were engaged, at least one year and perhaps three to five years would be needed to develop a program of significant change in the organization's design and functioning. A discussion of the approach will illustrate.

During this developmental period of time, an intensive inspection of problem-solving processes within the organization would be made, resulting in setting recommendations for new methodologies. The organization development process depends on a collaborative orientation to management, in that the methodology by which the organization is developed and enhanced is through teamwork between various levels of decision-makers. Importantly, the target in general is the organizational culture, either as whole or within a department or division. Deal and Kennedy[52] and Schein[53] have considered the nature of culture with implications for how it is changed. Gray and Starke define culture as including "accepted patterns of behavior, norms, organizational objectives, value systems, the technology used to produce goods and services—in short, all factors that allow us to differentiate one organization from another."[54] Briefly, organizational development focuses first on the goals and values system but rapidly moves to a consideration of all subsystems simultaneously.

The organizational development approach targets the formal work teams, asking them to self-analyze their activities, often with the use of a *change agent*.[55] This is someone who will guide the change process, usually either an internal or external consultant (a behavioral scientist in some/many cases). Used this way, the linkage to the consultation function of the behavioral scientist is most precise. The consultant may use a single study with phases or a series of action researches to assist the organization in defining its change goals and in monitoring its progress toward those goals. Action research first involves identifying organizational problems, then collecting and analyzing data on those problems. Specific actions are initiated to address the identified problems, with a follow-up evaluation determining whether or not those actions were successful. This follow-up is then used to feed back data to the initial action research effort to generate another round of problem identification and change strategies.

Most prominent of the behavioral science functions used in organizational development are those of research and consulting. Action research is sometimes seen as a part of a larger organizational development strategy. Consultants are usually engaged for the purpose of problem solving and/or changing organizations—a natural and appropriate developmental activity.

CASE TWENTY-SIX: THE PAROLE OFFICER RECORD PROBLEM. Management has a chronic challenge with information systems in almost all organizations. Designing and developing the first generation of the system is difficult because of hardware, software, and people problems. Creating successful ongoing operations is equally difficult. Behavioral scientists can and do get involved in information systems work, often through the organizational-development–oriented consultation function. How does information system development relate to subunits within the court systems?

McCleary analyzed "How Parole Officers Use Records" in order to demonstrate that the information contained in them reflects not only parolee behavior, but data derived from the interaction of parolee, parole officer (PO), and the work system. He notes in opening that:

A parole bureaucracy uses its records to classify and process men released from prison. Assuming only this internal use, parole records should give an accurate description of parolee behavior according to the classification criteria. In fact, parole records are more likely to reflect the needs and problems of parole officers (POs). I attribute this bureaucratic dysfunction to the discretion allowed POs in gathering and reporting information. In most cases, the PO himself decides what information will actually go into the official record. By exercising editorial discretion, the PO can suppress information that might make his job difficult or include information that might facilitate work goals or objectives. This is how POs use their records.[56]

His analysis produced five reasons for underreporting (not using the information system to its full extent):

1. Full reporting cuts into the probation officer's "free" time.
2. Full reporting places the probation officer in jeopardy.
3. Probation officers believe that the Department of Corrections evaluates their performance favorably on the basis of low caseload return to prison rates.
4. Full reporting may result in "busy work" for the probation officer.
5. A probation officer may restrict his options by reporting a violation.

The PO was found to use records for three purposes: "[to] (1) initiate a record to threaten or coerce a parolee, (2) initiate a record to eliminate a troublesome parolee, or (3) initiate a record that will protect himself and his Department of Corrections superiors."

The study had two major conclusions. As demonstrated by the study, the records obviously do not reflect actual parolee behavior. There is a significant error in the collection and presentation of the data.

A second, more important implication concerns the role of the bureaucracy in the various uses of records. Career contingencies in the Department of Corrections are such that Probation Officers are rewarded for producing "bad" records and punished for producing "good" records. The Department of Corrections realizes some political benefit from the dynamic operation of these contingencies but it does so at the price of a straightforward loss of data. That the Department of Corrections can classify and process men released from prison even in a total information vacuum suggests that the Department of Corrections per se makes no decisions of any consequence. Classification decisions are instead left up to the street-level bureaucrat, that is, to the Probation Officer and to other criminal justice agencies.[57]

Although more implied than directly stated, this work is a prelude to revision of the information system through the intervention of the behavioral scientist.

Comments and Follow-up Work.   This case demonstrates the behavioral scientist's skill as an analyst of the behavioral aspects of information systems development. This is the diagnostic step of an information system review.[58] The work is here carried out as applied research, much in the nature of a qualitative evaluation.[59,60] It is quite possible (and frequently is the case) for the behavioral scientist to be called in as a consultant to management in response to an identified information systems problem (e.g., poor data, or data irrelevant to management decision-making needs). Either the expert or the process consultation functions would be used. The latter would engage the parole officers in an interactive planning process through which consultant, parole officers, and management would collaboratively redesign the information system. The whole process is an organizational development one designed to increase the usefulness of the data system to management and to the organization as a whole.

In this general topic area, behavioral scientists could:

1. Research the actual management uses of the parole record, conducting a systems analysis of the flow of information and the purpose of the record for various users, concluding with recommendations for modification of the record or the use process.
2. Conduct an educational seminar for parole officer managers on the primary and secondary use of record data for case management and performance reviews.
3. Consult with parole office management, helping to develop a design for an organizational-development–oriented evaluation based on parole record data (involving staff in the process and using the report to create a change plan for future system refinement).
4. Consult with management regarding the use of parole record information as it currently exists, role-modeling how to feed back and analyze data for staff.

The use of data leads us quite naturally to a concern for controlling the organization's activities, the final area of management work.

Control

The last aspect of the management subsystem involves control. Controlling is "the managerial function of measuring and correcting performance of activities of subordinates in order to assure that enterprise objectives and plans are being accomplished." Control is the mechanism by which management determines whether performance is progressing according to the intended overall plan, with inclusion of the individual objectives established for specific aspects of the court organization. According to Koontz, O'Donnell, and Weihrich, control processes are somewhat generic to all organizational systems. For example, Koontz et al. note that:

> Control techniques in systems are essentially the same for case, office procedures, morale, product quality, or anything else. The basic control process, wherever it is found and whatever it controls, involves three steps: (1) establishing standards, (2) measuring performance against these standards, and (3) correcting deviations from standards and plans.[61]

The first step in establishing control is defining and establishing the standards for the court organization in every aspect of its work. There is increasing consensus among experts that this is done more effectively if standards are established through a participative process. The process should involve both the executive management team and the technical people who will be responsible for helping the organization achieve the standards.

Once standards are created, measuring performance against these standards is the next step, which requires a data system. Much of the work involved in developing and operating control systems is focused on the design, implementation, and use of data systems. When information systems are fully operational, they are the basis for management's varied, detailed, and exacting involvement in control processes.

The last step of the control process, an integral one to the information development and acceptance phase, is using the information to correct deviations from intended plans. This involves analysis of the data, presentation of results to users, and construction of a response plan. In this way the information system is used to manage the organization in a general sense and to produce a continuing organizational development process, department by department.[62]

* Control systems design and use are part of the organizing responsibility of the executives in the managerial subsystem. But review of performance (e.g., of judges and other personnel) is a primary example of the essence of control work. The organizing managers in the managerial subsystem must ensure that a control system exists. For our purposes, the control activity involves both the design and the actual use of the control system, with both aspects having work opportunities for behavioral scientists.

CASE TWENTY-SEVEN: JOB PERFORMANCE EVALUATION. One of the tasks for management is evaluation of individual and group job performance. This is a function for which behavioral scientists could be called in on a consulting basis to assist management. If there had not been any work done on developing the performance system, behavioral scientists would be involved in an "organizing of the control system" activity. However, that is not likely to be the case in many organizations in the 1980s. Most behavioral scientists would be engaged as consultants or applied researchers to assist in revising a troubled system, or to further develop the existing system (e.g., for improved productivity). Both methods and whole approaches are suitable subjects. The following case is one example of the survey method and a general methodological review.

Koebel presented an analysis of the results of a survey that was designed to evaluate judges.[63] The purpose of Koebel's study was to conduct and then critically examine an evaluation survey of judges in Louisville, Kentucky. The study was first to evaluate the judges, and then to provide an "evaluation of the evaluation" on six points related to quality control, questionnaire design, and differences between lawyers. The study used a survey of attorneys' opinions for the data on judicial performance.

A twenty-seven-question evaluation form was mailed to 2000 lawyers, who were asked to respond only if they had substantial professional contact with the judge.

The average number of responses to each judge was 270. The questions were grouped into four broad categories: judicial temperament, court management, judicial integrity, and legal ability. There were five possible responses to each question: No Opinion, Very Likely, Likely, Unlikely, and Very Unlikely. Fourteen questions were expressed as positive attributes, and thirteen were expressed as negative attributes.

One result of the study was to begin to identify a method by which judges could be examined as to their performance, albeit somewhat indirectly. There was some contribution to performance review, as the results are one indicator of quality. Accuracy of the indicator was a concern.

There were no consistently negative evaluations on any individual question for all judges as evaluated by any given respondent; thus a punitive bias in response could be eliminated. The questionnaire design allowed for the evaluation of seventeen judges. Response rate decreased according to how far back a position was placed in the questionnaire sequence; but since this decrease was minute, it was considered inconsequential. This indicated that the questionnaire was sufficiently accurate to be reliably used as an evaluation tool. A last result was a finding of differences between lawyers. A self-selected sample with too few or too many lawyers in a particular category, or the length or size of practice could produce biased results, but these biases are thought to be minor. Self-selected samples were recommended as the methodological finding.

Comments and Follow-up Work.   This case presents a methodology for developing data on judges' performance in the court. It is an illustration of the behavioral scientists' contribution to developing the methodology and procedures while simultaneously collecting information specifically useful to one court's management control efforts. The plan presented here was not suggested to be the total control system for judicial management, only one aspect of it. Multiple indicators generated by multiple methods would be the most desirable judicial control design.

In this case as in others the applied research and consulting functions are closely linked, particularly when the consultants work in a research mode (e.g., expert consultation using a scientific process model). Readers should keep in mind that judges are only one of the personnel groups in the court organization. Public defenders and prosecutors might use an adaptation of this model, expanding its utility.

In addition to these possibilities, behavioral scientists could:

1. Research the job performance systems now in use in a local court system, comparing them to state-of-the-art systems in national use.
2. Educate court administrators in systems used in industrial settings, recommending systems that have been/can be used in the court organization.
3. Consult with management, helping to revise a performance review system that has been labeled "unfair" by employees (or conduct a

survey to secure employee suggestions about alternatives or redesign possibilities).

There are many areas to control, including such specific decisions as competency.

CASE TWENTY-EIGHT: CONTROLLING COMPETENCY DECISIONS AND COSTS. Most courts have a significant problem in determining whether defendants are competent to stand trial, as illustrated earlier in Case 6. Behavioral scientists can contribute to solving this problem in two ways. First, they can be involved through the assessment and diagnosis function. They provide assessments of defendants' abilities that are used in the court's decision making. Second, they can be asked to examine the strength of the process used to determine competency. This is a procedural process evaluation that requires a consulting role, one oriented more toward improving the management and control of the competency process than to delivering services. It is the latter concern for which this next case is presented.

Roesch examined the methods used by mental health professionals to determine a defendant's competency to stand trial.[64] Through the review he hoped to "provide a better understanding of decision rules that mental health professionals have used to determine competency to stand trial," and to determine if lengthier psychiatric examinations would improve the accuracy of competency decisions. The author noted that most state laws allow courts to call on mental health professionals for recommendations concerning competency. However, many professionals are unaware that few courts disagree with their recommendations. Even with this implied power over decision making, few states give the professionals specific guidelines for the assessment. Professionals are simply called on to determine whether the defendant has sufficient ability to consult with his lawyer with reasonable understanding; whether he has a rational and factual understanding of the proceedings against him.

In the study, the author analyzed court data, comparing differences between groups of defendants who were found to be incompetent and competent, respectively. The data used were developed from a large study of legal and mental health issues and procedures related to competency in North Carolina. One group of subjects included individuals initially found incompetent, treated, and later returned to court as competent. In the other group, subjects were individuals found competent immediately. The study's total data base included information about demographics, length of present hospitalizations, prior hospitalizations, psychiatric diagnosis, and narratives from hospital reports such as the mental status examination and the diagnostic conference report.

Roesch found several differences between competent and incompetent defendants: "incompetent defendants were usually seen as psychotic or mentally retarded but competent defendants were not; incompetent defendants were described as confused, hallucinating, delusional, etc., while competent defendants were described as having no major symptoms.'' Roesch also presented the observations about the reports that were sent back to the courts. Most importantly, the reports often contained comments irrelevant to competency, comments that were unsubstantiated.

Finally, Roesch found evidence to suggest that the amount of time spent in the hospital for evaluation may not improve the accuracy of competency decisions. He suggested that an interview alone, which could be conducted in a noninstitutional setting, would be sufficient for decision making in most cases.

Comments and Follow-up Work. In many court systems, the procedures and processes used to establish competency are quite elaborate and expensive. In this example, a behavioral scientist examined the procedures with one quite significant result. He found that a single interview would be useful and sufficient for decision making in most cases. This could significantly impact on the time involved in making the assessment. The benefits to the court are apparent—cost savings and considerable administrative efficiency are realized.

Behavioral scientists' involvement in this work topic raises another issue as well. Quite simply this is an aspect of the court that should be tightly managed and carefully controlled. The finding of incompetency can be an absolutely significant event (if not the most significant event) in an individual's life. Should not the decision be *reviewed* and *reevaluated* on a regular basis? Patients have a right to a fair and impartial determination of their competency. That right depends on a rigorous procedure complete with standards and a formalized process. Behavioral scientists can contribute both research and consulting action to this most difficult topic.

In addition, behavioral scientists could:

1. Research the extensiveness of the competency process in several courts, relating the procedures to costs, in follow-up to and in comparison with the above case.
2. Conduct an educational seminar for judges and attorneys on the latest approaches to competency review and the potential cost savings of a revised procedure.
3. Consult with management on the design and implementation of a new competency review system throughout the state, using a participative process involving staff currently following the existing procedures.

Control is a key activity of management, one that has many behavioral components. Its nature makes it an important area for behavioral science work.

SUMMARY

This chapter reviewed the functions of behavioral scientists in four court subsystems: goals and values, structure, psychosocial, and managerial. Examples were presented of behavioral scientists' work in the areas of organizational philosophy and values; the structure of special services; individual and group dynamics; and planning, organizing, leading, and controlling the court organization.

Key elements in each subsystem are defined and examined for behavioral scientists' intervention potential. Work in the management subsystem is currently popular, although the other subsystems are equally important.

Goals and values involve the philosophical aspects of court and corrections organizations. What guides them in assigning importance to their tasks, and even in deciding what their tasks are? Are goals and values formally or informally transmitted? These initial questions provide work opportunities for behavioral scientists. The first case example examined the consistency of program and philosophy. Both the research and treatment functions of behavioral scientists were used in an interdisciplinary manner. The second study focused on the philosophy–policy–practice problem in parole selection elements. The authors constructed a decision matrix to identify empirically the practical and/or operational results of parole policy, using the data to improve the policy.

Four major components of the criminal justice system—law enforcement, prosecution, courts, and corrections—share a common set of structural elements. A short list includes: formalization, specialization, standardization, hierarchy of authority, decentralization, complexity, professionalism, and personnel configuration. These structural elements contain a wide range of work possibilities, especially with regard to education and training, consultation and research, and development. Formal studies of the arrangement, size, and technology of court structure could provide suggestions for maximizing the efficiency and goal achievement of the court's organization. One case example reported on a study concerning court boundaries with reference to prisoners' rights. Traditionally, the courts were not intervening in corrections matters, but their move into rights protection has caused changes in the corrections system and has extended the court's own structural boundaries. Behavioral scientists' functions could include management consultation and evaluation.

The psychosocial subsystem is individual behavior, and attitudes and values, including the "informal organization." Behavioral scientists have a long history of involvement in this area, particularly through social psychology. Essentially, behavioral scientists investigate and reinforce the importance of understanding group dynamics in the court system. The previously reviewed plea negotiations problem in Chapter 2, concerning reactions of police to pretrial negotiations, also illustrates the possible use of survey research to reveal the more informal reactions that need to be addressed in solving the problem. The sensitive nature of most personal and personnel problems can be defused by the consultant/mediator role of the behavioral scientist.

The first psychosocial subsystem case example examines delinquents' perceptions of their presiding judge. The perceptual data could be used to initiate a "dynamic process" of personal change. While certainly not part of the formal court agenda, these findings can be important for setting up the subsequent treatment. The second case concerned jurors' biases. This is currently an area of active work for behavioral scientists. The study showed that authoritarian jurors as a group convicted more often than equalitarian jurors as a group. Both applied research and assessment functions were used.

The management subsystem in the courts involves coordinating activities, management of personnel, and the development and operation of performance and control systems. The court's philosophy and action are influenced by its management team's relations with its organizational environment. Behavioral scientists can provide assistance in the traditional areas of planning, organizing, and controlling various parts of the court system. Innovative techniques are appearing for managing schedules, witnesses, and jurors, planning new courthouses, and managing existing space. Behavioral scientists can find opportunities for providing education and training, research, and consultation in the planning, organizing, directing, and controlling tasks of management. Significant problems in these areas have already been addressed. Studies have examined bail practices, overcrowding, court clinics, ways to expand personnel, and leadership issues. Organizational development work in court organizations is a new and potentially productive area.

The cases illustrate that behavioral scientists have functional opportunities in many of the subsystems, ranging from organizing and delivering assessment and treatment services to providing applied research and consultation to various management groups including judges and court administrators.

The diversity of the activities now engaged in provides evidence that the traditional areas of, for example, clinical assessment, expert testimony, and treatment are too limited for modern behavioral scientists. Both their work to date and their opportunities indicate that their use in these systems is and should be multifaceted.

REFERENCES

1. Kast, F. E., and Rosenzweig, J. E. (1979). *Organization and Management*. New York: McGraw-Hill.

2. Ibid.
3. Ibid.
4. Ibid.
5. Ackoff, R. L. (1974). *The Concept of Corporate Planning*. New York: John Wiley.
6. Kast and Rosenzweig. Op. cit.
7. Ibid.
8. Nir, Y., and Cutler, R. (1973). The Therapeutic Utilization of the Juvenile Court. *American Journal of Psychiatry,* 130 (10), 1112–17.
9. Gottfredson, P. M., Hoffman, P. B., Sigler, M. H., and Wilkins, L. T. (1975). Making Paroling Policy Explicit. *Crime and Delinquency,* 21, 34–44.
10. Holten, N. G., and Jones, M. E. (1982). *The System of Criminal Justice*. Boston: Little, Brown & Co.
11. Ibid.
12. Daft, R. L. (1983). *Organization Theory and Design*. St. Paul, Minnesota: West Publishing Co.
13. Kalmanoff, A. (1976). *Criminal Justice: Enforcement and Administration*. Boston: Little, Brown & Co.
14. Holten and Jones. Op. cit.
15. Kast and Rosenzweig. Op. cit.
16. Kutak, R. J. (1975). Grim Fairy Tales For Prison Administrators. In G. C. Killinger, P. F. Cromwell, and B. J. Cromwell, *Issues in Corrections and Administration*. St. Paul, Minnesota: West Publishing Co.
17. Holt v. Sarver, 309 F. Supp. 362 (E.D.Ark., 1970).
18. Hamilton v. Schiro, Civil No. 69-2443 (E.D.La., June 25, 1970).
19. Morris v. Travisano, 310 F. Supp. 857 (D.R.I. 1970).
20. Sostre v. Rockefeller, 312 F. Supp. 863 (S.D.N.Y., 1970).
21. Ziegenfuss, J. T. (1984). *Law, Medicine and Healthcare: A Bibliography*. New York: Facts on File.
22. Kast and Rosenzweig. Op. cit.
23. Lipsitt, P. D. (1968). The Juvenile Offender's Perceptions. *Crime and Delinquency,* 14 (1), 49–62.
24. Buckout, R., Weg, S., Reilly, V., Frohboes, R. (1977, September) Jury Verdicts Comparison of 6 vs. 12 person juries and unanimous vs. majority decision rule in a murder trial. *Bulletin of the Psychonomic Society* Vol 10(3) pp 175–78.
25. Ibid.
26. Kast and Rosenzweig. Op. cit.
27. Ibid.
28. Holten and Jones. Op. cit.
29. Ibid.
30. Ruben, H. T. (1976) *The Courts: Fulcrum of the Criminal Justice System* Pacific Palisades, Calif.: Goodyear 1976.
31. Koontz, H., O'Donnell, C., and Weihrich, H. (1980). *Management*. New York: McGraw-Hill.
32. Mudd, S., and Ziegenfuss, J. T. *Lutheran Social Services—East Region: Long Range Plan*. Lititz, Pennsylvania: Lutheran Social Services.
33. Roesch, R. (1976). Predicting the Effects of Pretrial Intervention Programs on Jail Populations: A Method For Planning and Decision-Making. *Federal Probation,* 40, 32–36.
34. Koontz, O'Donnell, and Weihrich. Op. cit.
35. Koontz, O'Donnell, and Weihrich. Op. cit.
36. Kaslow, F. W. (1979). The Psychologist as Consultant to the Court. In J. J. Platt and R. J. Wicks (eds.), *The Psychological Consultant*. New York: Grune and Stratton, pp. 166–67.

37. Suarez, J. (1972). Psychiatry and the Criminal Law System. *American Journal of Psychiatry*, 129, 293–97.
38. Ibid.
39. Kaslow. Op. cit.
40. Laben, J. K., and Spencer, L. D. (1976). Decentralization of Forensic Services. *Community Mental Health*, 12 (4), 405–14.
41. Ibid.
42. Ibid.
43. Huse, E. F. (1979). *The Modern Manager*. St. Paul, Minnesota: West Publishing Co.
44. Ibid.
45. Ibid.
46. Marx, G. T. (1975). Alternative Measures of Police Performance. In E. Viano (ed.), *Criminal Justice Research*. Lexington, Massachusetts: D. C. Heath.
47. Ibid.
48. Andrews, D. A., Young, and Wermeth, . (1973) The Attitudinal Effects of Group Discussions between young criminal offenders and community volunteers. *J. of Community Psychology* 1(4), 417–422.
49. Koontz, O'Donnell, and Weihrich. Op. cit.
50. Saks, M. J., and Hastie, R. (1978). *Social Psychology in Court*. New York: Van Nostrand Reinhold.
51. Gray, J. L., and Starke, F. A. (1980). *Organizational Behavior: Concepts and Applications*, 2nd ed. Columbus, Ohio: Charles E. Merrill.
52. Deal, T. E., and Kennedy, A. A. (1982). *Corporate Cultures*. Reading, Massachusetts: Addison Wesley.
53. Schein, E. (1983) The Role of the Founder in Creating Organizational Culture. *Organizational Dynamics*.
54. Gray and Starke. Op. cit.
55. French, W. (1976). Organization Development: Objectives, Assumptions and Strategies. *California Management Review*, 12 (2), 23–46.
56. McCleary, R. (1977). How Parole Officers Use Records. *Social Problems*, 24 (5), 576–89.
57. Ibid.
58. Ziegenfuss, D. G., and Ziegenfuss, J. T. (1984). *Health Information Systems: A Bibliography*. New York: Plenum Press.
59. Patton, M. Q. (1978). *Utilization Focused Evaluation*. Beverly Hills, California: Sage Publ.
60. Patton, M. Q. (1980). *Qualitative Evaluation Methods*. Beverly Hills, California: Sage Publ.
61. Koontz, O'Donnell, and Weihrich. Op. cit.
62. Ziegenfuss and Ziegenfuss. Op. cit.
63. Koebel, C. T. (1983). Evaluating Judges: An Analysis of Survey Results. *Evaluation Review*, 7 (5), 659–83.
64. Roesch, R., and Golding, S. C. (1980). *Competency to Stand Trail*. Urbana: University of Illinois Press.

PART II
BEHAVIORAL SCIENTISTS IN CORRECTIONS

Part II will examine the functional opportunities for behavioral scientists in the corrections organization. It matches the five functions of behavioral scientists (assessment and diagnosis, treatment, education and training, research, and consultation) against the five subsystems of the corrections organization (goals/values, technical, structural, psychosocial, and managerial). Each subsystem is explored, with cases of completed work and suggested follow-up topics identified.

4
BEHAVIORAL SCIENTISTS AND TECHNICAL CORRECTIONS WORK

Chapter 4 begins an analysis of functional opportunities, focusing on the technical aspects of corrections organization work. This includes a review of behavioral scientist functions with respect to the following core aspects of correctional work: presentence activities; probation; and institutionalization, including admission, classification, treatment (such as clinical, addictions, educational, vocational, medical care, and community adjustment services), civil rights protection, abuse control, environmental management, and discharge. Community corrections and recidivism are also discussed.

This part of the book concerns the organizational structure and functions of corrections and the technical processes that are the main work of this aspect of the criminal justice system. Chapter 4 outlines work opportunities for behavioral scientists that are related to the technical aspects of providing correctional services. (See Figure 4-1). Before defining and discussing in detail the technical work of correctional services, it is useful to define what we mean by corrections as a whole, the context of organizations such as prisons. Holten and Jones[1] used as an introduction to their text on the corrections systems, an overview provided by Donald Newman. It is useful and worth repeating:

The term 'corrections' encompasses almost all post-conviction and post-sentencing interventions with offenders. In its broadest sense, corrections involves the use of such techniques as fines, jail sentences, imprisonment, probation, parole, and various combinations of incarceration and community supervision. Correctional systems are complex organizations, comprising much more than probation and parole field services and a few prisons. Modern correctional systems employ a wide variety of programs, facilities, and techniques for the classification, processing, treatment, control, and care of their charges. Within the ambit of correctional services are hospitals for the criminally insane, group counseling programs, work release projects, halfway houses, farms, forestry camps, diagnostic centers, schools, factories which produce goods for state use, special programs for narcotics addicts, sex deviates and physically ill prisoners, and even geriatric programs for those who become old and senile while under sentence. Maximum se-

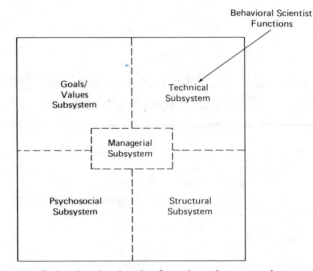

Figure 4-1. Behavioral scientist functions in corrections technical subsystem.

curity prisons are administratively linked with medium and minimum security facilities, with reformatories for young felons, and with training schools for juvenile delinquents. There are separate facilities and programs for female offenders, and the vast network of centralized prisons and other facilities is often incorporated with a wide variety of community based institutions and programs.[2]

From the above introduction it is apparent that the field of corrections is a vast and widely divergent system composed of many interacting parts. This chapter concentrates on the technical aspects of the correctional organization, with the structure, psychosocial, goals and values, and managerial subsystems the topics of Chapter 5. Behavioral scientists' involvement with corrections thus begins with some of the best-known of the correctional organizational activities (e.g., rehabilitation, probation, parole, and prison life). How does the technical work fit our organizational systems view?

In reference to our continuing use of the Kast and Rosenzweig model,[3] the corrections technical subsystem

refers to the knowledge required for the performance of tasks, including the techniques used in the transformation of inputs into outputs. It is determined by the task requirements of the organization and varies depending on the particular activity . . . the technical subsystem is shaped by the specialization of knowledge and skills required, the types of machinery and equipment involved, and the layout of facilities. The technology affects the organization structure as well as its psychosocial subsystem.

The technical subsystem of corrections as a whole is further divided into six major topics:

- Presentence activities, including diversion and investigation.
- Probation, including restrictions, revocation, and termination.
- Institutionalization, including such topics as reception/admission, classification, treatment, civil rights, abuse, environment, and discharge.
- Community corrections, including alternatives to prison programs.
- Recidivism.

This list follows the outline of Holten and Jones's well-known perspective on the criminal justice system. The list and subsequent descriptions of

Table 4-1. Corrections technical subsystem: Work opportunity table.

FUNCTIONS WORK TOPICS	ASSESSMENT AND DIAGNOSIS	TREATMENT	EDUCATION AND TRAINING	RESEARCH	CONSULTATION
Presentence activities					
Probation					
Institutionalization					
• Admission					
• Classification					
• Treatment					
*clinical					
*addictions					
*education					
*vocational					
*medical care					
*community adjustment					
• Civil rights protection					
• Abuse control					
• Environmental management					
• Discharge					
• Community corrections					
• Recidivision					

the components have been adapted and expanded from the Holten and Jones outline, with the addition of such issues as prisoners' rights and concerns for environment and abuse.

Throughout we are concerned with the functions of behavioral scientists within these various technical activities and components. The full range of behavioral scientists' functions will be visible here, including assessment and diagnosis, treatment, education and training, research, and consultation. Table 4-1, a work opportunity table, depicts the topics that are the potential points of behavioral scientists' involvement.

PRESENTENCE ACTIVITIES

Presentence activities are technical services provided by correctional agencies and individuals prior to the formal sentencing of the accused. Holten and Jones define presentence activities as follows:

> Corrections agencies, especially probation departments and programs, often become involved in cases before the accused is sentenced. In some cases they assume responsibility for persons diverted from traditional processing. In others, they perform a presentence investigation of defendants and prepare a report for use by sentencing judges.[4]

Presentence activities that are generally present in most correction systems are diversion and presentence investigation.

Diversion is defined as "the suspension at any point of formal criminal processing of an alleged offender and the referral of that person to a treatment program inside or outside the criminal justice system. Successful completion of treatment results in dismissal of the case; violation of conditions set at the time of diversion may result in reactivization of the case."[5] Diversion is an activity by which the correctional system is able to provide the accused with an opportunity to obtain treatment for a problem that has been responsible for his/her contact with the criminal justice system.

In many diversions that result in treatment or even additional assessment and diagnosis, behavioral scientists have already established a significant record of involvement. Increasingly, behavioral scientists are brought into the diversion activity by virtue of their consulting and education and training roles. Behavioral scientists have been asked to provide consulting opinions as to the probability of successful acceptance of treatment by the accused. Alternatively, behavioral scientists might be asked to provide education and training programs related to the types and appropriateness of new alternative-to-prison programs. The opportunities are quite varied.

The second presentence activity involves investigation. Presentence investigation usually results in "a report on the background of a convicted offender for the purpose of aiding the judge in the evaluation of a proper sentence."[6] Here the behavioral scientist is involved in assessment and diagnosis. The purpose of the background review is to establish the facts of the case, including any circumstances that may have led the accused to the inappropriate behavior that has caused his/her contact with the criminal justice system. This is a traditional assessment function and one in which many behavioral scientists participate. While activity by behavioral scientists relating to the preparation of the report is quite well established and generally known, behavioral scientists may also provide other services in presentence investigation work.

For example, behavioral scientists could research the impact of various presentence report elements, including an examination of the degree of comprehensiveness of the report, the various factors in it, and the contribution of those factors to the increased prediction capability of the report as a whole. Additionally, behavioral scientists might become involved as educators and trainers. They would assist in teaching correctional personnel how to develop presentence reports, including how to obtain the best information from relevant personnel (e.g., by increasing the effectiveness of their interviewing techniques).

Finally, Behavioral Scientists might be asked to give expert testimony in relation to the presentence report (e.g., testimony related to the dangerousness of a mentally disabled criminal offender). Two case examples will illustrate, with the first addressing the question of dangerousness.

CASE TWENTY-NINE: THE DANGEROUSNESS and DIVERSION PROBLEM. A typical problem confronting correctional personnel at the presentencing period is uncertainty about the potential dangerousness of the accused. Is the accused person in need of immediate incarceration to protect the client and the community? This has been particularly troublesome for the correctional system, as it involves the deprivation of liberty for the accused. Liberty for the client and community safety concerns are equally important, creating administrative problems.

In an example of behavioral scientist involvement in this problem, Kozol, Boucher, and Garofalo reviewed the diagnosis and treatment of dangerousness in a 1972 report.[7] Their article reports a ten-year study of the diagnosis and treatment of dangerous offenders. "Dangerousness" was defined by the authors as "a potential for inflicting serious bodily harm on another." The authors discuss the importance of an ability to reliably identify dangerousness, distinguishing who will and will not commit bodily harm again. This importance is related to the fact that determination of dangerousness is relevant to sentencing practices, to involuntary mental hospitalization, to other dispositions following conviction, and to preventive detention. Multiple uses at critical decision points mean that high reliability is a must to guarantee fairness.

The staff at the Center for the Diagnosis and Treatment of Dangerous Persons, Bridgewater, Massachusetts, feel that diagnosis is their most difficult problem. Dangerousness cannot be attributed to a single factor and is not detectable through a routine psychiatric examination. "There are no rigid criteria of dangerousness; there are only clues . . . frames of reference are not fixed, nor are they proposed as a rigid schema for examination; rather, they are a guide for the clinician. . . ."[8] In their view diagnosis is a clinical judgment that is based on collated data comprised of clinical examinations, psychological tests, and a reconstruction of the offender's life history. The clinical examinations are made independently by at least two psychiatrists, two psychologists, a social worker, and others. Psychological tests supplement the diagnostic procedure, with one test or a combination of tests used, depending on the specific case. Certain tests (e.g., the Rorschach) are used to define aspects of the offenders' "ego status," such as their perception of human relationships and modes of dealing with anxiety.

Treatment of all committed persons is mandatory, with the approach based on contemporary psychiatric and psychological theory. Individualization is the major emphasis of treatment, but group therapy is an integral part of the process. Drugs, hormones, or other chemical methods are not used.

In conclusion, the authors found that with the Center's methods, dangerousness was reliably diagnosed and effectively treated with a recidivism rate of 6.1 percent. However, they suggest the need to improve diagnostic and therapeutic competence to ensure that fewer dangerous people are freed and fewer nondangerous people are institutionalized.

Comments and Follow-up Work. This study illustrates the behavioral scientist's involvement in the assessment and diagnosis of dangerousness and in the treatment of the problem. The authors were called in to conduct this review as part of an education and training function for correctional personnel, and on a consulting basis to address the current status of the dangerousness problem. Thus, we have several behavioral scientist functions demonstrated here. These functions are particularly critical at the presentencing point of the criminal justice system. While the contribution to, and the involvement in, assessment, diagnosis, and treatment are readily apparent from the report, it is not difficult to see how these experts on dangerousness might be called upon to provide education and training programs for clinicians at other facilities. Additionally, since they appear to have developed a quite successful methodology, they could act as consultants to assist other facilities in developing a similar program, and/or in identifying some of the strengths and weaknesses of another facility's existing dangerousness prediction process.

In addition to these activities, behavioral scientists could:

1. Research the significance of the dangerous problem in their local community.

2. Provide educational programs on dangerousness to judges and attorneys, including innovative approaches to measurement and control.
3. Provide expert consultation regarding the dangerousness of an offender with an educational purpose, not just an advocacy one.

There are certain types of violence that are especially troublesome and frightening to the community, as the next case indicates.

CASE THIRTY: THE SEX OFFENDER. A second problem, equal in severity and difficulty to the dangerousness problem and certainly related to it, is that of what to do with the sex offender. Obviously, sex offenses have quite a sensitive and significant impact on society. Diversion and presentence disposition of this group are extremely troublesome problems. Behavioral scientists might be called on to design, develop, and operate programs for sex offenders or, as in this particular example, evaluate an existing program.

Dix reported on the evaluation of several aspects of the California Mentally Disordered Sex Offender Program.[9] This program allows a sex offender to be committed to the Department of Health for an indefinite period as an alternative to sentencing under the applicable penal code. If committed, the offender undergoes a battery of tests and in six months will be classified as either an "A" or a "B" patient. An "A" patient is "cured" and may be sentenced under the penal code. A "B" patient is not recovered, but is not further treatable and remains a danger to the health and safety of others. A "B" patient may be either sentenced or returned to the Department of Health for an indefinite period. Almost all mentally disordered sex offenders are committed to the Atascadero State Hospital (about 400 to 425 per year), most of them either child molesters or rapists.

The evaluation found that offenders processed as mentally disordered sex offenders were institutionalized for a shorter length of time than they would be if they were imprisoned under the penal code. Ambiguities in determining a definition of "dangerousness' created difficulties. The examiners looked mainly at the offender's past record (with no real examination of his present mental state) and were unable to predict who would become a repeat offender.

Comments and Follow-up Work. Here we have a continuing example of the "dangerousness problem." Offenders were referred to a program that theoretically offered them some treatment. But the program was not able to develop a capability to predict dangerousness. The evaluation indicated that the offenders were able to secure, in effect, a "lesser sentence" than if they had been imprisoned under the penal code. For those persons interested in goal attainment—full punishment or retribution—the evaluation indicated that the offenders were not receiving it.

The evaluation also identified difficulties in the current assessment process. If the evaluation conducted was a "formative" one (designed to provide process development data), it would enable the program to benefit from the feedback of the report results, making adjustments that would correct weaknesses.

This subgroup of offenders presents still other topics of concern. Behavioral scientists could:

1. Establish an innovative treatment program for sex offenders (e.g., one based on a peer assistance model).
2. Provide direct clinical treatment services to sex offenders.
3. Educate attorneys and judges on the latest thinking about treatment and control of these offenders.
4. Consult with management on the design of a regional program for sex offenders using local resources.

Slight offenses in this area may sometimes secure the offender probation in conjunction with treatment. Probation is considered next.

PROBATION

Probation is "a form of sentence whereby an offender may remain free of confinement so long as he obeys certain conditions imposed by the sentencing court and probation authority."[10] Probation is a mechanism by which the accused may escape imprisonment in an institution of one sort or another. As a brief expansion, it should be noted that: "probation may result from a sentence to prison that is suspended by the judge in lieu of a period of supervised probation, or it may be the status to which the offender is directly sentenced by the judge. The length of the probationary term may be shorter or longer than the appropriate prison or jail term would have been. State laws vary on this point."[11] There are a number of points at which the behavioral scientist could become involved in the probation aspect of the corrections system.

First, there is the point of initial decision, whether or not to grant probation. Sample activities for behavioral scientists might include involvement in: the identification and review of probation criteria; the identification and review of clients awarded probation; and the exact nature of the probationary decision, including the specific restrictions that may become part of it. In this introductory discussion of the topic, three aspects of probation identified by Holten and Jones are discussed:

- Restrictions
- Revocation
- Termination

Each is illustrated by a combined case report of behavioral scientist work.

Probation Restrictions

The purpose of restrictions or conditions on probation is to establish guidelines for identifying and shaping the kinds of behavior that are expected of the probationer. The purposes of restrictions or conditions are listed as the following:

- To define the limits of the behavior during the probation period.
- To identify the future pattern of behavior toward which the probationer must work.
- To ensure that the probation response is appropriate to the crime committed by the probationer.

It is clear from this brief statement of purposes that there are opportunities for the behavioral scientist to become involved. Behavioral scientists could help to develop the processes by which offender behaviors are changed, or they could examine a court's total set of probation conditions to determine whether they are consistent with the intended purpose of positive change and development for the offender.

In terms of both the process by which the conditions are developed and their substantive content, Holten and Jones cited the following point made by two commentators:

> Kerper and Kerper note that courts have ruled that some conditions are illegal, and they cite a California Appellate Court ruling that probably represented prevailing attitudes when it prohibited conditions which (1) had no relationship to the offender's crimes; (2) related to conduct which is not illegal; and (3) required or forbade conduct which is not reasonably related to the offender's possible future criminal behavior.[12]

As this quotation indicates, the process by which the conditions are developed and their ultimate outcome should be relevant to the probation conditions' purposes. There must be a relationship to the crime, appropriate limits to behavior, and an expectation that the conditions will lead to desired behavior in the future.

The process by which these conditions are arrived at should involve a multidisciplinary data set on the basis of which prosecutors, defenders, and judges collaboratively attempt to define what is most useful for an individual client. While the primary responsibility ultimately lies with the court, input from both prosecution and defense provides multiple perspectives for developing the set of conditions that will be most conducive to achieving the intended purposes of probation.

The outcome of probationary restrictions is actually an increased likelihood or probability that the probationer's behavior will be consistent with and operate within the defined boundaries of the law and the social system of which he/she is a part. This outcome is achieved by enabling the probationer to continue to live within society rather than be incarcerated. The case to be presented illustrates one type of behavioral scientist contribution to this outcome. It will link the restrictions discussed here and the revocation and termination aspects discussed next.

Probation Revocation

When the probationer is not living up to the terms of the probation (i.e., the conditions and restrictions as stipulated in writing by the court), probation can be revoked. Clearly, commission of a second crime is relevant grounds for the ending of the probation period. However, as Holten and Jones note:

The grounds for revocation of probation include more than the commission of another crime, although they obviously include that. The other grounds are referred to as *technical violations*. Revocation on these grounds requires that some illegal conduct be shown but this is obviously a vague requirement. Of course, violation of a specific condition of probation is sufficient grounds, but perhaps also is marginally illegal conduct not specified in the conditions.[13]

This quotation states that specific violation of specific conditions will end the probation. That is the point of the conditions in the first place—to shape behavior. Violation by marginally illegal activities that appear to be leading to additional crimes in the future, and/or are creating a pattern of behavior that is inconsistent with the intention of probation, can also be used as documentation for ending probation.

The result of revoking probation is essentially the termination of an alternative-to-prison initiative. The probationer was given an opportunity to create a behavior pattern that would enable him/her to adjust to society. The result of the revocation is a renewed effort to establish a "treatment/ correctional plan" for the individual offender that will result in changes of an inappropriate behavior pattern. Since the original conditions and restrictions of probation did not achieve this objective, there is a need for a new individual goal-planning process that produces new guidelines for the offender.

When offenders abide by the conditions, the probation is eventually ended, our next topic.

Termination of Probation

In addition to revocation, probation may also end simply by termination resulting from the *absence* of the probationer's illegal or inappropriate behavior. Holten and Jones notes that "probationary sentences may be terminated prior to the expiration of the probationary period. The court may act on a recommendation by the probation officer to permit early release of the offender, or it may allow the full period to run out, in which case the offender is automatically released."[14] These are formal discharges of the probationer from probation status. Discharge is intended to be total, which may include judicial, legal, administrative, and social or case work discharge.[15,16]

Behavioral scientists might become involved here at a number of points. For example, they could assess the status of probationers at the termination of the period, or become involved in research studies examining the nature and characteristics of probationers who have successfully completed the probation period. Potential activities are closely related to those identified for other aspects of probation, with one such case illustrated next.

CASE THIRTY-ONE: THE PROBATION EVALUATION. Probation has been a core element of the criminal justice system for some time. Correctional management is continually looking for ways to develop the system further. An evaluation of the existing process or a new initiative can make a valuable contribution to this process. Consider the following case.*

In 1983, the Middletown Probation Department instituted a new program whereby probationers would collaborate on the development of their probation conditions. This participative approach to conditions development was thought to result in more relevant conditions and greater commitment to them from the probationers. The probation department director asked for a first-year review of the program to determine how it was developing and to secure a preliminary review of the initial results.

Two behavioral scientists led the formation of a team to conduct the review, which they defined as a "formative evaluation" designed to contribute to program development.[17] The five-person team used the management consulting approach to evaluation and organizational development, reviewing philosophy, program, costs, management, and other departmental linkages (see Ziegenfuss and Lasky[18,19]). Evaluators were present during the sessions that were used to develop the conditions for 125 probationers during a three-month period. They examined data on two groups: (1) those with probation revoked, and (2) those terminated after full term with no incidents. A beginning analysis was made of differences between probationers with the collaboratively developed probation condition and

---

*Fictitious case.

...ose without it. Strengths and needed changes were fed back to the program director and staff in a positive, constructive way. The team was able to describe fully the program model and its level of implementation. The description of the implementation process was considered most helpful to others planning a similar program.[20]

Comments and Follow-up Work. This example illustrates a review of a probation experiment whereby increased collaboration was tried and evaluated. Here behavioral scientists are used in a program development role through their evaluation work. Their function would be as either consultants or applied researchers examining an individual organizational problem. This evaluative process could be used with many new programs as one ongoing approach to aid correctional system development.

The wide use of probation throughout the system makes it a key topic for scrutiny. Behavioral scientists could:

1. Provide educational and vocational assessment services to probationers.
2. Design a clinical program that addresses the job and community adjustment anxieties of probationers.
3. Research the success/failure rates of probationers of certain types (e.g., by age, sex) in the local community.
4. Consult with management on the design of a probationers' support group.

When probation and other alternative to prison programs fail, institutionalization of the offender is next. It can be and often is a direct stop without probation as a first corrective attempt.

INSTITUTIONALIZATION

There are many ways to punish offenders for crimes committed. One way is to incarcerate them in a prison or jail for a given length of time. Incarceration is literally imprisonment in a federal, state, or local correctional institution. As discussed here, incarceration is twenty-four-hour imprisonment in a residential facility operated formally as an institution for the criminal offender. Many aspects of the institution could become work subjects for behavioral scientists. The following list introduces some of the key topics. It is not an exhaustive list. Behavioral scientists may become involved in the following institutional areas:

- Admission
- Classification

- Treatment (including vocational, educational, psychiatric and addictive, and community adjustment)
- Civil rights protection
- Abuse control
- Environmental management
- Discharge

This list actually suggests that at almost each point in the institutionalization process (admissions, classification, treatment, etc.), behavioral scientists could act in one or more of their five primary functions (assessment and diagnosis, treatment, education and training, research, and consultation). The following discussions briefly introduce these tasks of institutionalization, with case examples of behavioral scientists' activity in each area.

Admissions

Admission to the institution is "the summation of administrative and clinical assessment procedures which result in the offender's being taken into the service system."[21] To this definition must be added the obvious point that it is the summation of judicial decision-making that leads to the specific decision to institutionalize. In the language of criminal justice, institutional admission is often called "reception." Reception by the institution may be related to the court's need to hold an offender prior to disposition of his/her case and prior to sentencing; or, those convicted are being formally admitted to the institution to begin serving their sentences.

Admission to the institution is one of the first points of substantive realization for offenders that they will be incarcerated as a result of their behaviors. Using this "realization point" as an example, behavioral scientists may become involved in the treatment of admissions anxiety. With regard to the actual process of admission, behavioral scientists can contribute to the education and training of institutional personnel in various processes, including paperwork, orientation, and the management of initial psychosocial problems. They can also offer consultation regarding methods for increasing admissions efficiency, or research on the procedures needed to ensure that offenders are not inappropriately admitted.

There is a special need for concern about protecting the offender's rights at this point, as well as for managing his/her personal concerns about the transition from freedom on the outside to the inside and imprisonment. The separation from family, friends, and community can be particularly difficult and is sometimes the stimulus for unexpected and unwanted tragedy (e.g., suicide), although it does not seem to receive the attention in the literature that it deserves.

At the admissions point the institution takes the new "client" through the following procedural steps:

- Checking of papers from the courts.
- Disrobing and giving up street clothes for prison clothes.
- Fingerprinting and photographing.
- The history.
- The physical exam.
- The assignment of a prison number.
- Transfer to a reception block for one to three months for diagnosis and classification.

This diagnosis and classification process, a separate and particularly significant step in the process, is discussed next. The following case indicates one way in which behavioral scientists may become involved in the admissions process.

CASE THIRTY-TWO: THE ADMISSIONS PROCESS.   What are the appropriate criteria for admission to an institution? In mental hospitals these are fixed by the hospital. In correctional organizations the facility admits clients after the court has made the decision. Still the process of admission warrants scrutiny, particularly with regard to the match of offender with facility, as this case indicates.

In one court a young offender was sentenced to prison for stealing an elderly woman's purse.* During the process, the woman was slapped several times, receiving a badly bruised jaw. The judge was determined to be harsh as it was the third encounter, but he had few prison options. He sentenced the youth to six months in the county prison. Once there the youth was attacked repeatedly, became depressed about the poor conditions, and after four months committed suicide. During this time he was in a cell with another inmate serving time for aggravated assault.

Comments and Follow-up Work.   This case could be analyzed as to the reason for admission to this facility and the placement with that cell mate. What clinical referrals were made during the inmate's time of personal problem? Were clinical services even available? Behavioral scientists could analyze this from a clinical treatment perspective, asking what alternative behaviors would have prevented the tragedy.

Additionally, behavioral scientists could:

---

*Fictitious Case.

1. Research the role of the assessment reports in admissions, including how frequently, by whom, and with what decision impact they are used.
2. Research the psychological impact of admission on offenders, especially including the incidence of anxiety reactions and post-admission depression.
3. Provide a training program that includes offender orientation through a peer group model.
4. Consult with a management team that is evaluating the admissions process with respect to its technical efficiency and its contribution to beginning a rehabilitation process.

One question about the above case concerns the assessment and diagnosis of depression. Was it done, and were the results used? This brings up the whole diagnostic area.

Diagnosis and Classification

Diagnosis and classification involve two separate steps. Diagnosis is an individual assessment of the offender's current status regarding a variety of personal characteristics, including: educational level, psychological history, social history, personality state, and educational needs. Diagnosis is part of the preparation for classifying the offender for placement within the facility. Once diagnosis is completed (through a very wide choice of diagnostic tests, procedures, and overall approaches), the offender classification step follows.

Offender classification is defined as "the interviewing and testing of inmates to determine the level of security required for each of them and the kind of treatment to be employed. If the state operates institutions of various security levels (maximum, medium, and minimum), classification personnel may even choose the place in which the prisoner will be incarcerated."[22] While the focus of this description of the classification step is primarily on security, there is also some concern given to the inmate's individual needs relative to his/her educational, vocational, and psychological situation. These are matched with the various security levels (maximum, medium, and minimum) in order to attempt to secure a best fit of offender and level of security needed, consistent with the offender's personal status.

It is at this time that a treatment plan for the offender is developed. This plan in theory presents the purpose, process, and outcome of the treatment that the offender is to receive during his/her course of confinement. However, as others have noted, the treatment plan produced is typically heavily weighted in favor of the institution.[23] This is usually the case in other types of institutions as well (e.g., mental hospitals). Administrative needs for order and efficiency are given priority over the offender's personal needs for change and growth. They are competing needs over which reasonable people can have different positions.

The issue of treatment versus security and custody has come up in other conflicts between a client's service needs and institutional efficiency/demands (see, e.g., O'Connor v. Donaldson[24]). A considerable concern for many institutions' lack of treatment plans has been identified and cited as a severe weakness in the organization. One cause is lack of knowledge. But as noted by Ziegenfuss,[25] basic guidelines for individual treatment plans are being presented, such as those offered by Clayton:[26]

- The patient should be included in the development of the plan and goals;
- short-term and long-term goals that are achievable and reasonable should be set;
- the goals should be stated in behavioral and in observable and measurable terms;
- the patient's strengths should be considered as well as his problems and needs;
- who will do what and when should be clearly stated and every goal should have an anticipated timeframe.

These guidelines are important for their advice and as indicators of another work opportunity for behavioral scientists. While the diagnosis and classification step in institutionalization may sometimes include development of a treatment plan that meets these requirements, that is too infrequently the case. Since the plans are not created to begin with, the ongoing need for periodic review and adjustment of this diagnosis and classification is even more rare. There is little information identifying how often these processes occur.

Clearly, behavioral scientists can become involved in a number of areas directly related to these diagnostic and classification tasks. Behavioral scientists have traditionally participated in assessment and diagnosis as a prime activity. Their potential involvement here is obvious. It is also possible that they could become involved in development of the treatment plan for the inmate at the classification point. The following case is one example.

CASE THIRTY-THREE: CLINICAL TREATMENT. Regular and frequent work for prison behavioral scientists is the assessment and treatment function, provided primarily by clinical and counseling psychologists and psychiatrists. As a result of this work an often asked question is: how do offenders differ from other clinical populations? There is a need to identify both the needs and personality differences and the methods by which these offenders can best be helped. The following case report presents one method for making the assessment distinction.

Allen, Urso, and Burger cited numerous studies that have offered evidence for the constructive validity of Jackson's Personality Research Form (PRF).[27] The authors found that up to 1982 only one study had attempted to determine whether the PRF measures the same personality constructs in various subpopulations. The purpose of the study was to determine whether the form measures the same personality constructs for male legal offenders as for a normative male group.

For the study, 122 male prisoners were given the PRF as part of the initial psychology assessment they received upon entering the institution. Their results were then compared to those of Jackson's normative group of male college students. In addition to mean level differences between the groups, the researchers also found "interesting variations in the factor structures of the two groups." This suggested that the form measures "some group specific personality dimensions in the inmate sample."[28]

In conclusion, the researchers found that the PRF was equivalent for the two groups on only two factors. These findings are especially important to psychologists who use the PRF to assess offenders. Because it measures different personality dimensions for this group, the authors suggest interpreting the scale based on the prisoner personality factors they defined and not on the "factorial conceptual dimensions" suggested in the PRF manual. Such careful interpretation is important in, for example, prisoner classification, rehabilitation, and research on social deviancy. The authors stress that the PRF does assess several personality dimensions important in understanding and treating the offender. "Exemplary incorporation of psychometric principles in test construction and the significance of the personality dimensions it seems to tap among prisoners indicate that further clinical application and research of the PRF by correctional psychologists is warranted."[29]

Comments and Follow-up Work.   This case example is an excellent demonstration of the methodological contribution of behavioral scientists to assessment. Psychologists can review assessment instrument use and accuracy as it leads to and sets up the treatment function. Here the psychologists are examining one of the assessment tools to determine its trustworthiness in terms of separating offenders from other groups. The implications for their work lead directly into the treatment functions, also involving colleague behavioral scientists who are depending on the assessment for reliability and validity.

Behavioral scientists have other opportunities here as well. They could:

1. Provide direct clinical services on a part-time basis.
2. Research the use of total clinical program models in the prison as to frequency, effectiveness, etc. (e.g., the use of the therapeutic community model).

3. Provide an educational program for prison staff on the use of the milieu for rehabiliation, not punishment.
4. Consult with management regarding the redesign of the physical environment to increase its therapeutic orientation (e.g., day room arrangements, colors, lighting).

Diagnosis and classification are the prelude to treatment, our next topic.

Treatment

Treatment is defined simply as the total effort put forth by the institution to promote positive change in the individual offender. The definition is purposely broad in order to encompass specific treatments and the total use of the environment, as in milieu therapy. This holistically oriented effort might include psychological counseling, educational activities, vocational training, and general supportive counseling from both administrative and security personnel as well as the clinical staff. Following on the notion of specific treatment methods and the therapeutic use of the environment, the process can be considered to be occurring at both a micro and a macro level. At the micro level, there are individual counseling and group sessions designed to address each individual offender's problems. For example, some inmates are addicted to drugs or alcohol. An *individual program* of addiction rehabilitation can be designed, developed and operated for one or two offenders, or a group of offenders with an addiction problem can be treated through a program.

At the more macro level of treatment–rehabilitation, the institution as a whole provides a *set of programs* which are designed to address the prison population's needs. For example, there may be vocational training programs that offer a variety of job counseling and job training programs. Often there is a range of educational programs, beginning with the high school equivalency program and continuing through college and perhaps graduate school. In addition, there are addiction and mental health programs that address the mental health needs of the offenders. Last, there are programs designed to increase individual inmates' ability to adjust to the community, in recognition of the fact that their problems have often developed because of their inability to integrate themselves into a community system. As a result, some prisons operate programs designed to assist the offender to understand the difference between, or points of conflict with, his or her behavior and the community's social system prescriptions. This entire set of programs for the organization as a whole constitutes the macro level.

There is, of course, a wide range of treatment services that behavioral scientists can provide. The following introductions and case examples will highlight behavioral science activities in six areas:

- Clinical services
- Addictions services
- Educational services
- Vocational services
- Medical care
- Community adjustment services

These are convenient categories for identifying the range of treatment options, but they do have a considerable degree of overlap.

Clinical Services. The purpose of clinical services is to secure change in the individual offender's personal status, including his or her psychological functioning, personality, attitude positions, value systems, etc. The way in which these services are delivered is usually through a series of individual and group sessions designed with specific goals in mind. Under ideal circumstances, a treatment plan is developed identifying specific behavioral and/or attitudinal outcomes expected. The outcomes actually achieved are usually specified in terms of behavioral or personality changes. The following example provides a demonstration of a clinical psychology program in a correctional organization.

CASE THIRTY-FOUR: CLINICAL PROGRAM DEVELOPMENT. There are two levels to the clinical program development task: the individual and the program level. Both have design and service delivery dimensions. This case discusses program level issues related to one correctional clinical psychology program, particularly the training of new personnel to address both skills and manpower shortages.

In 1971, the University of Alabama started a graduate training program in correctional clinical psychology.[30] The program combines academic instruction, field consultation, research, and social activism, and was initiated to provide specialized instruction and clinical training that was built on a base of general and clinical psychology. The program was developed to address the fact that few graduate students in clinical psychology enter the corrections field, despite the job opportunities available. Additionally, those who do enter the field find themselves ill prepared for the clinical and research problems encountered.

The correctional psychology curriculum requires twelve hours of specialization courses, including courses on correctional psychology theory, research, and program development. The students are also required to complete an internship in a correctional or criminal justice setting in which there are appropriate psychologist supervisors and role models. Before the internship year, students are placed in summer jobs within justice agencies or other related settings. Training assignments are also made to projects within the University's psychology department that are related to criminal justice research and program development. Students also write a dissertation on related topics.

The Center for Correctional Psychology functions administratively as a part of the University's psychology department which is the chief coordinator of the training program. It has eight major activity areas. First, it offers active consultation by faculty and graduate students to correctional systems, legal agencies, and law enforcement groups. Second, it offers in-service training by Center faculty and graduate students to personnel in law enforcement, the courts, and correctional agencies. Third, it answers hundreds of inquiries annually for advice, information, and opinions about the development of correctional psychology projects and activities. Fourth, special projects are undertaken, some of which have evolved into major program activities. Fifth, it issues and distributes publications on specific, technical issues relating to corrections psychology. Sixth, its students and/or faculty members edit two journals on law and psychology: *The Law and Psychology Review,* and *Criminal Justice and Behavior: An International Journal of Correctional Psychology.* Seventh, both professional personnel and students are involved in both preparation and presentation of expert testimony. Finally, it conducted a major prison classification project. As part of a court-mandated reorganization of prisons, the Center was given the task of reclassifying all prisoners in Alabama's prison system. This involved interviewing, assessing, and classifying 3192 inmates.

Comments and Follow-up Work.   This program, based at a university, provides an example of the linkakge of academic behavioral scientists with practice-oriented correctional organizations. A wide range of services is discussed in the report. They illustrate the kind of work that behavioral scientists can contribute to correctional organizations, beginning primarily with a training orientation. However, the Center itself is engaged in research in clinical services and in consultation. It does offer manpower support for all five of the behavioral science functions, from treatment to research. This center's activities demonstrate the multifunctional capability of behavioral scientists under the direction of a single organization.

How would behavioral scientists extend the work in this area? They could also:

1. Research the nature and amount of clinical services provided in a local corrections facility.
2. Design and implement a clinical internship program for doctoral clinical/counseling psychologists.
3. Consult with management to develop a contract mechanism for the use of outside clinicians in the clinical program.
4. Consult with management to develop a reimbursement mechanism for third party payment of clinical fees.

There are various aspects of the whole notion of treatment that can be considered beginning with assessment, the topic of the next case.

CASE THIRTY-FIVE: CLINICAL ASSESSMENT.   A second clinical task, at the individual client level, involves identifying and classifying inmates' needs. One problem frequently discussed, although not very openly, is homosexuality. Two authors examined the utility of two psychological tests for identifying homosexuality in a prison population.

The purpose of the study was to assess the applicability of two tests of homosexuality in a sample of convicted offenders (the Minnesota Multiphasic Personality Inventory and the 16 Personality Factor).[31] Two inmate groups were compared, one being a group of known homosexuals. They were diagnosed on the basis of institutional reports, presentence reports, psychiatric and psychological reports, and reports from other institutions and clinical agencies. The second group was composed of heterosexual inmates with no history of homosexuality according to any of the reports. The average ages of the men in both groups were similar, and both groups were tested in the routine testing program of the institution. The researchers examined which factors the two groups differed on, and which ones they agreed on. Study findings indicated that certain scales on the MMPI were able to diagnose homosexual behavior in prisoners, supporting other recent studies on homosexual samples.

Comments and Follow-up Work.   This study provides an example of the behavioral scientist's contribution to the assessment of the individual clinical needs and clinical status of inmates within the institution. Consider the possible follow-up to this study. Once a significant number of homosexual males or females could be identified, a clinical counseling program could be designed to address their needs. Clinical behavioral scientists could help them to change, if that is the inmates' interest, or to adjust to their situation within the institution. The functional demonstrations here are clearly assessment, diagnosis, and treatment, with some aspect of applied research.

In related work, behavioral scientists could:

1. Provide clinical assessment services that are targeted specifically at subgroups of the corrections population (e.g., female alcoholics, violence-prone offenders, child abusers).
2. Research the variety of assessment techniques available and their effectiveness relative to certain subgroups such as those just mentioned (e.g., female alcoholics).
3. Conduct an educational seminar for clinical/counseling staff on the new assessment techniques available.
4. Consult with management regarding the integration of the corrections assessment system with that of community service agencies and local hospitals (e.g., to increase staff resources and technical capability).

One final example will complete the clinical illustrations.

CASE THIRTY-SIX: CRISIS INTERVENTION. There are many on-going conflicts and pressures within the correctional organization. These often create crises for both individual inmates and for whole inmate groups. What kinds of mechanisms are used to intervene in the crises?

Marquis and Gendreau reported on a crisis intervention program.[32] Inmate personality "crises" were divided into three main categories: short-time blues, rough times due to outside and/or inside peer pressures, and crises due to administrative decisions with which inmates disagree. Medication is often prescribed to control the crisis, but there are limits to the positive contributions of medication, and there are negative side-effects. This article proposes an alternative program of relaxation–self-control procedures. This technique, which incorporates physical exercise, requires that the inmate systematically relax various parts of the body, keeping detailed behavioral follow-up charts. The procedure had been in use for about six months. The researchers found that approximately 70 percent of the inmates felt that the procedure helped them to alleviate stress and to reduce crises reactions. The study also found that the successful inmates no longer sought medication for help.

Finally, the authors listed four side-effects: use of the technique encouraged medical/psychology liaisons; its use (with its fairly immediate effects) increased acceptance of the professional staff by the custodial staff; it is now taught on a group basis, within the framework of a "life skills" course; and it is economical from a manpower standpoint because it can be administered by staff other than psychologists.

Comments and Follow-up Work. This particular report illustrates how behavioral scientists developed a program to address a critical institutional need: the management of stress and its impact on individuals within the offender population. The study can be considered applied research. But, it is also within our definition of the treatment function, particularly with regard to crisis intervention treatment. The example also illustrates the multiple utility of behavioral science work, in this case demonstrating benefits for offenders and staff and toward administrative order and maintenance of a more therapeutic environment.

Additionally, behavioral scientists could:

1. Design and develop a crisis intervention program that leads to short-term treatment for offenders (integrating a clinical crisis response with continuing treatment).
2. Research the crisis intervention capabilities of correctional units within their region, including the extent to which they are linked to the community social services system.
3. Conduct an educational seminar for clinical staff and management on why and how crisis intervention and ongoing treatment should be integrated.

4. Consult with management and inmates on the development of an inmate-run crisis intervention program.

Crisis intervention is only one type of treatment. Other special types such as addictions may also be considered as areas of work.

Addiction Services. Although some persons would consider addiction services to be a subset of general clinical services, a specific body of knowledge and a set of approaches distinguish it from general correctional clinical work. Behavioral scientists' involvement in addictions activities include a wide range of issues such as the definition of goals and values relating to what constitutes addictions, the variety of approaches to treating the problem, and the measures of success. There is much debate on many of these topics. For example, some addictions treatment groups consider clinical and counseling psychology directed toward producing personality change to be a fundamental requirement of the treatment process. Others consider addictions to be primarily a behavioral problem with an associated medical linkage. With the latter position, the task is to create methods for intervening in the drinking or drug-taking behavior, not to prescribe additional hospital-based medical methods or medicines.

The potential task for the behavioral scientist is again dual. At the program or organizational level, the task is the design and development of systems for providing addictions treatment. At the individual level the task is to assess the individual need for those services, to provide them, and to monitor and research their outcomes. Organizational and individual client problems are abundant, with many of them combinations of the two levels.

CASE THIRTY-SEVEN: THE ADDICTION PROBLEM. A significant problem within the inmate population in many or most prisons is addiction to both drugs and alcohol. The addictions are present at arrest, continue in the prison, and are fostered by the prison culture. Two different methods for addressing the addiction problem are briefly highlighted here.

Winick presented several illustrations of programs that address the needs of drug offenders.[33] The first example is Treatment Alternatives to Street Crime (TASC). This is a federally funded program for those who are drug-dependent and have committed a criminal act. The purpose of this program is to break the addict's crime–prison–drug dependence cycle. Treatment is introduced as soon as possible after the person is arrested; if the treatment is successful, the charges are dropped. If there is a trial, the offender may be sentenced to treatment or may be put on probation ''with the stipulation that he will submit to treatment.''

The second program is that of Synanon, a therapeutic community for treating drug users. It was founded by a former alcoholic in 1959 in Santa Monica. The community is based on a combination of approaches, also referred to as "the concept." Ex-addicts are the primary staff who act as "role models for residents. There is strong insistence on abstinence and severe penalties for backsliding, graded work activities . . . regular encounter group therapy and perception of the drug dependent person as an emotionally immature individual who must conconcentrate considerable personal growth into a relatively short time."[34] The programs are residential and usually long-term in length.

Comments and Follow-up Work.   Addiction programs are increasingly varied with regard to their outpatient and inpatient components, both programs within the prison and those in the community that are used prior to entering the prison. The above two programs are brief introductory abstracts of only two of the many alternatives. Behavioral scientists have been active in several roles, including assessment and diagnosis of the addiction problem, treatment in programs such as the two presented, and evaluation of the success of the programs in an applied research function (see, e.g., DeLeon[35] and Ziegenfuss[36]).

What other subjects could be investigated? Behavioral scientists could:

1. Research the incidence and prevalence of addictions in corrections at a local, state, or national level.
2. Research the relative effectiveness of addictions program models in corrections (e.g., therapeutic community models vs. individual counseling vs. methadone programs).
3. Design an addictions program for inmates in local facilities using addiction service resources already available in the community.
4. Consult with management to develop a strategy and specific programs for addressing the addictions problem from treatment to prevention.

Addictions treatment can be provided in somewhat new ways, as can other clinical services. The next section addresses the education needed by inmates, both in an intellectual sense and in a psychosocial sense.

Educational Treatment.   Behavioral scientists can and do become involved in the design, development, and operation of educational programs for offenders in institutions. These programs often begin with an assessment of the educational needs of offenders, including the evaluation of the offender's status in specific areas (e.g., daily living skills, reading comprehension). Behavioral scientists could be active in designing model programs. This would necessitate their working on the presentation of objectives and priorities; methods for discriminating among the characteristics of participants, the selection of participants most likely to succeed; and evaluation of the process and outcomes of treatment.

Behavioral scientists might also become involved in examining the academic achievement of released prisoners, including the analysis of such topics as the participants' backgrounds, educational achievements while in prison, post-release educational achievements, and overall academic development. Of particular interest with regard to intra-institutional educational efforts are the division of program content between cognitive and psychosocial work, inmate motivation toward education, and the relationship of the educational programs to other services.

Program-level issues would include considerations of curriculum such as the specific topics in academic, vocational, and psychosocial areas, and the personnel to be used. For example, one current debate is about whether to use correctional personnel or professionally qualified educators as instructors. The impact of that decision may determine whether the program becomes certified—if only certified instructors can be used. This in turn may affect both the acceptance of inmates who wish to continue their education in formal systems outside of the institution, and how well prepared they are to do so.

Behavioral scientists might also make some examination of the barriers that block the educational process within institutions, including public views of the prison purpose as punishment, and not as an opportunity for development. Additionally, there have been difficulties with minimal funding and with correctional officer conflict. Officers can feel both threatened and jealous as prisoners realize an opportunity to become more educated than they are. Other program development barriers also exist, including cultural and practical pressures that generate resistance to the program (e.g., anti-education values and the need for security).

In short, there is already considerable involvement of behavioral scientists in addressing the educational needs of persons in institutions. But there is much room for expansion. The following list identifies further topics for work:

- Goals analysis
- Values change
- The social functions of education
- Selection
- Measuring abilities and interests
- IQ testing
- Situational testing
- Teaching methods for reading, writing, and arithmetic
- Resistance dilemmas
- Inmates as students
- Teacher/student ratio
- Educational attitudes

- Equivalency diplomas in prison
- Evaluating program effects

As is apparent from the list, nearly all of the well-known topics in the educational field apply to the institutional population and their programs. Opportunities for the involvement of behavioral scientists as educators are as unlimited as the education field itself.

CASE THIRTY-EIGHT: NEW TREATMENT EDUCATION CONCEPTS. Behavioral scientists have been active in developing new ways of thinking about treatment across fields[37] and about the treatment process. One debate that has been quite vigorous is: what exactly is treatment? Is it basically education about one's behavior, or does it consist of some other process? The former point of view is a recent development, stemming from the medical model–psychosocial model paradigm debate. The following example of some new thinking by a psychiatrist is illustrative of this development.

Maxwell Jones recently wrote about the correctional-system use of an educational approach he calls social learning.[38] He presented examples of what is meant by social learning, which first involves the staff. According to Jones, before social learning can be used for inmates, staff members must be trained and experienced in the process too. This process includes open, two-way communication among group members, regular meetings for open discussion, "interaction without fear of reprisal," and increased trust among group members.

In this particular project, Jones was a facilitator to a staff training group. In that capacity, his role was to train the staff members to "deal with their own interpersonal conflicts, share information, and solve problems by a process of interaction and social learning. . . ." The staff members, in turn, act in the same role for inmates.

In the second illustration, the author describes the "asklepieion experience," in which a psychiatrist developed a sort of therapeutic community in a maximum security federal prison. The psychiatrist, Martin Groder, gained permission from authorities to allow him to use some twenty-five volunteer inmates to evolve their own treatment program. No prison officers were involved with forming the group; the only non-inmates were Groder and two mental health staff members. The inmates lived in a special unit, were given lectures, and began using "confrontation groups." At any time of the day or night, they could meet to discuss behavior, problems, etc. They also had regularly scheduled meetings with the same type of open discussions. Jobs around the unit were allocated according to merit, and basic rules were strictly enforced (no gambling, no drugs, etc.). In essence, the group established its own culture within the prison. The peer group, without outside interference, made and lived by its own rules and discussed and adopted different types of treatment to suit its members (e.g., gestalt, behavior modification). Although the project was successful, it was stopped after a period of time because it never received full support from the prison's upper administrators and the federal correctional system as a whole.

Comments and Follow-up Work.   These two examples provide illustrations of behavioral scientists' functions in the treatment area, both in the design of a new treatment program and in the thinking about alternative ways of conceptualizing treatment. Also useful is the presentation of start-up and continuation difficulties. The problem of nonsupport from administration is a common one with innovative programs of any type. Behavioral scientists could be engaged in another role in this kind of program development experience, through examining the reasons why they think that the program was not continued. This is program implementation research, of which there has been little to date. Scheirer's book is a good example of the opportunities in this direction.[39]
Additionally, behavioral scientists could:

1. Research the linkage of clinical treatment with educational strategies designed to increase the personal development of offenders.
2. Design and pilot test treatment models that combine clinical work, classroom education, and job orientation and skills training into an integrated whole.
3. Conduct an educational seminar with local educators on the special educational needs of offenders.
4. Consult with management as the process specialist leading the development of an educational program for delinquents sponsored by the local school district and integrated with the total corrections program.

Closely allied to this general educational work is the specific area of vocational treatment.

Vocational Treatment.   In this work, the behavioral scientist is essentially extending the treatment function to the vocational area, often with an educational approach. There is a need to teach offenders all aspects of the work system, including specific skills, self-awareness of their own interests and abilities, career awareness, attitudes toward work, beginning skills and competencies, employability skills, and job and career goal planning. As a part of this system, there are significant concerns about the unrealistic expectations that are sometimes generated in vocational planning and treatment. Thus there is a need to work through the problem of vocational adjustment in terms of real goals and expected accomplishments. Finally, there is a need to examine the linkage between vocational adjustment and recidivism, particularly in light of the increased interest in and concern for the employability of offenders.

As in the other aspects of treatment, vocational topics can employ behavioral scientists in assessment and diagnosis, treatment, education and training, research, and consultation. A single case illustrates one area of work.

CASE THIRTY-NINE: VOCATIONAL TREATMENT.   There has been much work published regarding employment training within institutions. However, there has been relatively little addresssing the work experiences and needs of clients once they are out of prison. The following presents the results of one review.

Shenk, Williams, and Ziegenfuss reported on an exploratory cost–benefit review of a community-based offender placement program.[40] The program uses in-prison therapy and outside placement to solve a vocational problem. The problem, which stimulated the creation of the Offender Development Service (ODS), was a complex web involving nonworking inmates, costs and fines that could not be paid, lack of contribution to the community's economy, and inmates returning to prison with accompanying costs of arrest, trial, and incarceration.

The ODS program provides therapy and employment training and assistance for offenders soon to be released from prison, and for offenders on probation and parole. The program was designed to integrate therapy, employment services, and follow-up in one total service approach. While in prison the offender receives in-depth individual, group, and family psychological counseling. To enhance "employability," offenders are given assistance in their job search, including interview and application training as needed. After employment, twenty-four-hour crisis intervention and follow-up are provided to avoid problems and to assist the offenders' smooth transition into society. The inmates' problems are defined as partly personal and partly a function of their difficulties in establishing an economically self-sufficient life-style. When inmates become economically independent, the benefits extend beyond them personally, contributing to the community's social stability and tax base. The program as a whole benefits the prison's already existing service network and range of training opportunities.

Comments and Follow-up Work.   This program illustrates the use of behavioral science work to contribute to the successful reintegration of the offender into the community. The role here was a consulting/evaluative one in which the behavioral scientist conducted a preliminary evaluation of the program with a cost–benefit orientation. Although somewhat summative in nature, the evaluation was used to continue the program's development, defining both its strengths and its areas of need.

There are other subjects for work in this area. Behavioral scientists could:

1. Research the cost benefit contribution of a vocational training program for offenders, extending the work that has been done (e.g., on a local or national level).
2. Review the existing literature on the benefits of vocational treatment to offenders, creating a seminar for management and fundors such as county commissioners (who might financially support program development).
3. Consult with management in the process of development of a corporate advisory group that would guide the vocational programs efforts to link with the private sector.

Inmates not only need educational and vocational help; medical needs are also present.

Medical Care.   One basic consideration of the overall treatment effort for prison inmates is medical care. This care can be described as including treatment for medical conditions already fully developed, intervention in developing problems, and prevention of problems such as addictions, cancer due to smoking, and other health problems common to the population as a whole. Medical care provision has been notoriously poor in correctional organizations throughout the United States.[41-45] This problem has recently gained increased attention, and various proposals have been presented to address the issue. Behavioral scientists can become involved in helping to design and develop prison medical care delivery systems.

Obviously, physicians, nurses, and allied health personnel are the key people involved in delivering the services. But, behavioral scientists have many roles to play within the delivery system's design, development, and operation. For example, behavioral scientists may contribute methodological skills for a needs assessment of the inmates' medical problems. This would be done through an applied research or consulting function. As a follow-up, behavioral scientists could conduct a services assessment, evaluating either the process or the results of existing medical services, documenting what services and physical capabilities are currently available and how they affect the inmates.

The following case example is a linkage of the medical care subject and a subsequent topic, the rights of offenders. It is certainly indicative of the challenging design and development problems in which behavioral scientists could become involved.

CASE FORTY: PRISON MEDICAL CARE DESIGN PROBLEMS.   One problem facing nearly all facilities is establishing a mechanism for delivering medical care to inmates. It has been nortoriously difficult to recruit good medical practitioners to provide these services, which have typically been grossly underfunded. The problem then becomes: how can we design a system for providing medical care to inmates that is of acceptable quality and quantity? The following case recognizes and reviews this problem, with some accompanying recommendations.

Ziegenfuss discussed the medical care system in prisons in terms of whether or not it is a discriminatory service based on inadequate quantity and quality.[45] Citing reports written in the 1970s, he reviewed the provision of medical services in prisons and the increasing advocacy and intervention activities of the courts. This analysis cited several studies that revealed serious questions about the quality and quantity of correctional medical care provided. The traditional problem-solving approach would be to provide more and better care within the same structure. Consideration of altering the present intra-institutional delivery system was examined in this article, primarily the use of the community's medical and health care system through contracts and other means. Importantly, problem resolution was defined in terms of service system design and redesign.

The analysis produced a set of continuing development needs, including the following research-and-development–oriented ones. There is a need for:

1. Analyses of the technical problems of community hospitals providing prison care.
2. Designs for the administrative structure of shared services with the prison's administration.
3. Analyses of community medical personnel's willingness and attitudes toward rendering prison care.
4. Models of grievance programs for prison medical care.
5. Legal analyses of the liability issues related to shared services (prison care in a community hospital).
6. Comparative studies of the cost of prison-based and community-based care.
7. Analyses of the political and organizational development barriers to implementation.
8. Models for analyzing the success or failure of the programs.[46]

This list of "work needs" establishes a task agenda for redesigning the prison medical care system. The recommendation by the author was that an acceptance of responsibility by community hospitals should be fostered. This requires much dialogue between prison and community medical and health care systems personnel. The above list of items must be addressed in order to complete the work which could be undertaken by a group of task forces organized as a planning project.

Comments and Follow-up Work.   The eight tasks suggested above are a blueprint for behavioral scientists' involvement in the prison medical care problem. While some of the tasks are extra-disciplinary (e.g., legal), the behavioral scientist can become involved in the overall design work and in specific phases of the implementation of a new program (e.g., either formative or summative evaluations). This is an example of behavioral science analysis of an organization systems problem with the identification of additional task opportunities.

Behavioral scientists could also:

1. Research the types and extent of medical care available to offenders in local facilities.
2. Research innovative designs tested for contracting medical care responsibilities to local hospitals in place of a separate prison medical care program.
3. Consult with local hospital representatives and corrections management on the development of a task force to address treatment needs and collaborative action.

All of these treatment services are to prepare the inmate for better adjustment on return to the community. This is the area of community adjustment, considered next.

Community Adjustment. This behavioral science activity involves providing programs and direct services to inmates in order to increase the match of their behavior with the requirements, norms, and guidelines of the community in which they are currently living, or would like to live. Behavioral scientists' work in this area might include the following:

- Analysis of community citizens' expectancies regarding typical problems, acceptance/rejection, etc.
- Analysis of post-release employment, expenditures, income, job type, social support, and living situation.
- Relationship with community programs, including work release, halfway houses, mental health centers.
- Job search and cultural integration as a whole.

The above list indicates that a wide range of topics under the broad label "community adjustment" provide ample opportunities for behavioral scientists' involvement.

Since the broad area of community adjustment has received increasing attention, the question is: do we know enough about this important phase of treatment in corrections work? Reintegration of former residents of institutions of all types (e.g., the retarded and mentally disabled as well) is considered to rest on strong social support during the initial period of reentry. Behavioral scientists can assess and define both the supports that now exist and the needs for additional programs such as discharge planning and follow-up monitoring.

CASE FORTY-ONE: COMMUNITY ADJUSTMENT TREATMENT. How does the correctional organization help former inmates to adjust to the world outside the institution? Some institutions have made no attempt to aid adjustment, while others have been quite vigorous in their attempts and their varieties of approaches. The following case discusses this problem with respect to juveniles.

Newman presents a definition and general information on juvenile aftercare.[47] The author defines the process as "the release of a child from an institution at the time when he can best benefit from release and from life in the community under the supervision of a counselor." As a review of the existing situation, data from a survey of state-operated special aftercare programs were presented. Forty states have programs. One of the findings was that juvenile aftercare has no clear organizational pattern; it may be the responsibility of a public welfare agency, the institution itself, or some other unit. In only thirty-four states did the state department running the juvenile institutions also provide aftercare services.

There were other findings that indicated needs. Although standards require accurate reporting of parole and aftercare, few states had any reliable procedure for collecting even simple data. The authority to release juveniles from state institutions is given to various people, groups, or agencies, including parole boards, departments of public welfare, or youth authorities. The average length of aftercare varies, and the trend seems to be to keep girls under supervision longer than boys. The standard minimum education for aftercare workers should be a bachelor's degree in the social or behavioral sciences and one year of work in a related field. While nearly all states reported having such requirements, few actually enforced the requirements. In-service training programs were not provided. The average caseload per worker was much higher than recommended.

The author found that: "In short, supportive, sustained and positive implementation of an aftercare plan is, more often than not, rare."[48]

The author noted the following implications and/or suggestions from the survey:

1. Clear lines of responsibility and authority for aftercare are needed, and the trend is toward state-operated programs.
2. A statewide reporting system and research are essential for planning, program development, and agency effectiveness.
3. The trend is toward employing qualified counselors with skills in group treatment and casework, with "a sustained and enlightened staff development program" necessary.
4. Aftercare planning should begin immediately after commitment.
5. Staff members need alternative resources, and the trend is toward community resources (youth employment services, etc.) and the use of substitute homes (foster homes, group care, etc.).

Comments and Follow-up Work.   The author analyzed the status of juvenile aftercare services in this country. This analysis was followed by presentation of a "goal plan" for continued development of aftercare systems. The items on the goal plan indicate that the needs are both organizational and individual-staff-related. The behavioral scientist works here as a consultant of sorts, actually creating an organizational treatment plan for discharge system development following an assessment of the existing situation.

With the same work orientation, there are other subjects. Behavioral scientists could:

1. Evaluate the extent to which prison clinical treatment addresses community adjustment, especially including post-discharge contact and support.
2. Conduct an educational seminar for community service agencies, outlining the community adjustment needs of offenders and identifying which agencies could make what kind of contribution to meeting those needs.
3. Consult with management to assist in the design of a multi-agency community adjustment program that reflects an area-wide, integrated approach to meeting offenders' needs for adjustment assistance.

All services must be rendered in compliance with professional norms and legal guidelines, the following topic.

Civil Rights Protection

There has recently been much interest in the civil rights of the inmate, that is, those rights provided for in the U.S. judicial system. What are they, and how do they involve behavioral scientists? In a recent review of patients' rights, Ziegenfuss listed the following topics under the heading of civil rights:[49]

- Competency
- Discrimination
- Driver's license
- Education
- Labor and compensation
- Voting
- Marriage and divorce
- Privacy
- Religion
- Sexuality

- Custody
- Contracts

The literature involving the above list is voluminous. The key point here is that inmates do have civil rights, and that there are various and conflicting views about the extent of these rights in various situations and at various federal, state, and local prisons.

Increasingly, it is being recognized that the true problem for the future is that of how to design and redesign health and human service systems so that they are consistent with the demands of civil rights (see Ziegenfuss[50]). With this view, the question is: how do we develop effective correctional programs that are consistent with civil rights guidelines such as freedom of religion, rights to education, contracting, and the others? Solving the design problem involves essentially a best match between rights and such program areas as treatment, management, philosophy, and physical environment. The potential involvement of behavioral scientists in this task is enormous. Ziegenfuss has identified a list of eighty-three work/research topics for a start.[51] The following case is certainly only one of many examples.

CASE FORTY-TWO: CLIENTS' RIGHTS. There is extreme difficulty in legally defining *what rights* to *what kinds* of *treatment* inmates actually have. As a result it is typically most difficult to make a determination as to whether a given organization is in violation of an inmate's civil rights—either certain rights in general as noted above (labor, marriage, etc.), or rights to very basic treatment within the institution. The following example describes one behavioral scientist's involvement in an inmates' rights case.

Brodsky[52] described a psychologist's involvement in a class action suit brought against the Mayaguez Industrial School in Puerto Rico. The suit alleged that the rights of the juveniles housed at the school were being violated because the school had insufficient staff members, no treatment program, unsafe and unsanitary living areas, extreme disciplinary measures, etc. Brodsky was asked to inspect the school at two different times. Both times he found conditions similar to those identified in the suit.

For example, in one part of the institution (the Center for Intensive Treatment), he reported that boys were locked in their cells for extended periods of time ranging from weeks to years. There were toilets but not wash basins. The boys had no recreation time, and they could not pariticpate in any of the institution's educational or vocational classes. After interviewing twenty-four of the boys who were in isolation, the author reported most of them were depressed, insomniac; were afraid they might lose emotional contact; or expressed the feeling that they were being strangled or asphyxiated. Additionally, the author found that beatings by guards were common. There were no organized counseling or treatment, no classification system for placement use, and no accountability measures for the staff.

Several times consent decrees were negotiated between the Department of Social Services and the plaintiffs, but each time the judges denied them. Finally, in 1981, six years after the original complaint was filed, the trial was under way. Brodsky gave testimony as to what he had learned on his visits to the school. In the cross examination, three major questions surfaced: "Did the school experience cause the emotional distress in the boys?" "Did the language difference interfere with objective understanding and assessment?" "Did the boys successfully exaggerate because they knew the inspector might help improve their living conditions?" At the time the article was written, the case was still under consideration by the court, and few changes had been made at the school.

Brodsky concluded by discussing the slow process of correctional change. He stated that the legal process and the courts must be the vehicle for change, not the social scientist. The effectiveness of the psychologist (or other social or behavioral scientist) depends on truly being an outside evaluator. Similarly, if the internal change process of the institution does not work, outside pressure must be used to spark change.

Comments and Follow-up Work.   This case presents an example of the behavioral scientist in several roles. He was brought in to evaluate the existing situation in the institution—in effect, a consulting function. However, the topic under concern was really the assessment and treatment process within the organization. Thus, the behavioral scientist was providing an "*assessment* of the assessment" function, as well as an examination of the extent and quality of the *treatment* processes within the organization. The problems identified in this institution are not unlike those experienced in many public institutions in the United States and elsewhere. With regard to the absence of services and the civil rights problem described here, behavioral scientists have an extensive agenda for work in almost all of their functions for decades.

Specifically, behavioral scientists could begin with the following. They could:

1. Research the clients' rights problem that have been raised about certain treatments in prison (e.g., involuntary behavior modification programs), identifying those that are inappropriate or borderline and therefore not recommended for use in their region.
2. Provide an educational seminar outlining the purposes of clients' rights and some methods for avoiding conflicts.
3. Consult with management on litigation avoidance strategies with regard to clients' rights (e.g., on the development of a prisoner complaint program).

4. Consult with management on the redesign of organizational policies and procedures to make them more consistent with clients' rights demands.

A civil rights concern of many advocates involves abuse. Since it is a particularly difficult and a now somewhat known problem, it is addressed separately.

Abuse Control

Abuse has been a concern for major institutions of all types, from mental health facilities to prisons to nursing homes. It is now accepted that abuse does occur and that there are two types, physical and psychological. In a previous publication, Ziegenfuss defined the problem as follows:

> There are essentially two types of abuse. Physical abuse is the hitting or striking of a patient, or in some way physically abusing the patient's person. Psychological abuse is the verbal and environmental pressures on patients which produce some harm to the patient's emotional status or psychological well being.[53]

The abuse question thus concerns both the physical and the psychological, or organizational, climate. The debate about the extent of the abuse is vigorous, but both sides are right, as the following comment suggests:

> Currently, there is an open debate regarding how much abuse exists within treatment settings such as state mental hospitals (or prisons). Unfortunately, the conflicting but appropriate answer is that there is far more abuse than some people believe but significantly less than others believe. One advocacy group found abuse to be the most frequent rights violation complaint. Another found it to be the third highest category.[54]

Patients and inmates have much in common when they are institutionalized in large facilities. The issues of abuse that are identified as problematic for patients are typically similar for inmates. The following list is illustrative:

- The provision of drugs and alcohol in return for favors from patients.
- The withholding of privileges in return for favors.
- Slapping and kicking when patients are thought to be no longer manageable.

- Handling patients physically (e.g., restraining them) when other means are possible.
- Maintenance of indecent physical facilities.
- Verbal harassment (threats, etc).
- General threats of harm if patient will not behave "appropriately."

The list is made longer by the misplaced creativity of the staffs and fellow residents of the institutions.

The sources for abuse are generally considered to be staff, the environment as a whole, or the treatment program itself. Each of these sources can generate different types of abuse. *Staff persons* contribute physical abuse through hitting or other means. The *environment* of the facility can become extremely oppressive with overcrowding, unsanitary conditions, and other physical problems. Last, the *treatment program* can be abusive in that it exerts undue pressure on inmates, or strips them of their dignity through certain treatment techniques; for example, some behavior modification programs would be so classified.

Behavioral scientists have been involved in several roles with regard to the abuse problem. There have been attempts to assess the extent of abuse and to devise methods for diminishing abuse within the organization (e.g., complaint programs).[55] We need first to understand the forces that create and support abuse.

CASE FORTY-THREE: ABUSE. The abuse problem is a significant one for both managers and clinicians within the institution. The question is: how should it be addressed? The answers are usually derived according to the source or cause of the abuse problem. Following the above comments about the three-part derivation, responses are usually directed at staff, at the environment, or at the treatment program. Rarely is there an integrated plan for reducing abuse involving all three causative factors. As an indication of the environmental aspects of abuse (the total organizational climate problem), the following case points out some of the difficulties inherent in an evaluation of this topic.

Bigelow and Driscoll conducted a study to determine how the power used by a facility affected the rehabilitation of the inmates.[56] The study was conducted at a federal correctional center for young men who had committed major crimes. Three categories of variables were used: status, power, and involvement. Under status, all members of the facility were categorized; inmates were considered rank and file, while authorities, supervisors, etc., were categorized as elite. Two types of power were studied: coercive power uses force or threatens force to "limit the behavioral alternatives of the inmates"; normative power uses persuasion and suggestion to influence behavior. The third variable, involvement, assessed the inmates' degree of participation in the organization, with the classification varying from alienation to commitment. The researchers began with the view that inmates working with staff who use normative power techniques tend to be more cooperative and to see the authorities as working models. They also propose that "effective resocialization of the inmates occurs under these conditions."

The researchers chose ninety-seven inmates from a rehabilitation-oriented institution. Of these inmates, fifty-nine were from the prison dormitory, where rank-and-file/elite relationships were based on coercive power. Thirty-eight inmates were from workshops, where noncoercive power was predominant. All of the inmates were given a questionnaire consisting of six scales: coercive power scale, cooperative attitude scale, cooperative norms scale, work values of the elite scale, work value of the subject scale, and a leadership scale.

The results supported most of the researchers' hypotheses. First, inmates working with the less coercive elite developed more cooperative attitudes than the coerced inmates. A more coercive elite was associated with less cooperative leadership, group norms, and attitudes among its rank and file. The less coercive elite was perceived as a better model for learning socially adaptive work values. The last hypothesis, only vaguely supported by the data, was that the less coerced inmates assimilate more socially adaptive work values than the more coerced.

In conclusion, although the data did show a positive association between less coercion and certain rehabilitative factors, they did not show that the noncoerced inmates were any further along in the actual rehabilitation process. This is important, since the major objective of the facility is to rehabilitate. However, at the very least, the study did show a close relationship between lack of coercive power, inmate involvement, and rehabilitation. Therefore, it offers support and a suggestion for the use of noncoercive techniques by prison authorities.

Comments and Follow-up Work.   This is *not* an abuse study and should not be considered as such. However, we can adapt our thinking of it by considering how coercive the institution as a whole can become, asking at what point coercion becomes "environmental abuse" that undercuts rehabilitation. Essentially, the linkage the behavioral scientists sought here concerned the contribution of coercion to rehabilitation. To the extent that an extremely coercive environment undercuts rehabilitation, we have a somewhat "abusive situation." Although this is perhaps a bit of an intellectual "leap," abuse could be considered to be operational here in the sense that the coercive environment tends to undercut the treatment objective of the institution, that is, provided that one exists.

This also directly raises the question: is an environment that is contratherapeutic or contrarehabilitative abusive? Have we established an institution for inmates that is designed (overtly or covertly) to be abusive of them in terms of generating environmental pressures that counteract rehabilitative work? While certainly not an example of "purposeful-obvious" abuse, this environment does represent the subtle, inadvertent type that often exists as a part of the organizational setting.

How could behavioral scientists become involved in this problem? They could:

1. Conduct a survey of staff and inmates inquiring into the level of abuse by identifying it in other, less emotionally loaded terms (e.g., "environmental negatives," "staff pressures," "treatment program inappropriateness," or other terms that clarify the nature of the problems present).
2. Conduct an educational seminar on abuse for the staff of the organization.
3. Consult with management on the design and implementation of anti-abuse strategies (e.g., staff education, complaint program, disciplinary measures) with the full participation of the inmates and staff in order to make them collaborative strategies.

Abuse can be set up by the environment although the effects are often very subtle. What is the environment? The next section discusses this subject.

Environmental Management

The concern for the environment is a concern for both the physical and psychological aspects of the institution that create the "context" in which the inmates exist. In an extension of patients' rights demands, inmates could construct a list of demands for environmental rights for the following reasons:

The general purpose of environmental rights is to ensure that the setting in which patients are treated meets minimal standards. There are four specific purposes.

- to ensure that the physical setting is appropriate
- to ensure that the setting supports therapeutic goal intentions
- to ensure that the setting does not undermine patient dignity and respect
- to ensure that the setting promotes the safety and humanity of patients while they are in treatment. . .[57]

The elements of the physical setting, the environment in which inmates are imprisoned, might include the following:

- Dining areas
- Grounds
- The level of restrictions in the setting
- Lighting
- Physical effects and private space
- Adequate ventilation

In addition to this illustrative list, other aspects of concern in the environment could include such topics as construction materials, fire protection, safety procedures, sanitary conditions, heat and electric specifications, emergency power, and shelter in case of other emergencies.

In addition to the physical characteristics, several behavioral scientists have begun to identify psychological characteristics of the environment.[58] These have to do with the psychosocial context in which the inmates live on a day-to-day basis (i.e., the therapeutic environment[59]). For example, is the climate characterized by fear, by threats, by extensive control from the legal authorities? Obviously in a prison institution the answer is yes. But some institutional environments are more subtle and have less of some of these characteristics than others. Several behavioral scientists have begun to measure those characteristics in a wide range of institutional facilities. This aspect of the environment is obviously a good match with behavioral scientists' interest in psychological and psychosocial aspects of people, groups, and organizations in interaction. The following case illustrates one behavioral scientist's work in this area.

CASE FORTY-FOUR: ASSESSMENT OF THE INSTITUTIONAL ENVIRONMENT. To date, there has been little consensus about an exact set of characteristics for the institutional environment. However, some behavioral scientists have been taking the lead in trying to establish what those characteristics are and how they relate to both inmates and staff working in the institution. The following example is illustrative of some of the work in this area.

Farbstein developed evaluation instruments to be used to determine the effects of the design of correctional institutions on behavior.[60] Seventy-one architects and seventy-one jail administrators were surveyed. In developing a standardized set of instruments, the intention was to create a mechanism for comprehensive environmental review that was quick and efficient enough for use. The analytical approach was to produce information useful to individual institutions and to extract multi-institutional data concerning common environmental influences on behavior. The instruments included attitudinal and environmental perception data, behavioral observations, record information about the physical setting, organization type, and style, and archival data. Portions of the data from two case studies involving 145 inmates and 42 officers were presented.

Comments and Follow-up Work. This article is illustrative of some of the leading work in this area. Although it is at a fairly early stage in its development, it is part of the ongoing research on man/environment relations that has received increasing attention in the last ten years. Some of the leading questions are: (1) what is the behavioral response to certain designs of institutions, and (2) how can those designs be used to create the behavioral responses that are most beneficial to both the individual inmate and to the management of the facility? Behavioral scientists are just beginning work in this area, as approaches and instruments are still being developed. It is therefore a research function with somewhat limited and tentative applications to date.

The relative newness also means that there is opportunity to open new subjects and create new applications. Behavioral scientists could:

1. Assess the environment of a local correctional facility with a positive constructive approach that yields specific suggestions for improvements that are feasible for the facility.
2. Survey the literature on correctional environment design, passing on to the local facility management suggestions based on pilot work tried elsewhere.
3. Consult with management on the development of an environmental redesign group composed of staff and inmates charged with the task of creating recommendations for improvement (e.g., an interactive participative system redesign group[60]).

Concern with the environment is increasing constantly now. Behavioral scientists should be at the forefront of the concern.

Discharge

Discharge is the final point of interaction between the inmate and the correctional system and is formally defined as "the point at which the inmate's active involvement with the program is terminated and the program no longer maintains active responsibility for the inmate."[61] Discharge involves a series of steps and as a process can be understood in terms of the prisoner's parallels with patients. The steps include the following:

- notice of the intent to discharge provided to [inmate], family and relevant others
- review of accumulated treatment progress information and an analysis of the current status of the [inmate]
- a hearing to secure the [inmate's] version of his current status
- a review of the discharge plan developed with [inmate] participation

- settlement of all administrative and court issues related to the release of the [inmate]
- the actual release of the [inmate].[62]

As noted by Brakel and Rock,[63] discharge can be differentiated into three components: clinical, administrative, and judicial discharge. The clinical discharge is the "point at which the [inmate's] active involvement with the clinical program ends." Administrative discharge involves release from the administrative entanglements of the care system, including settlement of all monies, forms, release statements, and so on. The judicial discharge is "the point at which the [inmate's] involvement with the court is terminated and the court no longer maintains an active responsibility for the patient."[64]

Using this definition of discharge with clinical, administrative, and judicial aspects, the range of involvement potential for behavioral scientists is considerable. For example, they could examine the process by which discharge is planned with regard to the clinical program. Does it ensure that clinical gains made within the prison are transferred to the inmate's setting on the outside? Additionally, the inmate's concern with the discharge process could involve the linkage between the prison and the court system. What are the criteria by which discharge is established, and are those criteria binding for all participants?

The following example indicates one area of concern, the furlough program.

CASE FORTY FIVE: THE DISCHARGE–FURLOUGH PROBLEM. A question that many administrative and correctional managers are concerned with is whether or not there are ways to utilize the discharge process (or parts of it) to enhance the treatment plan for the inmate. One mechanism that has been used is a furlough program by which inmates are given a "practice discharge." The following case example illustrates the issues.

To evaluate the furlough program, an analysis was conducted of the rates of recidivism for individuals released from Massachusetts State Correctional Institutions in 1973 and 1974.[65] The study question was: is furlough an effective correctional method? Inmates who had experienced one or more furloughs during their incarceration were studied to determine whether they were less likely to be reincarcerated within one year of their release from prison than similar types of inmates who did not participate in the furlough program. The subjects of the study were 1719 males who were released over a two-year period. The first experiment involved 610 furlough and 268 nonfurlough subjects released in 1973. The second experiment involved 621 furlough and 220 nonfurlough subjects. The results of both experiments indicated that the home furlough program contributed to a significant reduction in recidivism rates. The authors believe that programs such as this furlough process can be effective in reducing repeated criminal behavior of released prisoners.

Comments and Follow-up Work.   This is a very good example of behavioral science research on a program component, an evaluation of furlough impact on individual, organizational, and societal objectives. Both the individual and society have a stake in reduced criminal offenses, as does the correctional organization that wants to demonstrate its effectiveness. Although it is difficult to be sure that all extraneous conditions are controlled for, it appears that the furlough program did contribute to a reduction in criminality following release. This information is useful in program planning and prison management. The furlough program is providing a valuable service for both inmates and society, and as a result is deserving of both clinical and administrative support. The study illustrates the blending of treatment and administrative analyses in an applied research context.

Behavioral scientists also could:

1. Provide treatment services directed to the period when an offender's adjustment problems are often most severe.
2. Survey the community to identify the amount and nature of discharge services available to offenders, including the extent of service integration and cross referral (e.g., job counseling linked to family system support).
3. Consult with management on the design of a discharge follow-up plan, including support groups.
4. Evaluate existing discharge planning in order to identify strengths and weaknesses.

Discharge means discharge into the community. There are corrections programs already in the community that are sometimes linked to the separate residential institutions.

COMMUNITY CORRECTIONS

Community corrections are those activities of the correctional system that exist in the geographic confines of the community. This is noninstitutional criminal justice corrections, which is, by definition, outside of the boundaries of the penal institution. Within the institution's control, several different kinds of community-oriented programs have been discussed, including work release and furloughs. Community corrections includes, in addition to these, the alternatives-to-prison programs that are created to help such groups as addicted and mentally disabled offenders. Many of these programs are identified under the label "halfway houses" and are deserving of further discussion.

Halfway houses have a rather long history in this field, and are used primarily as a means for helping inmates make the transition from inside the prison to outside. There are significant differences in approach across a wide range of therapeutic and clinical support. These differences can be considered to constitute a continuum. On the more intensively therapeutic end of the continuum, the program may have clinical psychologists and clinical social workers along with aides and counselors available on a day-to-day basis to provide individual and group counseling. At the less intensive therapeutic end of the continuum, there are few professionally trained staff available. Primary staff may consist of a "house parent," who attempts to organize and administratively coordinate the boarding-home-like administrative process. With light staffing, the inmates pretty much manage themselves, with little reliance on external staff for clinical support and "treatment."

Behavioral scientists can become involved in assessments of community corrections programs on a variety of topics including the following:

- Identifying what community correction programs exist in a given community.
- Identifying what the needs for community corrections are.
- Assessing the effectiveness of community programs with regard to both treatment and administrative efficiencies.
- Examining the impact of community corrections programs (such as furloughs or halfway houses) on the inmate population in terms of recidivism, working stability, and quality of life.
- Consulting to community corrections organizations to further develop the processes and structures by which they operate.

The following example shows one of the areas in which behavioral scientists could become involved.

CASE FORTY SIX: INSTITUTIONAL VERSUS COMMUNITY CORRECTIONS.   There is considerable debate in the field about whether inmates are better served in community programs as opposed to institutional settings. Behavioral scientists can enter this debate from either a research or a development perspective. There is a need to collect additional data on the issue. There is also a need to evaluate what programs already exist using currently available information. The following example presents an analysis of the existing situation.

One study reviewed the current knowledge of the relative effectiveness of institutional and community-based programs for juvenile and adult offenders.[66] The evidence suggests that decisions are made about incarceration without considering whether community-based programs are as effective as institutional ones. A national assessment of institutional and community-based juvenile programs was conducted. The data highlighted similarities and differences in offenders' characteristics, program patterns, and outcomes. The results of the analysis indicate that variables such as race, gender, and state are critical in predicting the appropriate use of community or institutional placement. The knowledge of the comparative effectiveness of institutions versus community programs is not complete or adequate at this point.

Comments and Follow-up Work.   This article raises the question of whether or not inmates should be indiscriminately assigned to either institutional or community programs. Is there a differential inmate response to one or the other? Should we carefully select only certain inmates for inclusion in community corrections programs? Behavioral scientists in this case are presenting an overview of the existing literature. Behavioral scientists could also become involved in assessments for placement, in program evaluations, and in further applied research about how to integrate community programs with institutional ones.

For example, behavioral scientists could:

1. Research the relative costs of institutionalizing an inmate versus close community supervision with job or community service work.
2. In a comparative analysis of institutional versus community programs, research specific elements such as security, consistency with the mission, variety of clinical services available, presence of role models, etc.
3. Consult with management on the design of a community program that is fully integrated with the institutional, diagnosing strengths and weaknesses in the linkage (e.g., communication, discharge planning) and helping to assist with recommendations development.

One "bottom line" in corrections that is of concern to this institution versus community debate is the question of what the impact on recidivism is. As our final topic, recidivism also offers work topics.

RECIDIVISM

Recidivism has received much attention in the criminal justice literature. Its reduction is, in effect, a major goal of the correctional system. Stakeholders in the system are most concerned about how to ensure that inmates do not return to crime. There is a long, ongoing discussion about the recidivism rate, defined as "the number of ex-prisoners who commit crimes and are returned to prison (or jail)."[67] Behavioral scientists can work with prison personnel to develop and/or examine data regarding recidivism rates. It is the applied research aspects of the behavioral scientists' work here that holds the most potential for a contribution to the correctional system. What relationships can behavioral scientists identify that would help the correctional system understand what kinds of programs, support activities, and psychosocial treatments will help offenders to avoid a return to prison?

The set of variables involved in a grand assessment of the contributing factors in recidivism reduction might include the following:

- Imprisonment, including length of sentence, types of institutions, psychological impact.
- Parole, including specialization, supervision.
- Casework and individual counseling, including type and extent.
- Skill development, including opportunities to practice, work release, male/female differences.
- Group methods as opposed to other methods, including milieu therapy and structured leisure time.
- Standard demographic influences such as age, offense type, living situation.
- Behavior record within the institution.

These are an introduction to the kinds of topics that could be addressed by research in this area. The following example identifies one behavioral scientist's initiative.

CASE FORTY-SEVEN: INSTITUTIONAL EFFECTIVENESS. The issue is basically: are institutions effective in keeping inmates from returning to prisons, or are they not? While this is a global question, it has very specific implications for institutions and their correctional activities.

Alper cited numerous studies documenting high recidivism rates among those released from various types of correctional institutions.[68] He provided descriptions of conditions of the institutions, noting that it should not be surprising that the people released turned quickly to crime. Conditions such as overcrowding, poor diets, lack of exercise time, little fresh air, and no access to sanitary facilities were typical examples. In his view, the longer a person is inside a prison, the greater the chances are that he will become attached to it once again.

His analysis next considers the reasons for the ineffectiveness of treatment programs, including such factors as overcrowding, that results in a lack of individualized attention. Institutions that do not emphasize rehabilitation, focus on confinement and conformity, and use primarily fear, only teach prisoners to hide their true feelings. Another cited reason for ineffectiveness is that prisoners are paroled because their in-prison behavior meets certain standards. Once outside, they revert to previous behavior because "inwardly the system of treatment or confinement did not alter the basic dynamics of their lives." The author concludes that the answer seems to be in finding alternative measures to imprisonment.

Comments and Follow-up Work.   In this review, the behavioral scientist discusses the total organizational effects of the institution including specific environmental conditions such as overcrowding. The effects *in total* are in his view responsible for producing recidivism. His perspective is that an individual action or two would not be sufficient to correct the problem. Instead a major organizational change is needed. The change as derived from some of the findings here could be from institutional to community corrections facilities. The transition would provide ample work for behavioral scientists in all the functional areas.

For example, behavioral scientists could:

1. Research the impact of a major change (e.g., new facility, new community program) on various aspects of offender services (e.g., access, range, impact on crime and recidivism).
2. Conduct an educational program in which various measures of overall organizational effectiveness are discussed and analyzed as to their relevance to certain kinds of subprograms (e.g., community, job placement, education).
3. Consult with management on the selection of a set of key results areas by which the organization's performance will be measured.

Organization performance indicators such as recidivism are difficult to define and hard to gain consensus on. But they represent key data for helping the organization determine whether it is doing the "right things" in the "right ways." Behavioral scientists have contributed and can increase their contributions in this challenging area.

SUMMARY

This chapter reviewed behavioral scientists' activities with regard to technical services issues in the corrections organization. These included: presentence activities; probation; elements of institutionalization, including admissions, treatment, civil rights, abuse, environment, and discharge; community corrections; and recidivism. In this chapter these "technologies" are considered the main work of the corrections organization. All five functions of behavioral scientists can be applied here.

Presentence activities involve diversion and investigation. Behavioral scientists have contributed investigative reports and assessments of the dangerousness of individuals. Further opportunities for research into sensitive problems involved in the disposition of offenders are plentiful. Alternative-to-prison program planning and clinical treatments are other traditional areas that offer opportunities.

Three aspects of probation are: restrictions, revocation, and termination. Much work is needed in the area of restrictions. Developing restrictions that shape the desired behavior is difficult and certainly not an exact science. Potential contributions in research, education, training, and consultation are great, with practically an open field for behavioral scientists. Revocation occurs when the terms of restrictions are ignored or broken, while termination means that restrictions are completed successfully. Comparisons of the two situations are helpful in attaining a best match between offender and restrictions.

Institutionalization has many technical aspects, including: admission, classification, treatment, civil rights protection, abuse control, environmental management, and discharge. Behavioral scientists traditionally contributed assessments at admission for the classification and treatment of offenders using a variety of clinical and vocational services. A newer clinical subarea is educationally oriented treatment designed to bring prisoners up to functional social levels as well as to develop job skills through an educational process. Behavioral scientists have contributed program designs here as well as in other treatment areas such as medical care and community adjustment. Civil rights protection was opened first by the legal profession, but is rapidly engaging behavioral scientists, who recognize the individual and organization behavior aspects.

Physical and psychological abuse are problems in many institutional settings. Starting with the forces that create and support abuse, the behavioral scientist can continue to address all aspects of the problem. Once identified, methods for correcting abusive situations must be found quickly and transmitted to the institution. As an outside evaluator, educator, and change agent, the behavioral scientist has an invaluable role to play through all five basic functions.

Environmental management is another relatively new technical concern. Architects design with people in mind and within the confines of building and safety standards. But the issue of just how much environment can affect behavior has only recently surfaced as a research area. Assessing and correcting institutional environmental impacts is truly a multidisciplinary problem.

Discharge has three components: clinical, administrative, and judicial. Discharge can end an offender's formal association with the correctional organization. A concern here is operating discharge programs to enable them to contribute to reducing recidivism rates. One method meeting with apparent success is a furlough program of practice discharges.

Community corrections includes work release programs, furloughs, and alternative-to-prison programs. A traditional program is the halfway house, which provides professional support in making the transition from prison to society. Program assessment is a major work area for behavioral scientists with an additional organizational development consultation role.

Reducing recidivism rates is a high-priority goal for the correctional system. The contributions here are primarily in the research area. Identifying successful programs and best-match opportunities between program and offender are two of the most obvious areas. Helping to design and develop model programs that reduce recidivism is another area of contribution.

The cases cited in this chapter are illustrative of the kinds of activities that could be directed at individual correctional problems. With some imagination, it is not difficult to understand how these functional examples would be applied to other technical aspects; for example, the evaluation process used in examining a treatment program could also be used to consider the treatment program in a community corrections system. The reader should be interested in trying to match the existing functional activities of behavioral scientists in one technical area with their potential for action in other areas as well.

Table 4-1 presented an overview of these technical concerns and an illustration of the behavioral scientist's generic functional impact.

REFERENCES

1. Holten, N. G., and Jones, M. E. (1982). *The System of Criminal Justice*. Boston: Little, Brown.
2. Newman, D. J. (1975). *Introduction to Criminal Justice*. Philadelophia: Lippincott.
3. Kast, F. E., and Rosenzweig, J. E. (1979). *Organization and Management*. New York: McGraw-Hill, p. 110.
4. Holten and Jones. Op. cit.
5. *Ibid*
6. *Ibid*
7. Kozol, H. L., Boucher, R. J., and Garofalo, R. F. (1972) The diagnosis and treatment of dangerousness. *Crime and Delinquency* 18, pp 371–392.
8. *Ibid*
9. Dix, G. E. (1976). Differential Processing of Abnormal Sex Offenders: Utilization of California's Mentally Disordered Sex Offender Program. *Journal of Criminal Law and Criminology*, 67, 233–43.
10. Holten and Jones. Op. cit.
11. Holten and Jones. Op. cit.
12. Kerper, H. B., and Kerper, J. (1974). *Legal Rights of the Convicted*. St. Paul, Minnesota: West Publishing Co.
13. Holten and Jones. Op. cit.
14. Holten and Jones. Op. cit.
15. Brakel, S. J., and Rock, R. S. (1971). *The Mentally Disabled and the Law*. Chicago: University of Chicago Press.

16. Lindman, F. T., and McIntyre, D. M. (eds.) (1961). *The Mentally Disabled and the Law*. Chicago: University of Chicago Press.
17. Ziegenfuss, J. T., and McKenna, C. K. (1979). Process Evaluation As A Tool for Organizational Development. Presented at Annual Meeting American Society of Public Administration, Baltimore Maryland.
18. Ziegenfuss, J. T., and Lasky, D. J. (1975). A Rationale for Evaluating the Quality of Services in Drug and Alcohol Programs: Purpose, Process, Outcome. *Drug Forum*, 5, 171–84.
19. Ziegenfuss, J. T., and Lasky, D. I. (1980). Evaluation and Organizational Development: A Management Consulting Approach. *Evaluation Review*, 45 (5), 665–76.
20. Scheirer, M. A. (1981). *Program Implementation: The Organizational Context*. Beverly Hills, California: Sage.
21. Ziegenfuss, J. T. (1983). *Patients Rights and Professional Practice*. New York: Van Nostrand Reinhold.
22. Holten and Jones. Op. cit.
23. Vetter, H. J., and Simonsen, C. E. (1976). *Criminal Justice in America: The System, The Process, The People*. Philadelphia: Saunders.
24. Donaldson v. O'Connor 493 F. 2d 504, 527 (5th Cir. 1974).
25. Ziegenfuss. Op. cit., see note 21.
26. Clayton, T. (1976). O'Connor v. Donaldson: Impact in the States. *Hospital and Community Psychiatry*. 27 (4).
27. Allen, J. P., Urso, N., Burger, G. (1982, October) Structure of Personality Needs in a Young, Deviant, Male Population. *Professional Psychology* 13(5) 744–51.
28. *Ibid* p. 745.
29. *Ibid* p. 750.
30. Fowler, R. D., and Brodsky, S. L. (1978). Development of a Correctional Clinical Psychology Program. *Professional Psychology*, 9 (3), 440–47.
31. Cubitt, G., and Gendreau, P. (1972). Assessing the Diagnostic Utility of MMPI and 16PF Indices of Homosexuality in a Prison Sample. *Journal of Consulting and Clinical Psychology*, 39, 342.
32. Marquis, H., and Gendreau, P. (1975). Short-Term Educational Upgrading on a Contractual Basis. *Journal of Community Psychology*, 3, 94.
33. Winnick, C. (1979). The Drug Offender. In *Psychology of Crime and Criminal Justice*. New York: Holt, Reinhart & Winston.
34. Yablonsky, L. (1965). *The Tunnel Back*. Baltimore: Penguin.
35. DeLeon, G. (1983). The Next Therapeutic Community: Autocracy and Other Notes Towards Integrating Old and New Therapeutic Communities. *International Journal of Therapeutic Communities*, 4 (4).
36. Ziegenfuss, J. T. and De Leon, G. (Eds). (1983). The Therapeutic Community and Addictions. *International Journal of Therapeutic Communities*, 4 (4).
37. Ziegenfuss, J. T. (1980). The Therapeutic Community: A Plan for Continued International Development. *International Journal of Therapeutic Communities*, 1 (2).
38. Jones, M. (1979). Learning as Treatment. In *Psychology of Crime and Criminal Justice*. New York: Holt, Rinehart & Winston, pp. 470–87.
39. Scheirer, M. A. (1981). *Program Implementation: The Organizational Context*. Beverly Hills: Sage.
40. Shenk, G., Williams, J., and Ziegenfuss, J. T. (1983). The Offender Development Services Program: Cost Savings and Benefits in a County Prison. Paper Presented at National Conference on Social Welfare, Houston, Texas.
41. Cancila, C. (1983). MD Seeks Better Standard of Care for Inmates. *American Medical News*, November 4, 1983.

42. Sandrick, K. (1981, May). Health Care in Correctional Facilities. *Quality Review Bulletin* 7 (5).

43. Sandrick, K. (1981, July). Health Care in Correctional Institutions in the United States, England, Canada, Poland and France. *Quality Review Bulletin,* 7 (7).

44. Goldsmith, S. B. (1972, November). Jailhouse Medicine—Travesty of Justice? *Health Services Reports,* Vol. 87.

45. Ziegenfuss, J. T. (1984). Medical Services in the Prisons: A Discriminatory Practice and Alternatives. *Federal Probation,* 48 (2), pp. 43–48.

46. *Ibid,* p. 48.

47. Newman, C. L. (1968). Juvenile Aftercare. In *Sourcebook on Probation, Parole and Pardons.* C. L. Newman (Ed.) Springfield, Illinois: Charles C. Thomas.

48. *Ibid.*

49. Ziegenfuss. Op. cit., see note 21.

50. Ziegenfuss, J. T. (1983). *Patients Rights and Organizational Models: Sociotechnical Systems Research on Mental Health Programs.* Lanham, Maryland: University Press of America.

51. Ibid.

52. Brodsky, S. (1982). Correctional Change and the Social Scientist: A Case Study. *Journal of Community Psychology.* 10 (2), 128–32.

53. Ziegenfuss. Op. cit., see note 21.

54. Ziegenfuss. Op. cit., see note 21.

55. Ziegenfuss, J. T., Charette, J., and Guenin, M. (1984). The Patients Rights Representative Program: Design of An Ombudsman Program for Mental Patients. *Psychiatric Quarterly.* 56 (1)

56. Bigelow, D. A., and Driscoll, R. H. (1973). Effect of Minimizing Coercion on the Rehabilitation of Prisoners. *Journal of Applied Psychology* 57 (1), 10–14.

57. Ziegenfuss, J. T. Op. cit., see note 21.

58. Proshansky, H. M.; Ittleson, W. H.; Rivlin, L. G. (Eds) (1970) *Environmental Psychology: Man and His Physical Setting.* New York: Holt Rinehart and Winston.

59. Moos, R. H. (1975). *Evaluating Correctional and Community Settings.* New York: John Wiley & Sons.

60. Farbstein, J., and Wener, R. E. (1982). Evaluation of Correctional Environments. *Environment and Behavior* 14 (6), 671–94.

61. Joint Commission on Accreditation of Hospitals. (1979). *Consolidated Standards.* Chicago, Illinois: JCAH.

62. Ziegenfuss. Op. cit., see note 21.

63. Brakel and Rock. Op. cit.

64. Ziegenfuss. Op. cit., see note 21.

65. Leclair, D. P. (1978), Home Furlough Program Effects on Rates of Recidivism. *Criminal Justice and Behavior,* 5 (3), 249–258.

66. Sarri, R. (1981). The Effectiveness Paradox: Institutional vs. Community Placement of Offenders. *Journal of Social Issues,* 37 (2), 34–50.

67. Kalmanoff, A. (1976). *Criminal Justice.* Boston: Little, Brown.

68. Alper, B. (1974). Prisons, Training Schools and Recidivism. In B. Alper, *Prisons Inside-Out.* Cambridge, Massachusetts: Ballinger.

5
CORRECTIONS GOALS, STRUCTURE, PEOPLE AND MANAGEMENT WORK OF BEHAVIORAL SCIENTISTS

This chapter reviews the behavioral scientist's activities in areas of the correctional organization that support and enable but are not technical services. The chapter is concerned with behavioral scientist activities in four organizational subsystems: goals and values, structure, psychosocial, and managerial (see Figure 5-1). These organizational areas were defined in Chapter 1 and reintroduced in Chapter 3 with respect to court organizations. The reader will not be asked to re-review the primary definitions of each of these individual subsystems. They are used again here with case examples identifying behavioral scientist work.

It should be noted that these four parts of the whole organizational system are the support for the delivery of the primary technical service work—punishment, treatment, rehabilitation, and support of offenders in the institution. This means that within the various subsystems there are a range of activities that must be undertaken in order to build the "whole" of the correctional organization. For example, in the managerial subsystem, the four traditional activities of management—planning, organizing, directing, and controlling—are necessary aspects of the correctional manager's tasks.

As we review the cases illustrating actual and potential behavioral scientist work in each of these subsystems, it will be apparent that this is a rich field for study and work topics. Figure 5-1 illustrates the subsystems topics that will be addressed as they fit into the Kast and Rosenzweig organizational systems model.[1] The remainder of the chapter will expand the cases, demonstrating opportunities that have already been exploited by many in the behavioral science field. They will be considered according to subsystem.

GOALS & VALUES

The first subsystem is that of goals and values. What are the goals of the correctional system? While correctional organizations differ, a sample goals set could be listed as follows:

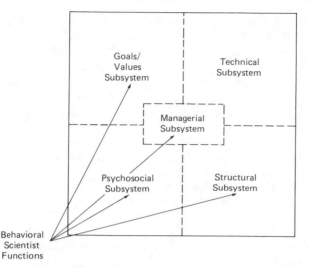

Figure 5-1. Behavioral scientist functions in corrections goals/values, structural, psychosocial, and management systems.

1. Punishment of offenders—retribution for crimes committed and deterrence from future crime.
2. Protection of community members—making society safe.
3. Reformative—securing adoption of the goals and values of society; that is, transforming the offenders' value systems.
4. Rehabilitative—developing offender skills, understanding, and knowledge through education and vocational training.[2]

The question is: do correctional organizations have all of these goals, some of the goals, or none of them? Are they stated explicitly by the correctional organization, and are they translated into operating objectives that help to direct the day-to-day activities of the corrections team? This is both an internal question and an organization–environment one.

These are forces existing outside the boundaries of the correctional organization that help to determine its goals. An analyst must study the forces that are shaping these operating goals, and the whole goal set of the organization. It is but one of the potential study topics illustrated by the first case.

CASE FORTY-EIGHT: GOAL PLANNING. Correctional organizations need to understand goal analysis for the purpose of planning for their organizations and for the development of services to individual prisoners. There must be a match between the goals of society and the individual goals of offenders struggling to integrate themselves into that society. Edith Flynn reviewed social planning issues with regard to this two-directional goals-and-values characteristic of the correctional organization.

Flynn believes that understanding the positive and especially the negative outcomes of previous policy and program decisions relating to social control is important in developing new policy guidelines for crime control.[3] This understanding creates a linkage between goals of previous activities (both their success and failure) and the work to be done in the future. In light of the failure of past policy, most current programs are now generating or using new criteria for decision making. Pressure for criterion change has been accompanied by several other needs, including:

- The need to bridge the gap between the results of research and those of practical action.
- The use of scientific and technical knowledge to help in goal planning and goal development.
- "Suggestions to policy makers promising ways to realize fairness and justice in administration of the criminal justice system."
- The need to make prediction research more responsive to the needs of the system.[4]

Historically, correctional philosophy was predominantly punishment-oriented, a situation reflected in the type of goals research. The single and focused goal of the system was to punish the offender.

More recently, the values and the primary goals of the system have shifted toward rehabilitation, emphasizing changing the offender's attitude. The most recent theoretical philosophy is characterized by the terms "resocialization and reintegration." This philosophy, or goal set, is based on certain assumptions, as follows:

- A great deal of crime can be seen as symptoms of failure and disorganization of the community.
- The way society responds to deviant behavior is an integral part of the crime and delinquency problem.
- Influencing future behavior is more desirable than imposing suffering and discomfort.
- Criminal law is not equally effective in dealing with all forms of deviant behavior.[5]

There is, therefore, a need for comprehensive social planning in the criminal justice field. Why?

The criminal justice system encompasses many levels (federal, state, local, private, etc.) with a consequent need for integrated planning and full-scale coordination. There is also a need for "well-defined objectives, definitions, standards, appropriate techniques for prevention and correction, and careful allocation of resources, meticulous research and program designs."[6]

Comments and Follow-up Work.   The author presented a model for comprehensive planning, crime prevention, and control. The above material raises the question of shifting goals and values, and is the primary concern in this subsystem of the organization. Behavioral scientists can become involved in analyses of this shift (as demonstrated here), or in identifying strategies and methods for assisting the process of goals/values change. For example, how do we help the staff of the institutions to participate in the goal-planning process? And if the changes are significant (e.g., from punishment/security to rehabilitation/treatment), how can behavioral scientists help the staff to accept and support the new goal set?

There are other work areas. Behavioral scientists could:

1. Research the extent of goal-planning use in corrections, including such individual techniques as management by objectives.
2. Present an educational seminar to clinicians and counselors that demonstrates similarities in the use of goal-planning techniques for individuals and for organizational units.
3. Consult with management on the design and implementation of a formal goal-planning system.

Mission, goals, and philosophy are key aspects of the organization, and must be thoroughly considered as a starting point in any anlyses of the use of behavioral science, The next case continues this consideration.

CASE FORTY-NINE: CORRECTIONAL PHILOSOPHY.   This problem of goals is related to and a part of a general correctional philosophy system. The last case linked philosophy and goals. A common belief about organizations is that a broad philosophy leads to certain specific goals of the system. The question is: do we need more debate on and understanding of the philosophy of corrections, the broad framework of which goals are a part?

William Amos reviewed some of the philosophical issues confronting the correctional system.[7] He began by evaluating the status of corrections philosophy in the United States, noting that it is affected first by a national "short term orientation." Americans tend to face problems quickly and expect to find solutions immediately. Second, he believes corrections philosophy is affected by the country's value system. These values include the belief that an individual's rights far outweigh those of society. Additionally, there is a certain awe of professionals and their contributions. He summarizes this national philosophy with: "if we had better training of professional staff and more money for programs, we could re-habilitate most people committed to correctional agencies."[8]

Amos proposes that the national philosophy be modified to include the premise that the behavioral science at this stage do not know how to rehabilitate criminal offenders. The behavioral sciences have increased our knowledge about corrections and have helped individuals, but they have not been able to develop a corrections model that would be suitable for national implementation. What is needed is a model that enables us to "place numbers of people and hopefully have them come out of the other end modified in their behavior and attitudes." For this and other reasons, behavioral sciences research has not met the national correction system needs.

Finally, Amos believes that correctional philosophy should not be based on rehabilitation, offering the following reasons and recommendations:

1. Medical and behavioral sciences do not have the capability to rehabilitate criminals on an organized and consistent basis.
2. Talking of rehabilitating people assumes these people were, in fact, once habilitated to social norms, values, and behavioral expectations.
3. We are too confinement-oriented and tend to confine many in correctional institutions for treatment beyond the capabilities of the institution (e.g., medical, social, and psychological misfits).
4. Those to be institutionalized should only be those sentenced for deterrence, for accountability, or as physical threats to society.
5. Courts should be given more structured and controlled alternatives to in-stitutionalizing.
6. The courts, parole boards, and public must realize that some people must be incarcerated for the welfare of society.
7. "We should work toward a more active use of community based programs for those who need not be placed in an institutional setting." Community correction programs work only for individuals who are willing to participate; they "do not work on a wholesale basis" but are only "one correctional tool among many."
8. Correctional institutions should not be evaluated on the basis of how well their clients perform in the community.
9. A national system of accreditation for insitutions should be established, and they should be required to offer a confined person the "protection, services and opportunity reflecting our belief in the dignity and nature of man." Along with this, a national inmates' bill of rights should be established with all states being urged to adopt and implement it. Finally, a program should be established to build a number of smaller institutions to allow us to get rid of our present "huge human warehouses."[9]

Comments and Follow-up Work.   Here we have an example of the most significant issues involved in the development of the mission of the cor-rectional organization. What is the *core* purpose of the organization—punishment and custody, or rehabilitation? Behavioral scientists are acting in an organizational analyst role here (applied research), contributing to the debate about misson and philosophy, and how these are reflected in the operations of both courts and correctional organizations. In terms of organizational systems planning, this analysis and definition of purpose is a key to realizing the future of the organization.[10-12] Competing missions must be confronted and debated.

Behavioral scientists can assist in creating the dialogue that must take place within the system between key stakeholders (e.g., managers, employees, community representatives). Behavioral scientists can be the "architects" of the planning and purpose-analyzing process; and they can do the work of the analyst, as Amos has done in this article.

Behavioral scientists also could:

1. Research the extent of staff support for a rehabilitation versus a punishment philosophy and/or the level of perceived intra and interpersonal conflict on this issue.
2. Present an educational seminar on the importance of staff attitudes to mission achievement, including philosophical consistency.
3. Consult with management in the design of a process and the choice of techniques for helping one unit (e.g., probation department) change from a punishment to a rehabilitation philosophy.

The development of consensus on mission and goals does not occur without some "differences of opinion." Debate is a healthy process for the organization, but extensive conflict can be divisive and destructive. The next case concerns this problem.

CASE FIFTY: GOAL CONFLICTS.   As noted in Amos's report, there are differences in philosophies and differences in the subsequent objectives and operations resulting from those philosophies. These conflicts emerge in organizations that attempt to achieve the multiple goals of correctional systems, punishment *and* rehabilitation. Some of these problems can be uncovered and discussed, in both a research and an educational contribution.

Klingemann, "investigated goal conflicts in five open, closed, mixed and public educational correctional institutions for juvenile delinquents and pre-delinquents.[13] Three hundred twenty two staff members completed the correctional practices questionnaire recording the percentage of daily work performed for administration, custody and treatment. Attitudinal data on correctional goals and the perceived causes of crime indicated that the majority of subjects supported education, training and therapy that is directed at legal conformity, or personal maturity and autonomy. The majority of subjects also agreed that remorse and deterrence were correctional goals; 53% held the opinion that habitual offenders are born criminals. A rather restrictive attitude toward inmates was typical of respondents when asked the ideal degree of inmate participation in different areas. A significant reduction of custodial activities was advocated with the subjects; *actual* time budget was compared with what they considered the *ideal* time budget. The results indicate that atonement, guilt, custody, and deterrence were related to the appreciation of work conformity as a means of rehabilitation. Overall findings do not support the hypothesis of the functional necessity of goal conflicts.''

Comments and Follow-up Work. Behavioral scientists here analyzed the variety of goal conflicts as they exist in several different types of correctional organizations. They are related to operational responses that identify the type of organization the facility will be—either custodial or treatment in orientation and activity. This is only one example of the work in this area. Behavioral scientists could:

1. Research the level of goal conflict in a local correctional facility by surveying clinicians, counselors, and educational and vocational specialists to identify specific examples and frequency, in preparation for change initiatives.
2. Present a seminar on goal conflict to prison guards using participative teaching techniques that allow and encourage them to confront their feelings about any therapeutic contributions they are expected to make.
3. Conduct management groups that foster communication between supervisors regarding goal conflict using policy and procedure examples that promote conflict between the therapeutic and punishment or security missions.

What kind of structure will ensure the attainment of these missions? The next section will address the structural question.

STRUCTURE

Structure was introduced in the opening chapter and was considered in Chapter 3 with reference to the work on court organizations. For review purposes Kast and Rosenzweig's definition is presented below:

Structure involves the ways in which the tasks of the organization are divided (differentiation) and coordinated (integration). In the formal sense, structure is set forth by organization charts, by position and job descriptions, and by rules and procedures. It is also concerned with patterns of authority, communication, and work flow. The organization's structure provides for formalization of relationships between the technical and the psychosocial subsystems. However, it should be emphasized that this linkage is by no means complete and that many interactions and relationships occur between the technical and psychosocial subsystems that bypass the formal structure.[14]

The cases illustrating behavioral scientists' work involving correction organizational structure include the following topics: probation and parole structures education and training individual job design, and environmental structure.

CASE FIFTY-ONE: PROBATION AND PAROLE STRUCTURE. Several structural questions confront correctional organizations, including, for example: how is the parole and pardon structure organized, who makes the decision, and on what basis? One question debated within the system is; who should have responsibility for this area? Should it be the institutional correctional staff, or should the decision-making structure be distributed among internal and external groups?

In one task force report on corrections, the organization of parole authorities was reviewed with special concern for the independence versus integration issue.[15] The report examined the current patterns in parole administration and organization. As one topic example, they found that parole decision-making for juveniles is internal; done within the incarcerating institution. The argument *for* this arrangement is that institutional staff are intimately familiar with the offender and the type of program he or she needs. The major argument *against* is that institutional staff members place too much emphasis on the offender's adjustment to institutional life, thereby establishing release policies that primarily fit the needs of institutions.

Parole decision-making for adult offenders is largely the responsibility of autonomous groups (e.g., parole boards). The argument *for* this structure is that it may be more fair to the offender, since these groups are without the vested interest of the institutional staff. The argument *against* this arrangement is that parole boards may be too sensitive to the problems of institutional programs and their overall goals.

The real issue is that the creation of a "division" of labor between institutional staff and autonomous releasing authorities is complicated by the growing use of partial release programs."[16] Attempts to promote closer coordination between institutional staffs and releasing authorities have generally identified the following as key problems. First, there is a need to create a structure that integrates the releasing authority with the centralized correctional agency, with the parole board appointed by that agency. Second, the power to release is held by the board that has general control over the entire correctional system, both in institutions and in the community. Third, the director of corrections serves as chairman of the paroling authority, whose members are appointed by the governor. Fourth, it is important to use coordinating committees including both parole board members and institutional officials. Fifth, the leading view among juvenile authorities is that "there should be a decision making body within a central correctional agency of the state that controls all releases to the community and return to institutions."[17] There are supporting reasons why.

Additional concerns involve the competence of parole decision-makers. First, are parole personnel in the juvenile field properly trained? Second, the decision-makers in the adult field are often political appointees who lack the appropriate background. Additionally, many are part-time parole board members whose major interest expertise are in other areas.

One solution to this problem would involve the creation of a full-time releasing authority. A second possible solution is to supplement part-time parole board members with parole examiners who would be fully trained and would provide professionalism in the structure. Qualifications and training of parole board members are a common problem. How does the system create a structure that will lead to resolution?

Some states now have job requirements that include a degree in behavioral science and experience in corrections. Other states require appointees to pass an examination in penology and criminal justice. One program consisted of a series of week-long intensive training programs, with publications and guides used to supplement the program activities.

A second approach to improving parole decision-making is through the use of professionals. The existing personnel structure would be altered to include professional parole examiners with the following responsibilities and changes resulting: (1) parole examiners would conduct interviews and hearings for the parole board which would then allow (2) the board to delegate power to the examiners to make certain decisions under the wide range of policies established by the board in turn allowing (3) the board to stay involved with broad-based policy questions, delegate some cases, and "act as an appellate body on the decisions of examiners." This structure includes in it personnel with the necessary skills and background. It would "secure examiners, with tenure, training and experience in corrections that could bridge the gap between parole boards and institutions more effectively." Finally, the use of examiners would reduce the need for increasing the size of parole boards to meet the increasing workload.

Comments and Follow-up Work. This case was presented in some detail, as it is a common one faced by many correctional organizations. Behavioral scientists could be involved here at a number of points. They could conduct a survey of programs across the country, identifying the range of structures used and their relative effectiveness (applied research). This information could be developed into a package of options that could be presented to managers in a training or informational session(s) (education and training). Behavioral scientists could be called in as consultants to identify the best of the options for one correctional organization (expert consultation). Also, they could be asked to provide consultation that would assist the organization in its efforts to change its structure (process consultation[18]).

What are the other possibilities? Behavioral scientists could:

1. Provide direct assessment and/or treatment service as a part of the probation and parole system in their local area, perhaps targeted at the post-discharge needs of offenders.
2. Conduct new research into client supervision models, examining particularly peer group methods.
3. Research the productivity and effectiveness of probation officers with very high caseloads, attempting to identify change and increased efficiency strategies.
4. Evaluate the impact of eliminating parole as a management strategy (costs/benefits) and as a rehabilitation strategy (diminished offender contact).

Since a key part of the problem appears to be the need to get more highly trained persons into the system, the organization's training structure takes on increased importance. How does the correctional system establish this needed educational structure? The next cast focuses on this problem directly, beginning with the needs of the clients—the offenders. A second case offers options.

CASE FIFTY-TWO: THE STRUCTURE OF TRAINING PRO-GRAMS. The education and training needs identified above in relation to parole boards are expandable to a generalized need for the correctional field as a whole, with particular relevance to inmates. That is, what is a viable structure for education and training programs that effectively contribute to the offender's development? The following report is given in detail, as it points out the wide range of issues and possible solutions.

The role of education and training in corrections is to help all offenders (regardless of their status in the system) to develop an ability to meet both the economic and the social requirements of the community in legal and socially acceptable ways.[19] For some corrections personnel, this translates to helping the offender obtain a high school diploma (or GED) and entry-level job skills. Others believe that the mission is expanded to include "not only academic and career education, but instruction in skills which stimulate and facilitate involvement in social, economic, and cultural pursuits and the ability to seek entry into and to take advantage of available opportunity systems."[20] The problem is that many prisoners require intensive and diversified programming, yet few institutions have sophisticated programs. Most county and local jails in the United States do not have any programs.

In the author's view, the flaw in correctional education stems from the assumptions that *all* prisoners have the same or similar educational aptitudes, interests, and needs and can *all* be served by the *same* limited programs. Additionally, most correctional education programs follow the worst of the public school models—the conventional classroom with the students seated in rows and the teacher at the front of the room, isolated from them. Many of the classrooms are poorly lighted, inadequately insulated, and even without paper and pencils. The vocational education programs are primarily focused on manual skills and rarely integrated with academic courses.

Correctional administrators and educators must begin to realize that the traditional methods are not working. Studies indicate that the post-release jobs of prisoners are generally not related to training they received in prison. Job loss after releases generally is not due to a lack of skills but to other non-job-content-related issues, such as poor attendance. The data are not just one-sided. Other studies have found a positive relationship between "a person's involvement in education and training programs while in prison, post-release employment in some jobs, and 'success' in staying out of prison."

Corrections must create an educational program structure that accounts for the prisoner's individual characteristics such as age, prior experience, interest, and aptitudes. Within this design challenge is the problem of dealing with staff and the public who feel that educational opportunities are actually rewarding law-breakers. These issues lead to a consideration of whether to change the traditional approaches significantly. For example, it may be necessary to move correctional education out of the prison facility, since security rather than program participation is usually the top priority in institutions. Some options were reviewed that would address these problems.

One suggested approach is an educational voucher system. The prisoner would receive educational vouchers guaranteeing access to educational services after the completion of specified time periods and the meeting of certain standards of conduct. With requirements met, the prisoner could take part in a program at a junior college of vo–tech school. Another choice would be a work—study arrangement, in effect a community-based apprenticeship. The United State Department of Labor has begun research on the feasibility of a voucher system. Cost considerations make the voucher idea attractive, since it costs more to incarcerate prisoners than it would to provide them with education and training opportunities that would reduce residential expenses.

A second approach involves viewing the prison as a specialized learning center where prisoners are grouped according to education and training requirements rather than by age, the nature of their crime, or where they live. This would ease the burden of trying to find one program that would serve the varying needs of every prisoner. According to the author, this approach only makes economic and social sense when other systems of community-based programming are not feasible.

A third approach involves increasing the use of educational technology in the traditional all-purpose institution. Prisons could use computer-assisted instruction, video tape systems, and other equipment to broaden the range of course offerings, which would also give the students greater schedule flexibility. With the new technology it will be important to maintain a balance between "machine related" education and the person-to-person contact that is still seen as the key to quality education.

Another approach, already used in some states, creates statewide school districts that include correctional institutions. This guarantees the prison a budget for staff, materials, and other resources just as it does for a regular school district. One qualifier for this approach is that prison schools cannot automatically and totally imitate public schools, as they have special student needs to address that differ significantly from those of public schools.

Approach five is introduced by the author with the note that many correctional administrators have comments on the large percentage of people in prison who do not belong there. If this is true, there should be more facilities that have security as a secondary priority, not the first. Instead of a secure prison, the facility could serve as "an education and training, reception, diagnostic and referral" center. Students would still be under the supervision of the authorities, but the primary goal of the institution would be "to provide education and training, diagnosis and prescriptive programming," not punishment and custody.

A final approach would be to use the nation's community colleges as resources for "relocating and redirecting correctional educational efforts." As one researcher suggested, community colleges could function as a diagnostic and testing center with staff acting as program developers and referral agents to other community institutions. In support of this approach, the American Association of Junior Colleges is interested in finding jurisdictions willing to use community and junior colleges as "precommitment diversionary centers . . . as facilitators in the delivery of any services necessary to divert the first offender from commitment to a correctional institution."

The author concludes by suggesting that if corrections administrators can agree that present education systems are inadequate, "we can then assemble some of the best theoreticians and practitioners in corrections and education to evolve new delivery systems".[21]

Comments and Follow-up Work. This case was presented at some length because it illustrates the wide potential of the behavioral scientist's contribution to the development of structural options for one aspect of the correctional organization—education. Here, the author reviewed the current educational structure, indicating some of its deficiencies. However, the larger contribution was the enumeration of alternative ways of organizing the educational component—the six approaches listed. As in the previous case, the behavioral scientist functions as an analyst of organizational structure. This function can be one of the applied researcher, or as a consultant. Should a correctional system be interested in moving to a new structure, expert and/or process consultation functions are possible uses of the behavioral scientist.

Behavioral Scientists also could:

1. Research the organizational arrangements under which training is provided to inmates (e.g., in-house staff, contracts with school districts, contracts with private providers) to determine the full range of options for their area.
2. Provide direct training services or organize colleagues in a group that will do so.

3. Consult with management in the creation of an evaluation design for the training programs in one or more facilities.
4. Lead an inmate group in an education program redesign effort that produces suggestions for revising the current education and training program.

The idea of solutions is the key. In some cases it is much easier to identify the problems than to suggest solutions. Structural problems must have alternatives, to be considered by both management and service staff. The next case presents further options for discussion and debate.

CASE FIFTY-THREE: EDUCATIONAL STRUCTURAL OP-TIONS.   Since education in prisons is now and will continue to be an important problem (especially via the renewed interest in the rehabilitation mission), a second case is appropriate. What are the mechanisms for structuring correctional education to make it more effective? Contracting educational services for the prisons to outside agencies is a fairly new attempt to create a mechanism for increasing the rehabilitation services to inmates.

Marquis and Gendreau identified three advantages of "contractual arrangements," including the following: short-term contracts can better meet the specific needs of the "student-inmate" population, outside teachers may be able to gain more respect than institutionally based teachers, and the contracting staff may be a part of the educational setting the inmate will move into after release from prison.[22] Their study examined the effectiveness of educational contracting to a community college. Inmate volunteers for the program had "normal" IQ's and most often a primary school education level. At the conclusion of the courses, academic and self-esteem changes were assessed. The results showed gains in arithmetic and spelling but little change in reading ability, with no increase in self-esteem.

In conclusion, the authors felt that "given the time involved, the fact no concrete reinforcers were contingent upon performance and the students were adults, some of whom had left school long ago, the academic gains compared favorably with operant achievement programs carried out with juvenile delinquents. However, despite the aforementioned advantages of a contractual system, this administrative experiment made clear that educational upgrading may be a slow process."[23] The experiment was successful but did not erase all questions.

Comments and Follow-up Work.   Behavioral scientists examined the structure of the educational system with specific reference to one alternative mechanism—contracting. This new structure was evaluated to determine its effectiveness and benefits with respect to the previous mechanisms. Either in a research function or in a consulting one behavioral scientists can help to both develop and test alternative structures.

In addition to these opportunities, the behavioral scientist could:

1. Research the correctional educational structures nationally, analyzing their strengths and weaknesses and matching this analysis with local situations to create a list of individualized recommendations.
2. Offer to create an alternative educational structure as a planning option for management.
3. Consult with management as advisor to an educational program redesign process based on staff and inmate input.

These cases have focused on educational program structure. But the structure of the correctional organization includes much more than the educational component. An issue cutting across all work areas in the organization is the structure of jobs, or job design. With high stress and other organizational climate characteristics making corrections work difficult, the design of the job is relevant to reducing burnout, maintaining personnel, and improving the quality of working life overall.

CASE FIFTY-FOUR: THE JOB DESIGN STRUCTURE PROBLEM. In creating organizational change, one question that arises is: how do we measure its impact on the structure of the organization, both as a whole and with respect to individual jobs? Do broad organizational change strategies have any impact on the structure; and, the follow-up issue: how does that structural change relate to the individual job level?

The purpose of the study by Repucci, Dean, and Saunders was to demonstrate the utility of job design variables as "evaluative measures of change in a state training school for adjudicated male delinquents."[24] The work is related to similar studies used by industrial psychologists examining "job enlargement" as a remedy for problems with workers in specialized jobs in industrial companies. In previous studies, researchers found that manipulating autonomy, variety, feedback, task identity, and informal contact could increase worker motivation, satisfaction, and performance. Other research found similar results, adding participation, information, and learning to the variables that could be manipulated. The present study was part of a larger project directed at changing the facility from "an internally oriented custodial facility to a community oriented rehabilitative one based on a social learning theoretical framework. . . ."

The subjects of the study were staff members with youth in residential living units (cottages). The test was administered two times by a research assistant as a part of a larger questionnaire on job satisfaction. The first time, fifteen staff members had been working in "social learning based" cottages, while twenty-four of the staff members were still working in "benevolent custody" cottages. At the second test administration (fourteen months later) all subjects were working in social learning cottages.

The results of the study confirmed the hypotheses on organizational change. According to the authors, these results support the idea that comprehensive program innovation was responsible for institutional change as measured by staff perceptions of their own jobs. If the assumption that staff perceptions and attitudes helps determine the type of service rendered, is accepted, then "programs that change these perceptions in a positive direction, thereby increasing worker satisfaction, should have beneficial effects for clients."

Comments and Follow-up Work.   Here behavioral scientists are involved in analyzing the effects of change on structure at the job level, using it as an indicator of larger changes. Since structure is a multilevel characteristic (from individual jobs to whole programs and units), behavioral scientists can be involved at different levels. Here the interest was in the effect of a program modification on the ways in which employees' jobs were perceived. The jobs were redesigned as a result of program level changes.

This case raises the issue of job design and its contribution to the quality of working life of organizational participants. Behavioral scientists also could:

1. Research the level of job satisfaction among correctional workers (e.g., guards, management), comparing these levels with other staff in other organizations.
2. Present an educational seminar on techniques for increasing job satisfaction through job design.
3. Consult with management on the creation of a job redesign group composed of employees with those jobs and oriented toward autonomous redesign of both the social and technical aspects of the job.

The program level changes are somewhat parallel to the notion of the environmental context of the program, at the whole organization level. What is the environment, both internal and external, and how does it affect correctional activities? The next case considers this question as an issue of environmental structure.

CASE FIFTY-FIVE: ENVIRONMENTAL STRUCTURE.   A new area in the development of institutional designs is concern for the environmental structure. This is developing under the general headings of man/environment relations and environmental psychology.[25] Physical environmental design is one structural aspect of the correctional institution that obviously requires work. Conditions are poor in many facilities and in need of both reconditioning and alternative designs.

The following is verbatim from the abstract of a conference report in this area: "Esser presents an outline of a conference sponsored by the Health Facilities Design, Health Services and Promotion branch of the Canadian Department of National Health and Welfare.[26] Much of the discussion focuses on the biosocial, health, psychological merits of windows, particularly in hospitals and detention centers where the sense of isolation caused by windowless rooms can lead to prolonged illness or suicide behavior. A model for window design incorporating user needs is presented."

Comments and Follow-up Work. This report illustrates the behavioral scientist's efforts in the area of man's relationship to the physical surround. This relationship is a fundamental concern in terms of basic research, but it is also very pragmatically grounded in day-to-day design questions. The conference reported on here is a demonstration of one aspect of the education and training function; it presents the field reports of new developments in this area (in the sense of technology transfer). One topic in particular (windows) is the focus of special concern. It is indicative of the type of topics that would and should engage behavioral scientists as sensitivity to physical designs and their behavioral effects grows.

In related projects, they also could:

1. Identify the anti-therapeutic aspects of their local correctional facility with specific suggestions for improvement.
2. Present an educational seminar on the contributions of environmental design to communications and to treatment generally.
3. Consult with management on the creation of an environmental monitoring group (composed of inmates and staff), with the responsibility for assessing and creating recommendations for an improved environment.

THE PSYCHOSOCIAL SUBSYSTEM

The psychosocial subsystem was discussed in the opening chapter and again in Chapter 3 with reference to court organization and management. The organizational concerns and topics in corrections are essentially the same as for the courts with the difference that the issues often involve residential institutions as opposed to juries and courtroom dynamics. For review purposes, the psychosocial subsystem definition of Kast and Rosenzweig is presented:

> Every organization has a psychosocial subsystem that is composed of individuals and groups in interaction. It consists of individual behavior and motivation, status and role relationships, group dynamics, and in-

fluence systems. It is also affected by sentiments, values, attitudes, expectations, and aspirations of the people in the organization. Obviously, this psychosocial subsystem is affected by external environmental forces as well as by the tasks, technology, and structure of the internal organization. These forces set the "organizational climate" within which the human participants perform their roles and activities. We would therefore expect psychosocial systems to differ significantly among various organizations. Certainly the climate for the person on the assembly line is different from that of the scientist in the laboratory or the doctor in the hospital.[27]

It is clear that this topic area is closely linked to the environmental questions and cases just reviewed. In this subsystem the individual and group behaviors resulting from the environmental and other structures are represented. Psychological and sociological analyses are a traditional area of work activity for behavioral scientists. The cases indicative of work in this subsystem include the topics of personality, attitudes, group leadership, stress, and organizational conflict. The first is personality.

CASE FIFTY-SIX: PERSONALITY OF THE PROBATION OFFICER. A long-standing interest in the psychosocial subsystem involves the question of whether certain personalities have a better "fit" with certain jobs and tasks than others. This question has been addressed for various personnel within the correctional organization. The following case example illustrates a justifiable concern for the probation officer and how his or her personality fits the job.

Goldsboro and Burbank presented the view that the probation officer's basic personality and how he uses it to help clients, is "his most potent therapeutic tool."[28] Their position is based on several assumptions: (1) that personalities can change, and therefore probation officers are made, not born; and (2) that the knowledge and skill needed to help bring out the best in an officer's personality are available. Criminal justice organizations are faced with two decisions stemming from their responsibility for the officers. What should the personality of the probation officer be like? And, how should the probation office be organized in order to achieve this development? That is, what is the relation between organizational structure and the staff personality that is the eventual result?

The probation officer should have "maturity and integrity which comprise the cardinal qualities of personality."

1. He must be able to form and sustain wholesome, interpersonal relationships.
2. He must be able to identify with a wide range of people.
3. He must be able to accept responsibility for the authority he carries.

4. He must be able to use it firmly but "tempered with judgment and understanding"
5. He must be able to work with aggressive people; he must have strength and some immunity in facing extreme aggression and hostility . . . ability to meet hazardous situations where the awareness of the need as well as the ability to take calculated risks is essential.
6. He must be able to work along with other agencies and people.
7. He must be able to and want to improve his performance on the job.

The atmosphere of the probation office and the morale of its staff reveal "the development of integration of purpose . . . and the level of performance and effectiveness in discharging its responsibility to clientele and community." Since the judges, or board of judges, set the tone for this atmosphere, they should have the same qualities suggested for the officers.

Given this objective, the role of supervisory staff is to help the officer assess the assets and liabilities of his personality. The focus of supervision should be on the officer's learning and performance on the job. The officer should be required to develop the ability to gain and maintain the personality traits listed above. The way he uses supervision will reveal his attitude toward authority, which will then be reflected in clients. He should learn to understand and discipline his own aggression and resistance to better help his probationers. He must learn to use the available knowledge and insight of other agencies and people. The officer must want to make constructive use of supervision and be concerned about his own level of performance.

Comments and Follow-up Work. This case demonstrates the behavioral scientist's interest in the individual personality of participants in the correctional organization. The functions demonstrated here are a combination of assessment and treatment functions. In the psychosocial subsystem, behavioral scientists can be concerned with how to assess the relevant personality variables that contribute to desired organizational objectives, especially to effective client relations. Although not specifically stated in the case summary, the issue is that those staff with "inappropriate personalities" would need to be "treated" to help them to adjust in the desired direction. Behavioral scientists could be involved at several points: (1) in the definition of the "ideal" personality, (2) in the assessment of the degree to which staff actually have that personality, and (3) in helping individual staff members to change their personality characteristics in order that there be a better match of job and person. This latter function may raise ethical issues, but these are at least somewhat ameliorated if the change is totally voluntary on the part of the staff, not coerced in any way by management.

What other personality-related work topics arise? Behavioral scientists could:

1. Conduct a personality assessment of the probation staff, matching personalities with job performance to determine whether prediction would be possible in the future.
2. Research the ethical issues of job selection based on personality characteristics and performance (see number 1 above), including reliability and validity issues.
3. Act as a clinical consultant to management, providing advice on how best to assist employees with personal problems (e.g., addictions, marital problems, child raising) that are affecting job performance.

Closely related to the personality issue are the attitude positions of staff—how they affect personality characteristics and eventually the clients.

CASE FIFTY-SEVEN: ATTITUDINAL PREFERENCES. A question that has intrigued analysts of the psychosocial subsystem is whether certain staff characteristics help to generate higher acceptance from clients than other characteristics. This has been discussed in terms of a variety of dimensions and variables, from authoritarian to democratic personalities to demographic considerations such as age. One concern involves the issue of male versus female staff preferences.

Holland, Levy, Beckett, and Holt presented one review of some of these issues.[29] The California Department of Corrections was seeking ways to ensure that employers were not restricted from certain duties or responsibilities because of their sex (except those duties involving observation or searching of unclothed members of the opposite sex). This study was conducted to investigate inmates' preferences for the sex of prison personnel. The researchers surveyed 386 randomly selected prisoners in four commitment categories. In the research group, 139 were male felons (criminal offenses jailed for custodial purposes), 81 were male civilly committed narcotics addicts (in treatment-oriented facilities), 77 were female felons, and 89 were female addicts. The survey consisted of forty-nine items designed to measure attitudes toward staff positions and duties.

The survey found that the inmates as a whole do not have a strong preference for staff of either the same or the opposite sex. However, when a strong preference was expressed, it was for opposite-sex staff members. Further, the results illustrated that for certain positions, all of the inmates had similar preferences (e.g., the majority preferred males for ground maintenance or chaplains, and females for nurses). This reflects common sex-role stereotyping, even though the subjects were instructed to respond with the assumption that the sexes were equally competent. The researchers also suggested that the addicts were generally less conservative than the felons.

Based on the study, the authors suggest that prisoners' attitudes should be assessed periodically "both in planning for specific changes and in attempting to maintain custodial environments that are maximally responsive to the legitimate needs of inmates."

Comments and Follow-up Work.   The study appears to be basic, a relatively straightforward concern with the sex preferences of prisoners. But the issues are much more complex than that. Is there a way to use this kind of data to help design a better psychosocial subsystem? If inmate preferences can be identified, at least one area of the subsystem can be designed to minimize conflict. For example, if female nurses are preferred, why not provide them if the candidates and personnel pool allow it? Or, if that is not possible, management would at least be prepared for conflict, expecting some resistance from offenders when male nurses are put on duty. Behavioral scientists could be involved in assessment work as shown here, or in education and consultation designed to overcome inmate preferences thought to be causing difficulties in the system.

Specifically, they could:

1. Research guards' attitudes toward drugs to determine whether addictions is covertly supported by staff.
2. Present an educational seminar to staff on the linkage of attitudes and behavior, using illustrations such as addictions and the negative impact of covert support.
3. Consult with management, presenting expert guidance on the range of attitude change techniques and when they may be used most effectively.

Attitude patterns and acceptance data suggest that some staff would be better leaders than others. Prediction is always a most difficult problem; but even if the data could not be used for prediction, they could at least contribute to leadership training, the next topic.

CASE FIFTY-EIGHT: GROUP LEADERSHIP TRAINING.   It is increasingly recognized by organizations of all types that groups are a key element of organizational productivity and process. One issue of psychosocial subsystem concern is group leadership training and an assessment of its effects on group dynamics.

Shapiro considered the group leadership training question.[30] The author was called in as a consultant to help organize and conduct a group conseling program at the federal correctional institution at Lompoc, California. His initial purpose was to train a group of leaders drawn from various staff members, including correctional officers, medical personnel, caseworkers, and people from industry, education, and the personnel department. The short-range objectives were to train group leaders and to develop staff-led voluntary inmate counseling groups. The long-range objectives were to reduce alienation among inmates and to improve staff–inmate relationships at all levels.

The content of the program consisted of four leadership training series. Each series involved eight group sessions. The rationale for the program was that the best way to become a group leader is first to have experience as a group member. The sessions involved discussion, feedback, technique demonstration, etc. In later series, certain inmates were selected to train to become group leaders.

An evaluation of the program was conducted based on the changes in pre- and post-attitude tests, individual interviews, and a crisis report written by one of the correctional officers. The evaluation showed that the training program and the inmate counseling groups were successful.

Comments and Follow-up Work.   This case demonstrates an intervention in the psychosocial subsystem of the organization by a behavioral scientist through the education and training function. The role was a combined one, with the behavioral scientist asked to provide an apparently "already-developed" training program. If this was the case (it is hard to be sure from the report), this is an example of purchase of service consultation. Training service and the developed/tested package are purchased from the behavioral scientist. When there is a program evaluation (such as this one) whose purpose is also to contribute to the professional training literature, an applied research function is present as well. The case demonstrates the range of functions that can be combined in a single activity set over a period of time.

For example, behavioral scientists could:

1. Assess the leadership skills of group leaders within the facility (e.g., middle-level managers) in order to identify training needs.
2. Consult with management in the creation of a group leadership skills training program.
3. Consult with group leaders to assist them in developing their own leadership evaluation plan.

One aspect of leadership is demonstrating stress management and teaching it to others. Stress is reflected in various psychosocial subsystem elements such as conflict and morale. The next case addresses this problem.

CASE FIFTY-NINE: STRESS IN THE SYSTEM.   It is no secret that correctional facilities are filled with stress for both inmates and staff. This stress is a part of the psychosocial climate of the system. How much there is and, more important, how it can be reduced in both volume and intensity are typical and much discussed concerns. Behavioral scientists have been and will continue to be involved, as the following study indicates.

Inwald's paper outlined several areas of difficulty in conducting research on officer stress that are based on characteristics unique to the correctional setting.[31] The paper provides guidelines for research that can be used to develop programs dealing with stress that may help improve attendance, decrease sick leave abuse, increase job performance, etc.

Unique characteristics of the correctional setting that create research problems are: accountability to governing politicians and the public at large, daily crises, and paramilitary structure. Actual problems encountered by researchers are: atmosphere that does not allow for disruption of routine (so researchers can interview or whatever); reluctance of administrators to make staff available; red tape involved with allowing access to outsiders; administrators' concerns that officer stress tests will result in negative reflection on them; and, on self-report inventories, flat-out refusal and/or denial of problems by some officers, and then overly willing officers whose responses are made to use stress research as a vehicle with which to condemn the administration.

Some aids for overcoming these problems are: make clear statements to management concerning the possible political and administrative advantages of stress research; develop research systems that could be used by those without a psychology background; schedule data collection times around daily routine; use trained, uniformed personnel to develop and gather information for assessment; and develop behavioral descriptions that will be non threatening to officers but will yield important information.

Comments and Follow-up Work.   The need for additional research can be addressed by behavioral scientists who identify both its direction and specific topics, with the use of approaches that bypass the problems listed. But the need also is for stress reduction training. The stress is present *now*, and must be addressed with an organizational response even if more research on its nature and characteristics is needed. Both research and training opportunities are apparent here.

Behavioral scientists could:

1. Assess the extent of stress in the organization unit by unit, to identify the change points according to highest stress.
2. Develop an educational seminar on stress management for correctional staff.
3. Consult with management on the design of a total organizational program of stress reduction, using both social and technical interventions (e.g., group sensitivity to stress training and job redesign).

One end result of intra-organizational stress is conflict. The dual missions of the correctional organization—punishment and rehabilitation—and the very nature of the work tend to create the potential for more conflict than other organizations might expect. The next case addresses this problem.

CASE SIXTY: ORGANIZATIONAL CONFLICT—GROUP LEVEL. All organizations experience conflict. Correctional organizations are potentially more conflict-laden than others. We do know that conflict exists, but we need additional information on how to assess and respond to conflict situations. Research will provide the information, while consulting behavioral scientists will translate the research into the answers available to date. That consulting function is demonstrated in this case.

Sebring and Duffee presented a case study in which two professors were called in as consultants to solve a "win–lose" conflict in a state correctional facility.[32] One purpose of the study was to increase "change agent understanding of the politics and dynamics of win–lose organizational and inter-organizational conflict." Their second purpose was to make known the organizational responses that result from ongoing win–lose conflict. In this case the consultants were asked by the state regional education director to assess the situation at a state correctional facility for women, which was reportedly having staff problems.

The professors began by gathering information, talking to staff members and researching the organizational structure. They found that the conflict at the facility encompassed several bureaucratic levels, but that it had begun as a combined personality and philosophy clash between two staff members. At the highest level, it resulted in conflict between the state bureau of corrections and the state department of education over control of vocational education funds for prison education. The overall result was "organizational paranoia" at the prison. Every individual was on one side or the other, and they all felt the "other" side was out to get them.

The researchers next attempted to diagnose the cause of the conflict. Using a "bureaucratic conflict model," they decided the problem began at the highest level and was "recycling itself" to the lower levels. Based on this assessment, the consultants decided that the best attack on the problem would be to work down, starting at the top. This would lead to intervention in the lower-level conflicts that had led the state bureau of corrections "to grow cautious about participating in organizational changes with the department of education."

The researchers also attempted to assess the unique characteristics of prisons that were creating management difficulty. The top three they noted were: "the intangible nature of treatment goals; differing and conflicting philosophies about appropriate ways to change inmate behavior; and multiple bureaucracies."

With the necessary data and assessment work complete, the consultants chose a process consultation approach to solve the problems. Their intent was to involve staff members in the problem analysis and problem-solving work of the institution. A series of meetings was held with the various people involved in the conflicts to discuss the problems, possible solutions, personal feelings, etc. These "feedback sessions" were to open the issues, but after just a few meetings, no progress was made. Neither side was willing to make any concessions; no agreements could be reached. Each side still blamed the other, with everyone remaining suspicious of everyone else. Even the consultants received anonymous phone calls, questioning and investigating their credentials and political leanings.

Finally, the consultants prepared a concluding report, stating that there were ongoing conflicts, that few inmates were beneficiaries of the educational programs, and that others were actually being harmed by the organizational conflict. They recommended that the vocational education funds be stopped until the problems were solved. They offered alternative recommendations, ranging from having a third party arbitrate a settlement appealing to both, to firing both sides and starting over. In the "post-intervention analysis," the consultant decided that all the factors involved in this particular case made it extremely difficult to resolve with traditional methods. Using the case example, they developed seven suggested strategies for conflict resolution.

Comments and Follow-up Work. The report here is quite clear in its identification of the behavioral scientists' functions. They were engaged as consultants to assess the situation and create a solution to the organizational conflict problem. Their approach centered on process consultation (see, e.g., Schein[33]). Using this approach requires that consultants engage the organizational participants in working collaboratively *with* the consultants to solve the problem. The behavioral scientists did not come in as "expert consultants" with all the answers. Instead they were to develop in collaboration with staff a process by which the organization could solve this conflict. Through that experience staff would learn how to solve other conflicts the might arise, without having to call in the experts again.

In related areas, behavioral scientists could:

1. Provide "treatment" to the organization by acting as its therapist–problem solver when conflict situations require a third-party mediator.
2. Assess the extent of interorganizational conflict, analyzing relations between the correctional facility and other organizations (e.g., various courts, community service agencies, government agencies).
3. Provide expert consultation on conflict resolution mechanisms such as ombudsman programs.

Conflict is ever present in correctional organizations and is therefore worthy of a second case review.

CASE SIXTY-ONE: ORGANIZATIONAL CONFLICT—INDIVIDUAL LEVEL. The extent of conflict in corrections and its disabling power suggest that conflict is a topic of prime concern for management. This next case involving conflict deals again with the individual level, the correctional officer in particular. It is tied to the organizational mission/philosophy problem, which is tracked right to the individual.

An article by Pogrebin and Atkins "suggests that correctional officers are perhaps the most influential correctional staff members as perceived by inmates.[34] Their ability to act as agents of prisoner resocialization has never really been recognized, nor have the problems of their experiencing role conflict through a custodial self-perception ever been resolved by managers of penal institutions. It is concluded that what is needed in current day correctional institutions is the restructuring of the correctional organization to recognize the guard both as an authority figure and a role model to inmates."

Comments and Follow-up Work. There are really two aspects of this case; one concerns structure, the other psychosocial factors. One behavioral scientist activity here is an analysis of the structure leading to conflict, an analysis that raises organizational design issues. This is assessment at the organizational level, based on an analysis of what happens to individuals. A concern not noted here but one that is a psychosocial topic, is the determination of what ill effects are felt by the officers as they attempt to handle this stress individually. Would they need treatment for stress, and/or education as to how to manage it? Both are additional behavioral scientist functions.

These are not the only work topics. Behavioral scientists could:

1. Assess the nature of the difficulty in a "personality problem" conflict between two department directors.
2. Provide service as a third-party mediator of internal personal disputes.
3. Consult with management to establish an internal mediation method with design involvement of staff at all levels of the organization.

Role conflict affects the individuals and the organization as a whole, weakening the psychosocial subsystem only as a start of the effect. The next case elaborates this point.

CASE SIXTY-TWO: JOB STRESS IN CORRECTIONAL INSTITUTIONS. The conflict that has been reviewed in the past several cases produces stress that negatively impacts both individuals and work groups. The following case identifies more specifically some of those impacts and a perspective for organizing and understanding the effects.

Brodsky reported as a part of his abstract of one study "that evidence is mounting that people working in correctional facilities experience a significant amount of stress in their jobs that might lead to high job turnover, high rates of sick leave, and troubled relations with inmates, other staff, and family members.[35] This article examines the stress experienced by these workers from a medical/anthropological and psychiatric perspective. It focuses on the structural and cultural parameters of work stress in the correctional environment. Data are examined from a diverse population of people working in corrections: people who are working and functioning well and those who dropped out of work because of work stress, people who worked in corrections for both long and short periods of time. . . ."

Comments and Follow-up Work.   This study illustrates the behavioral scientist as an analyst of stress in the psychosocial subsystem. This is a research or consulting role, but it closely parallels the "treating" function in the organization—a similarity to working with the personal problems of an individual in a clinical sense. The "illness" here is stress, which will have a negative impact on the organization as a whole and on its individual participants.

This topic area is a rich one. Behavioral scientists could also:

1. Research the causes of organizational stress and the responses taken by other organizations, matching stress type with response.
2. Create an educational seminar for corrections management, using the above review as a base.
3. Consult with management on the development of an ongoing stress evaluation program that supports a diagnosis–planning–action–evaluation cycle of continuing intervention in this problem.

Continuing with this thinking, behavioral scientists could explore the staff's attitudes toward stress. But this would be a subtopic of the staff attitude area, the next case subject.

CASE SIXTY-THREE: STAFF ATTITUDES.   The final psychosocial case links the concerns about conflict and stress to both staff and inmates. How aware are staff about the problems in the psychosocial system, and are they willing and able to see that inmates and fellow staff members obtain the help that they need? The following case addresses this awareness level.

Freeman and Johnson in an abstract of their study stated that they used 115 correctional officers (COS) who were administered a questionnaire assessing their health-related knowledge, attitudes, and practices.[36] The subjects reported generally negative attitudes in relation to their work and inmates. Low-ranking correctional officers were less likely than higher-ranking ones to be certain about the inadequacy of clearly inadequate mental health care for inmates. Rural correctional officers were more likely than urban ones to perceive inmates who complained of illness as faking. Subjects used first aid once every 2.6 years, on the average, but made referrals of mentally ill inmates about 2.5 times per year. Data suggest that the role of the correctional officer in health services needs reevaluation.

Comments and Follow-up Work. This case illustrates the behavioral scientist's work in assessing the degree to which correctional staff are actively engaging in the alteration of both individual and organizational health problems. It raises the question of whether inmates are getting the medical and psychiatric care they need. The referrals are not being made. But even if they were, the services have been found to be inadequate (see, e.g., Goldsmith,[37] Sandrick, [38,39] and Ziegenfuss[40]). The bottom line is that the psychosocial subsystem continues to be affected negatively by both staff and inmates who need treatment (from behavioral scientists and others), but who are not even getting the initiating referrals.

Behavioral scientists also could:

1. Research the educational level of staff and their attitude toward the conflicting aspects of the correctional mission (punishment vs. rehabilitation), adding other variables such as age, sex, and job position to determine the degree of, and persons with, attitude support for each aspect of the mission.
2. Research staff attitudes regarding expectancy of successful rehabilitation.
3. Create a training program that outlines attitudes and expectancy effects on goal attainment (e.g., the self-fulfilling prophecy of inmate failure).

These problems will involve management, which is a separate subsystem of the organization, as outlined below.

THE MANAGERIAL SUBSYSTEM

Behavioral scientists can be useful to corrections organizations management by serving a wide variety of functions within the managerial subsystem. As noted in the opening chapter, the managerial system "spans the entire organization by relating the organization to its environment, setting the goals, developing comprehensive, strategic and operational plans, designing the structure, and establishing control processes."[41] The managerial subsystem of the correctional facility links the goals, values, and mission of the organization to the structure and the psychosocial and the technical services that are provided. How does it do so?

There is considerable debate as to whether management generally is an art or a science. If we define it as an art, as Koontz, O'Donnell, and

Weihrich have done, management is "the use of underlying knowledge (science) and application of it to realities in a situation, usually with blend or compromise, to obtain practical results; managing is an art, but management is more properly used to refer to the body of knowledge—science—underlying this art."[42] When considered as a science, management involves the use of systematically applied concepts, theory, principles, and techniques.

With respect to corrections, this means that the managerial subsystem is involved with the traditional activities of planning, organizing, directing, and controlling the correctional organization. This can involve the behavioral scientist in a wide range of functions, including, for example, assistance in scheduling and staffing, analysis of various staff roles and functions, working with managerial and administrative resistance to change, and helping to identify structural requirements or needs for change. The structural work might include designing mechanisms that will help integration of various technical activities within corrections. This ensures that the management work is carried out in a way that will support the organization's mission; this is, punishment and rehabilitation for the inmates in the system and treatment assistance to needy individuals who come into contact with it.

There are many functional contributions that behavioral scientists can make in the managerial subsystem. The constraints are those of the boundaries of the system. The following examples will follow the four traditional activities of management:

- Planning
- Organizing
- Directing/leading
- Controlling

Each is related to the case work already discussed, but the linkages to management are as varied as the reader's understanding and imagination. The complex subsystems of the correctional organization produce unlimited possibilities for assisting management.

Planning

This is an increasingly recognized core component of the manager's work. Kast and Rosenzweig have defined plans and planning:

A plan is any detailed method, formulated beforehand, for doing or making something. Planning is the process of deciding in advance what is to be done and how. It involves determining overall missions, identifying key results areas, and setting specific objectives as well as developing policies, programs, and procedures for achieving them. Planning provides a framework for integrating complex systems of interrelated future decisions. Comprehensive planning is an integrative activity that seeks to maximize the total effectiveness of an organization as a system in accordance with its objectives.

Planning has an implication of futurity, and it implies that there is some skill involved in designing plans for objective accomplishment. In short, a plan is a predetermined course of action. Essentially, a plan has three characteristics. First, it must involve the future. Second, it must involve action. Third, there is an element of personal or organizational identification or a causation; that is, the future course of action will be taken by the planner or some other designated person(s) within the organization. Futurity, action, and personal or organizational causation are necessary elements in every plan.[43,44]

This quote defines both the breadth and depth of the work. The planning task is illustrated here with a single case representing some of the more active work in corrections management. Managers are increasingly interested in defining the organization's objectives and in relating that definitional work to both individual staff jobs and the technical work as a whole. The case illustrates the potential for behavioral scientist involvement in this interest.

CASE SIXTY-FOUR: MANAGEMENT BY OBJECTIVES. Management by objectives is an approach to both organizational planning and control. The objective-setting process is planning, as it is the point at which the organization defines its desired future through a system of objectives. Behavioral scientists can and do get involved in this activity, often through acting as facilitators in the planning process. Has management by objectives been employed in corrections, and how has it worked?

The author begins by briefly explaining that Management by Objectives (MBO) is a systematic approach to managerial problem solving and decision making, a process for directing both managerial and subordinate goal setting.[45] The purpose of the approach is to identify organizational objectives, setting measurable goals and "providing avenues for achieving them." MBO works on the assumption that people work best when (1) they understand what they are doing, (2) they understand why they are doing it, (3) they know where they are headed, and (4) they know what the final result will be. By providing all employees with a well-defined purpose and direction, MBO encourages self-management and increases motivation and satisfaction. The MBO approach starts with the assumption that the manager or supervisor is the key person in any organizational structure. It then guides managers in setting the goals and objectives that enable the measurement that demonstrates results and increased program effectiveness.

In the second section of the article, the author focuses on how MBO works in the correctional organization. It is noted that the approach has been slow to be used in correctional organizations, and three reasons for this are discussed. First, correctional personnel must meet the needs of the public. The lack of consensus in society regarding the proper treatment for offenders makes it nearly impossible to set goals and objectives that will suit everyone. This is easy to understand, since even among corrections personnel there is no consensus on the purpose. Some feel punishment is the goal; others, rehabilitation.

The second reason for the slow startup of MBO in corrections could be the lack of managerial sophistication of corrections personnel. "Although the importance of setting objectives has been increasingly emphasized in recent years, the objectives set have rarely directed achievement to specific identifiable and measureable goals and results." Corrections managers are not yet able to manage well. One solution is an MBO program because it provides the managers with the proper tools for problem solving, educating them during the process.

The final reasons for a lack of MBO in corrections is the misconception that it was designed and will only work for profit-making, commercial enterprises; it is not believed to be suitable for nonprofit, service-oriented agencies. MBO was developed in commerical enterprise, but it is quite applicable in nonprofit organizations. Many nonprofit organizations are successfully employing MBO because it helps increase effectiveness in goal accomplishment by imposing standards of accountability on managers. In some areas, correctional activities are identical to the activities of profit-motivated businesses. Some of these areas are personnel management, public relations, and program administration. Likewise, just as businesses strive for higher return on their financial investment, corrections strive for better returns on their resource investments. Savings are achieved, for example through lower overhead costs or by more effective crime prevention through improved rehabilitation techniques.

In summary, the author believes there is no apparent reason why MBO should not be implemented in corrections.

Comments and Follow-up Work.   MBO is a control and accountability tool, but it begins with the planning of the future through the construction of individual objectives and whole sets of objectives. Behavioral scientists can become involved in applied research to assess how many corrections groups are currently using MBO, or alternative planning and control techniques. The analyses presented here might be part of preparatory work for an education and training session on the use of MBO in planning. Last, behavioral scientists could surely be called in as process consultants to assist the corrections unit in the work of planning, including the development of objectives, and analysis of their accomplishment at year's end.

Additionally, behavioral scientists could:

1. Research the number of corrections organizations using MBO techniques.
2. Create with colleagues an MBO training program.
3. Consult with management on the implementation of MBO.

Once objectives are defined and the planning work is completed, the task is to organize the work structure. The next section identifies how behavioral scientists could get involved.

Organizing

Organizing is "establishing an intentional structure of roles in a formally organized enterprise."[46] It is the manager's task of ensuring that the parts of the organization are connected one to the other in a way that both supports and leads to goal accomplishment.

Organizing was introduced as a management activity to the court system. It is here exemplified by a team classification. However, it should be remembered that this is a key task of management, which is the creating of the structure of the system in a total sense. In that view it goes beyond the creating of the structure to include the integration of the psychosocial subsystem with goals, values, and technical task demands as well. Organizing is an arranging of the parts and acquisition of resources, *and* it involves an accounting for individual attitudes, feelings, and intergroup dynamics. The case example used here presents this multiple subsystem linkage problem.

CASE SIXTY-FIVE: ORGANIZING TEAM-CLASSIFICATION. One problem for the corrections manager concerns how to organize the individual units and the work activity groups. A narrow, technically oriented concern would focus on how to get the work done most efficiently. However, the managers cannot be narrow; they must be concerned about the social system, including both staff preferences and inmate acceptance. Thus, there is a need to develop a matching of performance needs and organizational receptivity in a human relations sense. The classification task is one sample topic.

Hepburn and Albonetti, in the abstract of their study, note that "team classification seeks to bring together various levels of correctional staff and the inmate to discuss and resolve issues pertaining to such matters as work and cell assignment, disciplinary action, furlough request, and merit time considerations.[47] The analysis of questionnaire data obtained from 1,295 inmates and 555 staff in Missouri's Adult Correctional facilities supported the hypotheses that team classification, when successfully implemented, is (a) positively associated with staff attitudes toward inmates, work assignments, and other staff and with inmate attitudes toward staff in both living and program assignment; and (b) negatively associated with staff punitiveness in role conflict and with inmate alienation. An effective team classification process that enables staff from various levels to work together and that permits the inmate to represent his interests in the decision making process, provides each member with a greater commitment to voice in and understanding of the institution's treatment of inmates. This, in turn, improves their perception of the living/working conditions within the institution.''

Comments and Follow-up Work. This case presents an analysis of the classification task, identifying the positive contributions of the team method. The work indicates that classification, which can involve behavioral scientists' assessments, has a positive effect on inmates when it is organized with multiple staff-person input and, most important, with the inmate's contribution than without team or inmate input. Through this analysis, behavioral scientists are making both a managerial contribution toward the "best way of organizing" and a treatment contribution, identifying a structure that fosters inmate acceptance and treatment purpose understanding. There is a significant need for additional work on redesigning the organization of corrections tasks, such as this one, where behavioral scientists will have multifunctional impact.

Behavioral scientists also could:

1. Research the extent of organizational reliance on the team approach in corrections nationally.
2. Present a seminar on team relations and team building to management and staff.
3. Consult with management to assist in designing and running a management retreat for goal planning and team building.

Will corrections management lead the staff into the team approach? The leadership issue is the next topic.

Directing/Leading

Management must both direct and lead the employees of the system. What does this mean? Kast and Rosenzweig offered the following explanation:[48]

Leadership is (1) a function and (2) a status grouping. Directors, executives, administrators, managers, bosses, and chiefs would typically be included in the category called leadership. . . .

The leadership function involves facilitating the achievement of group goals. In the modern organizations, the leadership functions can be (and often are) performed by several or many participants. However, praise or blame for success or failure is typically focused on the individual— the formal leader. . . .

Tannenbaum and Massarik summarize the relationship between leadership and influence systems by stating that leadership is "interpersonal influence, exercised in situations and directed, through the communication process, toward the attainment of a specified goal or goals. Leadership always involves attempts on the part of a leader (influencer) to affect (influence) the behavior of a follower (influencee) or followers in a situation."[49]

Managers of the correctional organization must use the planning work as a basis for creating the organization necessary to achieve jointly defined objectives, those to be accomplished to fulfill the organization's mission. Directing and leading includes influencing the staff and helping them to attain their objectives. It also means pointing them in the desired direction and informing them of the work activities to be done by the times targeted.

This work certainly requires an understanding of the purpose and value of participation and the need for management to lead the organization's change efforts. Since the organization is dynamic, the change process problem is an ongoing challenge. The first case in this area is an overview of some of the problems of leadership, while the second addresses the change problem.

CASE SIXTY-SIX: PRISON ADMINISTRATION PRAGMATICS. One problem for correctional administrators is trying to *reduce* the amount of theory they receive and *increase* the practical advice available on a day-to-day basis. Several commentators have attempted to make the transition from management theory to practical advice. The following case illustrates one such transition, with comments on the leadership effects.

William Hofstetter offered his views of some practical considerations of correctional management.[50] Based on his experiences as an adult and juvenile correctional clinical psychologist and program administrator for twenty years, he presented two observations. His first observation was that there is constant interaction among inmates, and that this interaction has a definite structure and systematic method. Second, the more involved an inmate is in his own rehabilitation, the more effective the outcome. Generally, Hofstetter feels that inmate participation in the administration of programs has not worked very well. Programs either are totally controlled by facility personnel, or they are taken over by inmates. There is a need for inmate participation to be clearly spelled out, including the extent of authority, power, direction, and limitation for each participant and for the entire group.

Hofstetter also reviewed several programs. One program established college-level courses offered in a large West Coast penitentiary. The purpose of the program is to give inmates the learning and social skills that would be needed to be successful at an outside university. The program is unsuccessful because of the inmates' increasing pressure for more and more freedom.

In the second example, an inmate housing unit was operated without direction from the administration. Inmate control was intended to increase the awareness of the problems of self-government. It was designed to enable the staff to assess the inmates' ability to deal with the factors necessary for survival outside of the prison. The program had been successful, at the time of writing, for five years, and is serving as a model for others.

Last, there are efforts to increase the amount of positive interaction between officers and inmates. Officers now wear civilian clothes instead of uniforms, which traditionally were symbols creating distance and alienation between the groups. There is also an attempt to end the inmate pass system, which has controlled inmate movement in the institutions. A review of this second program found that inmates liked it because they felt more independent. Officers were pleased because they no longer wasted their time filling out and stamping passes, and monitoring the whole process. The time that was saved by doing away with the pass system was used to establish a group therapy program.

Comments and Follow-up Work. There are several aspects of both leadership and behavioral scientist work here. The basic question underlying the program experiments was: "is less direction better?" For inmate development, correctional management must know when to support inmates' self-direction of their own programs. The housing unit apparently was successful. Behavioral scientists can be engaged to assess the degree of inmate participation and direction in the programs, surfacing recommendations for change. Here the manager was a behavioral scientist (clinical psychologist) with an interest in observing and commenting on aspects of the managerial task. He would be a highly useful member of a consulting team of behavioral scientists whose task was to assess, or develop, correctional management, particularly in organizations oriented toward involvement of clients.

Behavioral scientists could:

1. Present management with modern alternatives to the time-clock approach of time supervision.
2. Present an educational seminar outlining several practical motivational techniques for public sector employees.
3. Offer to assist management in the evaluation of employee work scheduling systems (e.g., for holiday and vacation coverage).

If change is required, a team approach may be used. This could be a change agent team.

CASE SIXTY-SEVEN: THE CHANGE AGENT TEAM. Many correctional managers become interested in systems development or find that they *must* establish a change process within the organization to address problems or new directions. Establishing this process requires change agents, either persons internal to the organization or external ones brought in from the outside. How is a team established, and what role do behavioral scientists have in either the development or delivery of this change process?

In a study entitled "The Internal–External Change Agent Team . . . " the authors presented a case study of a collaborative effort between country corrections personnel and a university to bring about change in the jail.[51] The project involved the Berkshire County House of Corrections (Massachusetts) and the University of Massachusetts School of Education at Amherst. The sheriff was searching for alternatives to the jail's traditional programs, which did not prepare inmates for successful reintegration into society. For the most part, inmates spend their time watching television and helping with menial work. The university was committed to "creating new types of learning communities and new systems for the delivery of services to the corrections field."

Working together, the overall goal of the collaborators became "the creation of a 'comprehensive program for the educational rehabilitation of offenders and a model for correctional institutional change. . . .' " This led to the development and implementation of a new education program. The model education program had three phases: (1) developing the processes of a participatory education program, (2) implementing and administering the new program, and (3) institutionalizing the changes to ensure that they were ongoing jail procedures that would not need intervention by outsiders for continuation. Both the university and the jail supplied staff for the project. The chief representative for the university (the external change agent—project director) had training and experience in counseling, group work, and organizational development. The chief representative from the jail (the internal change agent) was a correctional officer who had previously demonstrated interest in correctional reform.

During the first phase, each of the change agents worked on the potential or real obstacles inherent in the nature of each of their respective roles. For example, the external agent needed to establish her credibility within the jail, since outsiders are generally viewed skeptically. The internal agent had to address the alienation of his peers in the prison, who saw him as challenging values they supported. By the second phase, the change agents were able to work together on the administrative operation of many new programs developed at the completion of phase one. In the third phase, the two agents transferred roles (she became less involved as he took on more responsibilities), and the new changes began to stabilize within the institution.

According to the authors, the success of the internal/external change agent team "is dependent upon combining the energies of two people whose skills are complementary and whose particular liabilities are cancelled by each other's strengths".

This provides the team with leverage that neither as individuals would be able to gain. As the model education program progressed, the work responsibilities and roles of the two agents evolved. Initially, they had to build trust, as she was the conceptualizer, he was the learner. She was the program developer and he was the mediator between her and the jail. In the second phase, they began to depend on each other more as they shared leadership. Finally, they "traded bases of credibility". Originally, the external agent carried the weight of responsibility for the program, since she had greater prestige, being viewed as the outside "expert". Gradually, she transferred her specific skills and access to needed resources to the internal agent. Finally, she returned to her original role at the University while he became the administrator for the new system within the jail.

Comments and Follow-up Work. This case demonstrates the correction officer's interest in leading the organization to a new level of development through a change process. Behavioral scientists have been and are engaged in these roles, often as process consultants. They are brought in to help to identify the need for change and the specific topics e.g., in this case an alternative educational model.

They can also contribute by writing up the change effort so that it can be communicated to the rest of the behavioral science community. With that action, the case goes beyond a single success to being a possible model for other change efforts. For it to be successfully used as a model, there must be fairly detailed information as to the "behavioral dynamics" of the barriers and the change techniques. These were presented and discussed in this study, allowing the reader at least to have a strong introductory understanding of the nature of the process.

In addition, behavioral scientists could:

1. Research the types of change processes that have been used successfully in corrections.
2. Research the skills match needed in creating teams composed of internal and external change agents.
3. Provide change agent services to management on an as-needed and ongoing basis, beginning with a small pilot project.

How is the change controlled? This is a subpart of general organizational control, the next topic.

Controlling

Correctional managers must be concerned with keeping their organization on the correct path to a desired future. That is, they must *control* it at the individual unit and whole organization levels. Kast and Rosenzweig define the topic as follows:

The concept of control is quite general and can be used in the organizational context to evaluate overall performance against a five year strategic plan or specific performance against a production quota of 25 units per hour. It relates to both ends (outputs) and means (inputs and transformation processes). Thus, the theory of control is pervasive. . . .

The word control has several meanings, and, more specifically, several connotations that are meaningful to the discussion in this chapter. For example, it means (1) to check or verify; (2) to regulate; (3) to compare with the standard; (4) to exercise authority over (direct or command); (5) to curb or restrain. At least three relatively distinct lines of thought are apparent in this definition—(1) curbing or restraining, (2) directing or commanding, and (3) checking or verifying. All are significant for organization theory and management practice. However, we are primarily concerned with the third connotation of control.

Checking or verifying implies some means of measurement and some standard that can serve as a frame of reference in the control process. The planning function typically provides the necessary yardstick— hopefully explicitly, but if not, at least implicitly.[52]

Control mechanisms in organizations are many and varied. All, however, begin with some amount of information about progress toward the stated goals. This section will first consider two control-oriented cases: one on information systems development and one on program evaluaton. They are followed by a case about cost/benefit analysis in corrections programs, a topic of ever increasing interest in this resources-constrained time period.

CASE SIXTY-EIGHT: INFORMATION SYSTEMS. Without information it is not possible to know the status of the organization's progress toward goal attainment. Behavioral scientists can become involved in information systems design and/or in the process of implementation. The following is one case offering both design and start-up issues.

Chard reviewed the socio-psychological information system developed by the New York State Division for Youth.[53] The general objective of the system was to define the program processes and to determine the effectiveness of deliquency rehabilitation programs. The information system had three specific purposes. First, its purpose was administration and planning; that is, to keep up-to-date and usable information on all facilities for centralized management purposes. Second, the information system's purpose was to enable the division to assess cost-effectiveness. The system was to develop the data necessary to measure the overall cost-effectiveness of individual programs. Third, it was to be used for research, investigating four general evaluation-oriented questions: (1) How effective are programs in achieving their aims? (2) Which programs are suitable for whom? (3)

How should programs be modified to increase effectiveness? (4) What alternative programs should be added to, or replace existing ones?

The components of the information system included the following. A policy-making committee determines the scope of the socio-psychological information system, deciding who should have access to it. Programming personnel and a controlling group are responsible for the day-to-day operation of the system. The data files include information on youth, and models, programs, and patterns of utilization. A special research project component has established coordinated files for exploratory research. Last, reports are generated automatically or on demand for any of the users.

Comments and Follow-up Work.   This report identifies the development of one information system at the state level. The material presented here relates to the use of the data for planning, control, and research. Several evaluation questions are identified that can be used to establish the nature of the topics used to control the system (e.g., cost-effectiveness, modifications needed). Behavioral scientists can be involved in the design and development stages of these systems through a consultation and/or an applied research function. Furthermore, it is often the case that behavioral scientists staff and direct these programs on a day-to-day basis.

Where they are not staffing the program, behavioral scientists could offer other types of support. They could:

1. Assess the extent of user support for the current correctional management information system.
2. Evaluate the information feedback loop to determine whether the data are going back to those providing the original input in a time and arrangement that will allow them to take appropriate action.
3. Provide consultation to management on new analytical approaches for the information system.

Information is the basis for both *planning* the organization's future activities and *evaluating* how the progress is developing. The next case reviews the evaluation work of behavioral scientists.

CASE SIXTY-NINE: PROGRAM EVALUATION.   As the information system case indicated, the data generated are used for evaluation. Behavioral scientists have been active in evaluation work in a wide range of roles. Because of a number of organizational environmental trends (e.g., rising costs, an interest in accountability, new program developments) evaluation work has been steadily increasing in the past ten years. An abstracted next case illustrates one example of evaluation research work.

Vito in an abstract of the study presents the results of an evaluation of a correctional treatment program.[54] The program project Papillon was designed and implemented to meet the needs of the substance-abusing offender. It was based on the unit management concept (Smith and Fenton, 1978), whereby the treatment staff are situated within the general population of the prison. This arrangement grants the inmate less restrictive access to project staff while enabling the staff to study the inmates' behavior in the cell block. Special attention is given to the limitations of the research design, including (1) failure of the research design to follow a time series format, (2) failure to adequately measure treatment effects, and (3) erosion of the treatment effects. It is suggested that such limitations impinge upon the ability of the evaluation to generate conclusive evidence on project outcomes and may even be responsible for negative conclusions about correctional treatment programs.

Comments and Follow-up Work. Here the behavioral scientist was providing applied research on a treatment program in a correctional setting. While the work was clearly applied research, there is some need to have adequate scientific knowledge of the treatment aspects of the program. Although it is not clear from the report, other behavioral scientists could have been used as an advisory group, thus providing greater understanding of the treatment and the research designs needed to contribute even more to science. Evaluation work can provide an assessment of an individual program. And, if adequately related to other professional literature, it can contribute to the extension of knowledge about treatment program effectiveness generally. The latter results in some pushing of the applied work toward basic science.

Behavioral scientists also could:

1. Research the rise of qualitative approaches in corrections evaluation.
2. Provide program evaluation services as an individual or as the head of a team.
3. Consult with management on the design of a facility-wide evaluation program that is regular, continuing, and takes an organizational development approach.

Evaluations can consider costs as a part of the evaluation design. Other studies are directed at the cost issues specifically. The next case illustrates an interest in costs.

CASE SEVENTY: COST-EFFECTIVENESS. The organization must control the individual unit costs, or the whole organization will not be a viable one. There is another reason for reviews. Both the total program and individual treatment efforts need to be examined in terms of society's financial investment in this approach to criminal justice. The following report considers cost issues as they are related to an impact on criminal behavior.

Bloom and Singer reviewed the cost-effectiveness of correctional programs with two purposes.[55] First, their intent was to extend and refine the existing evaluation methodologies for measuring a correctional program's ability to prevent and postpone criminal behavior, including cost-effectiveness. The second purpose was to present a case study of an evaluation conducted at the Patuxent Institution in Maryland, in part because Patuxent is an atypical correctional facility. It offers an intensive program of medical, psychiatric, and therapeutic services to adult male inmates who are declared "defective delinquents." These inmates have committed crimes, and are deficient intellectually or have emotional disorders. Inmates were given indeterminate sentences, and were released when Patuxent staff decided they were cured.

On a per-inmate basis, Patuxent has more psychiatrists, psychologists, and social workers than any other prison in the United States. The standard procedure at Patuxent encourages participation in psychological and medical treatment programs, academic and vocational education, recreation, and work assignments. Inmates' progress is determined by their response to these programs and is rewarded by "incremental privileges."

Because of rising costs at the institution the Maryland Legislature asked for a third-party evaluation of the facility. This study was a reanalysis of data from that evaluation.

To determine Patuxent's cost-effectiveness, the researchers compared it with a conventional prison, an alternative to Patuxent. Differences examined included: average length of imprisonment, the probability of rearrest following release, and the time from release to rearrest. Program output was measured in terms of crimes postponed and prevented.

Conceptually, this is the difference between the behavior of inmates released from Patuxent and what would have occurred had they been sent to prison instead. Operationally, this difference was estimated by comparing the experience of a sample of Patuxent offenders with that of a comparable group of prison inmates. Based on statistical tests, the authors estimated that 76 percent of the typical Patuxent inmates are rearrested. This is generally about eight percentage points less than if they had gone to prison (84 percent rearrest). Additionally, the time before rearrest was about one year shorter for prisoners than for Patuxent inmates. The conclusion: Patuxent offers preventive and postponement benefits in comparison to prison.

As a second part of their report, the researchers described the methods used for their cost calculations. The calculations focused on the cost of constructing, maintaining, and operating the facility and lost earnings of offenders confined. In their conclusions, the authors stated that Patuxent, because of its expenses, can only be justified in terms of its rehabilitation benefits, its prevention and/or postponement of crimes. The extra costs of the facility could yield the same or far greater benefits if used in other facets of corrections. As they were using this whole-program approach, they had no way of determining which part (or parts) of the overall program are responsible for its effectiveness.

Based on the study, the Maryland Legislature was undecided. In order not to end the successful, yet somewhat "non cost effective" program, they made three modifications. The legislature altered the commitment criteria to include the offender's ability and desire to benefit from the treatment. They also required that each inmate be given a treatment program that was individually designed, with progress determined by achievement of goals in that treatment plan. Last, they ended the indeterminate sentence and ruled that no prisoner could be held beyond his original sentence.

Comments and Follow-up Work. This case involves behavioral scientists in the key management area of cost-effectiveness. They assess the program from the cost point of view in order to provide the legislature with an answer to the question of whether to continue funding. This requires a close examination of treatment methods; but the function involved is essentially a consulting one, with applied research as the identifier of the type of work. The expert consultants are brought in to develop and carry out an evaluation of the program. It is a summative evaluation, designed to provide a performance review to determine continuation. As noted in the case, the data collected were not primarily directed at helping the program to develop (i.e., there was little formative evaluation information).

This type of work can be expected to expand as all types of public programs begin to focus on the costs of programs and the possible alternatives. Behavioral scientists will have many increased opportunities in research and consultation. For example they could:

1. Research the uses of and approaches to cost/benefit analyses of corrections programs.
2. Provide an educational seminar on the behavioral aspects of cost analyses (e.g., the psychological orientation to conserve) and how to build them into the corrections culture.
3. Consult with management on the design of practical cost/benefit studies.

The management area, like the other areas of the corrections organization, has offered many work opportunities.

SUMMARY

This chapter is concerned with the other four corrections organization subsystems (goals and values, structure, psychosocial, and managerial) that are supportive of the delivery of the primary technical service work discussed in Chapter 4. Goals are addressed first. They consist of punishment, protection of the community, and reformation and rehabilitation of the offenders. Analyzing goals is the first step in planning for structures that will incorporate them. New goals of "resocialization and reintegration" require comprehensive planning that must make the goals acceptable as well as operational. One study concluded that behavioral sciences research has not yet met the national correction system needs for successful rehabilitation methods. Conflict arises from the multiple goals of the corrections system, which require behavioral science analysis and active involvement in resolution.

Structure is designed to differentiate and coordinate the tasks of the organization. For behavioral scientists interested in corrections, some organizational structure components of interest are: probation and parole structures; education and training; individual job design and environmental structure. In probation and parole, the basic who, what, and how of decision making provides a basis for analyzing the structure in terms of its future improvement and development. Behavioral scientists can survey programs, analyze effectiveness, and present training programs to managers that will improve their individual systems.

Education and training is a critical need for the whole corrections field. Having better-trained personnel is an objective for many organizations, and it is often more efficient to train existing personnel than to recruit and orient new people. The programs available to offenders must be examined for variety and suitability. Other types of training, such as job-related behaviors (e.g., being on time, relating to others on the job), need to be offered and emphasized. Even more nontraditional approaches are called for, such as a voucher system, or prisons designed as specialized learning centers. Changing the focus of some prisons from security and detention to education and prescriptive programming would suit the needs of those "who do not really belong in prison." These suggestions illustrate the variety of ways that behavioral scientists could contribute to improving structure through education and training.

The psychological aspects of job stress and organizational climate are also related to job design and structure. One illustrative study looked at changing the custodial focus of jobs to a community-oriented rehabilitative one ("job enlargement" for corrections personnel). The study showed that the program modification did change the way in which employees' jobs were perceived. Further work by behavioral scientists at all structural levels, from individual jobs to units, could alter the psychosocial nature of the corrections organization, subsequently improving job satisfaction.

Man/environment relations and environmental psychology are new areas that have some direct applications for corrections. The most obvious area for work is the physical environment of the prison. Poor conditions and overcrowding are at crisis levels. Solutions must be found in terms of the redesign of current facilities and planning for new ones.

The psychosocial subsystem involves analysis of individual and group behaviors. Work to date in this area includes: personality; attitudes; group leadership; stress and organizational conflict. Assessment, education, and training are the frequent functions. Some prepackaged programs are useful; in other cases process consultation is a better approach. Further research is needed to help the organization develop and maintain a healthy psychosocial subsystem for both staff and offenders.

The managerial subsystem links the goals, values, and mission of the organization to its structure, including the critical task work. In corrections, managers are involved in the traditional activities of planning, organizing, directing, and controlling the organization. All of these offer specific areas for contributions by behavioral scientists. For example, management by objectives has been successful for business but has been slow in appearing in corrections. Behavioral scientists can help managers through education and training. Maintaining supportive connections between the various parts of an organization is another important managerial task. This deals with more than technical efficiency, including also the match between tasks and personnel. Behavioral scientists can use all their functions to help achieve these goals.

Directing and leading includes influencing the staff and helping them to attain objectives, keeping directions, and meeting target dates for the completion of tasks. Behavioral scientists can address such questions as: how much leadership is necessary to develop good programs for staff and inmates? In some areas a change process is necessary, requiring either an internal or external change agent. Behavioral scientists can be used to determine what kind of change agent is necessary, and can be change agents themselves.

Controlling the organization means guiding it to a desired end. The mechanisms for control are varied, including program evaluation, data collection, and cost/benefit analyses. Behavioral scientists can be process consultants in program evaluations, trained data collectors, and analyzers of the data. The management subsystem in corrections, as a whole, is in need of new techniques, new personnel, and the willingness to try alternatives.

In all of the areas examined in this chapter, behavioral scientists have the skills to bring valuable contributions to the corrections organization. Ideally, they can work in the four subsystems (goals and values, structure, psychosocial, and management) to bring about constructive change in the corrections system.

This chapter concludes this examination of the functions of behavioral scientists in courts and correctional organizations. As before, the corrections examples indicate that behavioral scientists have been most active; but there is much work yet to be done, with ample opportunities for behavioral scientists to make significant contributions to the development of these organizations.

REFERENCES

1. Kast, F. E., and Rosenzweig, J. E. (1979). *Organization and Management.* New York: McGraw-Hill.
2. Holten, N. G., and Jones, M. E. (1982). *The System of Criminal Justice.* Boston: Little, Brown.
3. Flynn, E. E. (1973). Social Planning and the Concept of Reintegration. In E. Sagarin and P. E. J. McNamara (eds.), *Corrections: Problems of Punishment and Rehabilitation.* New York: Praeger.
4. Ibid.
5. Ibid.
6. Ibid.
7. Amos, W. E. (1974). The Philosophy of Corrections: Revisited. *Federal Probation,* March.
8. Ibid.
9. Ibid.
10. Ackoff, R. L. (1970). *A Concept of Corporate Planning.* New York: John Wiley.
11. Ackoff, R. L. (1974). *Redesigning the Future.* New York: John Wiley.
12. Steiner, G. A. (1979). *Strategic Planning: What Every Manager Must Know.* New York: The Free Press.
13. Klingeman, H. (1982). Conflicts in Correctional Institutions for Juvenile Delinquents. *British Journal of Criminology* 22 (2), 140–64.
14. Kast and Rosenzweig, Op. cit.
15. Task Force Report: Corrections. (1967). Organization of Parole Authorities. In C. L. Newman (1973), *Sourcebook on Probation, Parole and Pardons.* Springfield, Illinois: Charles C. Thomas.
16. Ibid.
17. Ibid.
18. Schein, E. H. (1969). *Process Consultation: Its Role in Organization Development.* Reading, Massachusetts: Addison-Wesley.
19. McCollum, S. G. (1976). New Designs for Correctional Education and Training. In G. G. Killinger, P. F. Cromwell, and B. J. Cromwell, *Issues in Corrections and Administration.* St. Paul, Minnesota: West Publishing, pp. 301–13.
20. Ibid.
21. Ibid.
22. Marquis, H., and Gendreau, P. (1975). Short-Term Educational Upgrading on a Contractual Basis. *Journal of Community Psychology,* 3, 94.
23. Ibid.
24. Repucci, N. D., Dean, C. W., and Saunders, J. T. (1975). Job Design Variables as Change Measures in a Correctional Facility. *American Journal of Community Psychology,* 4, 315–25.
25. Proshansky, A. M., Ittelson, W. H., and Rivlin, L. G. (1970). *Environmental Psychology.* New York: Holt, Reinhart & Winston.
26. Esser, A. H. (1980). Window Design: Considerations for Health and Well-Being. *Man–Environment Systems,* 10 (5–6), 291–94.

27. Kast and Rosenzweig. Op. cit.
28. Goldsboro, E. W. and Burbank, E. G. (1954). The Probation Officer and His Personality. In C. L. Newman, *Sourcebook on Probation, Parole and Pardons.* Springfield, Illinois: Charles C. Thomas, pp. 104–12.
29. Holland, T. R., Levi, M., Beckett, G. E., and Holt, N. (1979). Preferences of Prison Inmates for Male Versus Female Institutional Personnel. *Journal of Applied Psychology* 64(5), 564–568.
30. Shapiro, S. B. (1975) The Group Leadership Training Program at F.C.I. Lompoc. In R. E. Hosford and C. S. Moss (eds.), *The Crumbling Walls: Treatment and Counseling of Prisoners.* Urbana: University of Illinois Press, pp. 18–33.
31. Inwald, R. E. (1982). Research Problems in Assessing Stress Factors in Correctional Institutions. *International Journal of Offender Therapy and Comparative Criminology,* 26 (3), 250–54.
32. Sebring, R. H. and Duffee, D. (1977). Who Are the Real Prisoners? A Case of Win–Loss Conflict in a State Correctional Institution. *Journal of Applied Behavioral Science,* 13, 23–40.
33. Schein. Op. cit.
34. Pogrebin, M., and Atkins, B. (1982). Organizational Conflict in Correctional Institutions. *Journal of Offender Counseling, Services and Rehabilitation,* 7 (1), 23–31.
35. Brodsky, C. M. (1982). Work Stress in Correctional Institutions. *Journal of Prison and Jail Health,* 2 (2), 74–102.
36. Freeman, R. W., and Johnson, L. D. (1982). Health Related Knowledge, Attitudes and Practices of Correctional Officers. *Journal of Prison and Jail Health,* 2, (2), 125–38.
37. Goldsmith, S. B. (1972). Jailhouse Medicine—Travesty of Justice? *Health Services Reports,* 87, 767–74.
38. Sandrick, K. M. (1981). Health Care in Correctional Facilities. *Quality Review Bulletin,* 7 (5).
39. Sandrick, K. M. (1981). Health Care in Correction Institutions in the United States, England, Canada, Poland and France. *Quality Review Bulletin,* 7 (7).
40. Ziegenfuss, J. T. (1984). Medical Services in the Prisons: A Discriminatory Practice and Alternatives. *Federal Probation.* 48 (2) pp43–48.
41. Kast and Rosenzweig. Op. cit.
42. Koontz, H., O'Donnell, C., and Weihrich, H. (1980). *Management,* 7th ed. New York: McGraw-Hill.
43. Kast and Rosenzweig. Op. cit.
44. LeBreton, P. P., and Henning, D. A. (1966). *Planning Theory.* Englewood Cliffs: Prentice Hall.
45. University of Georgia, Institute of Government (1975). Management by Objectives in the Correctional Setting. In G. C. Killinger, P. F. Cromwell, Jr., and B. J. Cromwell, *Issues in Corrections and Administration.* St. Paul, Minnesota: West Publishing, pp.201–7.
46. Koontz, O'Donnell, and Weihrich. Op. cit., in definitions glossary.
47. Hepburn, J. R., and Albonetti, C. A. (1978). Team Classification in State Correctional Institutions: Its Association with Inmate and Staff Attitudes. *Criminal Justice and Behaviors,* 5 (1), 63–73.
48. Kast and Rosenzweig. Op. cit.
49. Tannenbaum, R., and Massarik, F. (1957). Leadership: A Frame of Reference. *Management Science* (October), p. 3.
50. Hofstetter, W. (1973). Practical Considerations on Prison Administration of Treatment Programs. In E. M. Scott and K. L. Scott (eds.), *Criminal Rehabilitation . . . Within and Without the Walls.* Springfield, Illinois: Charles C. Thomas, pp.53–56.

51. Gluckstern, N. B., and Packard, R. W. (1975). The Internal–External Change Agent Team: Bringing Change to a "Closed Institution." *Journal of Applied Behavioral Science,* 13, 41–52.

52. Kast and Rosenzweig. Op. cit.

53. Chard, R. (1973). Research Information Systems: Their Use in Prediction, Prevention and Rehabilitation. In E. Sagarin and P. E. J. McNamara, *Corrections: Problems of Punishment and Rehabilitation.* New York: Praeger, pp.115–25.

54. Vito, G. F. (1982). Does It Work? Problems in the Evaluation of a Correctional Treatment Program. *Journal of Offender Counseling, Services and Rehabilitation, 7 (1), 5–21.*

55. Bloom, H. S., and Singer, N. M. (1979). Determining the Cost-Effectiveness of Correctional Programs. *Evaluation Quarterly,* 3 (4), 609–27.

BIBLIOGRAPHY

PART I: COURTS

Apfelbaum, E. (1974). On conflicts and bargaining. In L. Berkowitz (Ed.), *Advances in experimental social psychology* (Vol. 7). New York: Academic Press.

Arens, R., Granfield, D.D. and Susman, J. (1965). Jurors, jury charges, and insanity. *Catholic University of America Law Review, 14*, pp. 1–23.

Arens, R. (1974). *Insanity defense.* New York: Philosophical Library.

Ares, C.E., Rankin, A. and Sturz, H. (1963). The Manhattan bail project: An interim report on the use of pre-trail parole. *New York University Law Review, 38*, pp. 71–92.

Asch, S.E. (1952). Effects of group pressure upon the modification and distortion of judgments. In G.E. Swanson, T.M. Newcomb, and E.L. Hartley (Eds.), *Readings in social psychology* (rev. ed.). New York: Holt, Rinehart & Winston.

Bales. R.F. and Borgatta, E.F. (1955). Size of group as a factor in the interaction profile. In A.P. Hare, E.F. Borgatta, and R.F. Bales (Eds.), *Small groups.* New York: Knopf.

Barland, G.H. and Raskin, D.C. (1973). Detection of deception. In W.F. Prokasy and D.C. Raskin (Eds.), *Electrodermal activity in psychological research.* New York: Academic Press.

Baron, C.H. and Hofrichter, R. (1976). Quality control moves to center stage. *New Directions in Legal Services, 1*, pp. 21–22ff.

Bartlett, F.C. (1957), *Remembering: A study in experimental and social psychology* Cambridge: Cambridge University Press. (originally published in 1932).

Bass, B.M. and Klubeck, S. (1952). Effects of seating arrangements in leaderless group discussions. *Journal of Abnormal and Social Psychology, 47*, pp. 724–727.

Bavelas, A., Hastorf, A.H., Gross, A.E. and Kite, W.R. (1965). Experiments on the alternation of group structure. *Journal of Experimental Social Psychology, 1*, pp. 55–70.

Bedau, H.A. (Eds.) (1967). *The Death Penalty in America* (rev. ed). Garden City, N.Y.: Doubleday Anchor Books.

Bedau, H.A. and Pierce, C.M. (Eds.) (1967). *Capital Punishment in the United States.* New York: AMS Press, Inc.

Bedau, H.A. (1977). *The Courts, the Constitution, and Capital Punishment.* Lexington, Mass.: Lexington Books.

Bem, D.J. (1966). Inducing belief in false confessions. *Journal of Personality and Social Psychology, 3*, pp. 707–710.

Berg, K.S. and Vidmar, N. (1975). Authoritarianism and recall of evidence about criminal behavior. *Journal of Research in Personality, 9*, pp. 147–157.

Berman, J. and Sales, B.D. (1976). A critical evaluation of the systematic approach to jury selection. Paper presented at 84th annual convention of American Psychological Association, Washington, D.C.

Bermant, G. and Coppock, R. (1973). Outcomes of six-and twelve-member jury trials: An analysis of 128 civil cases in the State of Washington. *Washington Law Review, 48*, pp. 593–596.

Bird, C. (1927). The influence of press upon the accuracy of report. *Journal of Abnormal and Social Psychology, 22*, pp. 123–129.

Boehm, V. (1968). Mr. Prejudice, Miss Sympathy and the authoritarian personality: An application of psychological measuring techniques to the problem of jury bias. *Wisconsin Law Review*, pp. 734–750.

Bower, G.H. and Karlin, M.B. (1974). Depth of processing pictures of faces and recognition memory. *Journal of Experimental Psychology, 103*, pp. 751–757.

Brakel, S.J. (1974). *Judicare: Public funds, private lawyers, and poor people*. Chicago: American Bar Foundation.

Brickman, L. and Lempert, R. (eds.) *The role of research in the delivery of legal services*. Washington, D.C.: Resource Center for Consumers of Legal Services, 1976.

Broeder, D.W. (1958). The University of Chicago jury project. *Nebraska Law Review, 38*, pp. 744–761.

Brown, B.R. (1968). The effects of need to maintain face on interpersonal bargaining. *Journal of Experimental Social Psychology, 4*, pp. 107–122.

Brown, E., Deffenbacher, K. and Sturgill, W. (1977). Memory for faces and the circumstances of encounter. *Journal of Applied Psychology, 62*, pp. 311–318.

Brumbaugh, L.J. (1917). *Legal Reasoning and Briefing*. Indianapolis: Bobbs-Merrill Co.

Buckhout, R. (1973). *A jury without peers*. New York: Center for Responsive Psychology.

Buckhout, R. (1974a). Eyewitness testimony. *Scientific American, 321* (6), pp. 23–31.

Buckhout, R. (1974, December). Eyewitness testimony. *Scientific American, 231* pp. 23–31.

Buckhout, R. (1974b) Eyewitness recall of facts about a person. *Bulletin of the Psychonomic Society, 4*, pp. 191–192.

Buckhout, R and Ellison, K.W. (1977, June). The line-up: A critical look. *Psychology Today, 11* (1), pp. 82–88.

Burger, W. (1974). Chief Justice Burger proposes first steps toward certification of trial advocacy specialists. *American Bar Association Journal, 60*, p. 171.

Byrne, D. and Clore, G.L. (1970). A reinforcement model of evaluative responses. *Personality: An International Journal, 1*, pp. 103–128.

Carlin, J.E. (1966). *Lawyers' ethics*. New York: Russell Sage Foundation.

Carlson, A.B. and Werts, C.E. (1976). Relationships among law school predictors, law school performance, and bar examination results. *Law School Admission Research*. Princeton, N.J.: Educational Testing Service.

Carlson, R.J. (1976). Measuring the quality of legal services: An idea whose time has not come. *Law and Society Review, 11*, pp. 287–318.

Carroll, J.S. and Siegler, R.S. (1977). Strategies for the use of base-rate information. *Organizational Behavior and Human Performance, 19*, pp. 392–402.

Chertkoff, J.M. and Conley, M. (1976). Opening offer and frequency of concession as bargaining strategies. *Journal of Personality and Social Psychology, 1*, pp. 181–185.

Cray, E. (1968) Criminal interrogations and confessions: The ethical imperative. *Wisconsin Law Review*, No. 1, pp. 173–183.

Crosson, R.F. (1967). An investigation into certain personality variables among capital trial jurors. *Dissertation Abstracts, 27*, pp. 3668B–3669B.

Cullinan, E. and Clark, H.W. (1966). *Preparation for trial of civil actions*. (3rd ed.) Philadelphia Committee on Continuing Legal Education of the American Law Institute.

D'Andrade, R.G. (1974). Memory and the assessment of behavior. In H.M. Blalock (Ed.), *Measurement in the social sciences*. Chicago: Aldine.

Davis, J.H., Bray, R.M. and Holt, R.W. (1977). The empirical study of social decision processes in juries. In J. Tapp and F. Levine (Eds.), *Law, justice and the individual in society: Psychological and legal issues*. New York: Holt, Rinehart & Winston.

Davis, J.H., Kerr, N.L., Atkin, R.S., Holt, R. and Meek, D. (1975). The decision processes of 6-and 12-person mock juries assigned unanimous and two-thirds majority rules. *Journal of Personality and Social Psychology, 32* (1), pp. 1–14.

Dean, J.M. (1974). *Illegitimacy of plea bargaining*. Federal Probation, *38*, pp. 18–23.

Dershowitz, A. (1971). Imprisonment by judicial hunch. *American Bar Association Journal*, *57*, pp. 560–564.

Dessions, G.H., Freedman, L.Z., Donnelly, R.G., and Redlich, F.C. (1953). Drug-induced revelation and criminal investigation. *Yale Law Journal, 62*, pp. 315–347.

Deutsch, M. (1949). A theory of cooperation and competition. *Human Relations, 2*, pp. 129–152.

Deutsch, M. and Krauss, R.M. (1960). The effect of threat on interpersonal bargaining. *Journal of Abnormal and Social Psychology, 61*, pp. 181–189.

Devlin, Rt. Hon. Lord Patrick (1976, April 26). Report to the Secretary of State for the House Department of Departmental Committee on Evidence of Identification in Criminal Cases, House of Commons, Chairman: Rt. Hon. Lord Devlin, London: Her Majesty's Stationery Office.

Diamond, S.S. and Zeisel, H. (1974). A courtroom experiment on juror selection and decision making. Paper presented at the annual meeting of the American Psychological Association, New Orleans.

Diamond, S.S. (1974). A jury experiment reanalyzed. *University of Michigan Journal of Law Reform, 7*, pp. 520–532.

Doob, A.N. and Kirshenbaum, H.M. (1973) Bias in police lineups—Partial remembering. *Journal of Police Science and Administration, 1*, pp. 287–293.

Dorcus, R.M. (1960). Recall under hypnosis of amnestic events. *International Journal of Clinical and Experimental Hypnosis, 8*, pp. 57–61.

Driver, E.D. (1968). Confessions and the social psychology of coercion. *Harvard Law Review, 82*, pp. 42–61.

Dunn, R.E. and Goldman, M. (1966). Competition and noncompetition and feelings toward group and nongroup members. *Journal of Social Psychology, 68*, pp. 299–311.

Ebbesen, E.B. and Konecni, V.J. (1975). Decision-making and information integration in the courts: The setting of bail. *Journal of Personality and Social Psychology, 32*, pp. 805–821.

Ebbesen, E.B. and Konecni, V.J. (1976). Fairness in sentencing: Severity of crime and judicial decision making. Paper presented at the annual meeting of the American Psychological Association.

Efran, M.G. (1974). The effect of physical appearance on the judgment of guilt, interpersonal attraction, and severity of recommended punishment in a simulated jury task. *Journal of Research in Personality, 8*, pp. 45–54.

Ekman, P. and Friessen, W.V. (1969). Nonverbal leakage and clues to deception. *Psychiatry, 32*, pp. 88–106.

Ellsworth, P.C. and Ross, L. (1976). Public opinion and judicial decision-making: An example from research on capital punishment. In H.A. Bedau and C.M. Pierce (Eds.) *Capital Punishment in the United States*. New York: AMS Press, Inc.

Emerson, C.D. (1968, Summer). Personality tests for prospective jurors. *Kentucky Law Journal*, (note) *56*, pp. 832–854.

Etzioni, A. (1974, November/December). Creating an imbalance. *Trial Magazine, 10*, pp. 28–30.

Falknor, J.F. and Staffan, D.T. (1954). Evidence of character: From the "crucible of the community" to the "couch of the psychiatrists." *University of Pennsylvania Law Review, 102*, pp. 980–994.

Feneck, N. (1977). Dogmatism and the ability to disregard inadmissible evidence. Unpublished doctoral dissertation. Hofstra University.

Fine, B.J. (1957). Conclusion-drawing, communicator credibility and anxiety as factors in opinion change. *Journal of Abnormal and Social Psychology, 54*, pp. 369–374.

Finkelstein, M.O. and Fairley, W.B. (1970). A Bayesian approach to identification evidence. *Harvard Law Review, 83*, pp. 489–517.

Finkelstein, M.O. (1966, December). The application of statistical decision theory to the jury discrimination cases. *Harvard Law Review, 80*, pp. 338–376.

Forston, R.F. (1968). The decision-making process in the American civil jury: A comparative methodological investigation. Unpublished doctoral dissertation. University of Michigan.

Forston, R.F. (1970). Judges' instructions: A quantitative analysis of jurors' listening comprehension. *Today's Speech, 18*, pp. 34–38.

Freedman, L.Z. (1960). "Truth" drugs. *Scientific American, 202*, (3), pp. 145–154.

Freud, S. (1959). Psycho-analysis and the establishment of facts in legal proceedings. In J. Strachey (Ed.) *Standard Edition of the Complete Psychological Works of Sigmund Freud*, Vol. 9 (p. 103). London: Hogarth Press.

Friedman, H. (1972). Trial by jury: Criteria for convictions, jury size and type I and type II errors. *The American Statistician, 26*, pp. 21–23.

Fried, M., Kaplan, K.J. and Klein, K.W. (1975). Juror selection: An analysis of voir dire. Chapter 2 in R.J. Simon (Ed.), *The Jury System in America: A Critical Overview*, Vol. IV, Sage Criminal Justice System Annuals. Beverly Hills: Sage publications.

Gallo, P.S. (1966). Effects of increased incentives upon the use of threat in bargaining. *Journal of Personality and Social Psychology, 4*, pp. 14–20.

Gardner, D.S. (1933). The perception and memory of witnesses. *Cornell Law Quarterly, 18*, pp. 391–409.

Gardner, M.R. (1976). The myth of the impartial psychiatric expert—Some comments concerning criminal responsibility and the decline of the age of therapy. *Law and Psychology Review, 2*, pp. 99–122.

Gaudet, F.J. (1938). Individual differences in the sentencing tendencies of judges. *Archives of Psychology, 32*, (230).

Gelfand, A.E. and Solomon, H. (1974). Modeling jury verdicts in the American legal system. *Journal of the American Statistical Association, 69*, pp. 32–37.

Gelfand, A.E. and Solomon, H. (1973). A study of Poisson's models for jury verdicts in criminal and civil trials. *Journal of the American Statistical Association, 68*, pp. 271–278.

Gerbasi, K.C. and Zuckerman, M. (1975). An experimental investigation of jury biasing factors. Paper presented at Eastern Psychological Association, New York.

Gerbasi, K.C. Zuckerman, M. and Reis, H.T. (1977). Justice needs a new blindfold: A review of mock jury research. *Psychological Bulletin, 84* (2), pp. 323–345.

Golden, J. (1973). Jury selection: Can personality and attitude testing help? *Social Action and the Law, 1* (1), pp. 7–8.

Gordon, R. (1968). A study in forensic psychology: Petit jury verdicts as a function of the number of jury members. Unpublished doctoral dissertation, University of Oklahoma.

Grether, W.F. and Baker, C.A. (1972). Visual presentation of information. In H.P. Van Cott and R.G. Kinkade (Eds.), *Human engineering guide to equipment design*. Washington, D.C.: U.S. Government Printing Office.

Griffitt, W. and Jackson, T. (1973). Simulated jury decisions: The influence of jury-defendant attitude similarity-dissimilarity. *Social Behavior and Personality, 1*, pp. 1-7.

Grossack, M.M. (1954). Some effects of cooperation and competition upon small group behavior. *Journal of Abnormal and Social Psychology, 49*, pp. 341-348.

Gulliver, P.H. (1973). Negotiations as a mode of dispute settlement: Towards a general model. *Law and Society Review, 1*, pp. 667-691.

Hagan, J. (1974). Extra-legal attributes and criminal sentencing: An assessment of a sociological viewpoint. *Law and Society Review, 8*, pp. 357-383.

Hamilton, V.L. and Rotkin, L. (1976). The capital punishment debate: Public perception of crime and punishment. Paper presented at 84th Convention American Psychological Association, Washington, D.C.

Hans, V.P. and Doob, A.N. (1976). Sec. 12 of the Canada Evidence Act and the deliberations of simulated juries. *Criminal Law Quarterly, 18*, pp. 235-253.

Harris, R. (1972, December 16). Annals of Law: Trial by jury. *New Yorker*, pp. 117-125.

Hawkins, C.H. (1962). Interaction rates of jurors aligned in factions. *American Sociological Review, 27*, pp. 689-691.

Hazard, J. (1962). Furniture arrangement as a symbol of judicial roles. *Etc., 19*, p. 181.

Hazard, G. (1963). *Research in civil procedure*. New Haven: Walter E. Meyer Research Institute of Law.

Henney, J.C. (1947). The jurors look at our judges. *Oklahoma Bar Association Journal, 18*, pp. 1508-1513.

Heumann, M. (1975). A note on plea bargaining and case pressure. *Law and Society Review, 9*, pp. 515-528.

Hoeberg, B.C. and Stires, L.K. (1973). The effect of several types of pretrial publicity on the guilt attributions of simulated jurors. *Journal of Applied Social Psychology, 3* (3), pp. 267-275.

Holbrook, J.C. (1956). *A survey of metropolitan trial courts in Los Angeles*. Los Angeles: University of Southern Carlifornia Press.

Horvath, F.S. and Reid, J.E. (1971). The reliability of polygraph examiner diagnosis of truth and deception. *Journal of Criminal Law, 62*, pp. 276-281.

Hovland, C.I. and Mandell, W. (1952). An experimental comparison of conclusion-drawing by the communicator and by the audience. *Journal of Abnormal and Social Psychology, 47*, pp. 581-588.

Hovland, C.I. and Weiss, W. (1951). The influence of source credibility on communication effectiveness. *Public Opinion Quarterly, 15*, pp. 635-650.

Hunter, R.M. (1935). Law in the jury room. *Ohio State Law Journal, 2*, pp. 1-19.

Inbau, F.E. and Reid, J.E. (1962). *Criminal Interrogation and Confessions*. Baltimore: Williams and Wilkins Co.

Institute of Judicial Administration. (1972). *A comparison of six- and twelve-member juries in New Jersey superior and county courts*. New York: IJA.

Institute of Judicial Administration/American Bar Association. (1977). *Juvenile Justice Standards Project: Standards Relating to Juvenile Delinquency and Sanctions*. Tentative draft, (b).

Institute of Judicial Administration/American Bar Association. (1977). *Juvenile Justice Standards Project: Standards Relating to Dispositions*. Tentative draft, (a).

Izzett, R.R. and Leginski, W. (1974). Group discussion and the influence of defendant characteristics in a simulated jury setting. *Journal of Social Psychology, 93*, pp. 271-279.

Johnson, D.M. (1955). *The Psychology of thought and judgement*. New York: Harper.

Johnson, R.N. (1976, December 12). The state and death. *The New York Times*, pp. 11, 44.

Johnson, C. and Scott B. (1976). Eyewitness testimony and suspect identification as a function of arousal, sex of witness, and scheduling of interrogation. Paper presented at 84th annual convention of American Psychological Association, Washington, D.C.

Jones, E.E. and Davis, K.E. (1965). From acts to dispositions: The attribution process in person perception. In L. Berkowitz (Ed.), *Advances in experimental social psychology* (Vol. 2). New York: Academic Press.

Jones, E.E. and Nisbett, R.E. (1971). *The actor and the observer: Divergent perceptions of the causes of behavior*. Morristown, N.J.: General Learning Press.

Jurow, G.L. (1971). New data on the effect of a "death-qualified" jury on the guilt determination process. *Harvard Law Review, 84*, pp. 567-611.

Kadish, M.R. and Kadish, S.H. (1971). The institutionalization of conflict: Jury acquittals. *Journal of Social Issues, 27*, pp. 199-217.

Kahn, R.L., Wolfe, D.M. Quinn, R.P., Snoek, J.D. and Rosenthal, R.A. (1964). *Organizational stress: Studies in role conflict and ambiguity*. New York: Wiley.

Kairys, D., Schulman, J. and Harring, S. (1975). (Eds.), *The jury system: New methods for reducing prejudice*, Philadelphia: National Lawyers Guild.

Kairys, D. (1972). Juror selection: The law, a mathematical method of analysis, and a case study. *American Criminal Law Review, 10,* p. 771.

Kalvern, H., Jr. (1958). The jury, the law, and the personal injury damage award. *Ohio State Law Journal, 19,* pp. 158-178.

Kalvern, H., Jr. and Zeisel, H. (1966). *The American Jury.* Boston: Little, Brown.

Kaplan, M.F. and Kemmerick, G.D. (1974). Juror judgment as information integration: Combining evidential and nonevidential information. *Journal of Personality and Social Psychology, 30,* pp. 493-499.

Katz, D. and Kahn, R.L. (1966). *The social psychology of organizations.* New York: Wiley.

Kelley, H.H. (1971). *Attribution in social interaction.* Morristown, N.J.: General Learning Press.

Kelley, H.H. (1967). Attribution theory in social psychology. In D. Levine (Ed.), *Nebraska Symposium on Motivation* (Vol. 15). Lincoln, Nebraska: University of Nebraska Press.

Kelley, H.H. (1973). The processes of causal attribution. *American Psychologist, 28,* pp. 107-128.

Kelley, H.H. (1965). Experimental studies of threats in interpersonal negotiations. *Journal of Conflict Resolution, 9,* pp. 79-105.

Kelley, H.H. (1966). A classroom study of the dilemmas in interpersonal negotiations. In K. Archibald (Ed.), *Strategic interaction and conflict.* Berkeley: University of California, Institute of International Studies.

Kelley, H.H. and Thibaut, J.W. (1969). Group problem solving. In G. Linzey and E. Aronson (Eds.), *The handbook of social psychology* (Vol. 4), (2nd ed.). Reading, Mass.: Addison-Wesley.

Kelman, H.C. (1961). Processes of opinion change. *Public Opinion Quarterly, 25,* pp. 57-78.

Kessler, J.B. (1975). Social psychology of jury deliberation. Chapter 3 in R.J. Simon (Ed.) *The Jury System in America: A Critical Overview.* Sage Criminal Justice System Annuals, Vol. 4. Beverly Hills: Sage Publications.

Kessler, J.B. (1973). An empirical study of six- and twelve-member jury decision-making processes. *University of Michigan Journal of Law Reform, 6,* pp. 712-734

Kidney, J. (1977, June 6). Lawyers—Can they police themselves? *U.S. News and World Report, 82,* pp. 33-35.

Klatzky, R.L. (1975). *Human memory.* San Francisco: Freeman.

Kline, F.G. and Jess, P.H. (1966). Prejudicial publicity: Its effects on law school mock juries. *Journalism Quarterly, 43,* pp. 113-116.

Kohlberg, L. and Elfenbein, D. (1975). The development of moral judgments concerning capital punishment. *American Journal of Orthopsychiatry, 45* (4), pp. 614-640.

Komorita, S.S. and Brenner, A.R. (1968). Bargaining and concession making under bilateral monopoly. *Journal of Personality and Social Psychology, 9,* pp. 15-20.

Krauss, R.M., Geller, V. and Olson, C. (1976). Modalities and cues in the detection of deception. Paper presented at the annual convention of the American Psychological Association.

Kraut, R.E. (1976). Verbal and nonverbal cues in the perception of lying. Paper presented at the annual meeting of the American Psychological Association.

Kubis, J.F. (1962). Studies in lie detection. Technical Report 62-205, Fordham University.

Labinsky, J. (1976). A traffic in legal services: Lawyer-seeking behavior and the channelling of clients. *Law and Society Review, 11,* pp. 207-223.

Ladinsky, J. (1963). Careers of lawyers, law practice and legal institutions. *American Sociological Review, 28,* pp. 47-54.

Lana, R.E. (1972). Persuasion of the law: A constitutional issue. *American Psychologist, 27,* p. 901.

Landy, D. and Aronson, E. (1969). The influence of the character of the criminal and his victim on the decisions of simulated jurors. *Journal of Experimental Social Psychology, 5*, pp. 141-152.

Larntz, K. (1975). Reanalysis of Vidmar's data on the effects of decision alternatives on verdicts and simulated jurors. *Journal of Personality and Social Psychology, 31*, pp. 123-125.

Lawson, R.G. (1970). Relative effectiveness of one-sided and two-sided communications in courtroom persuasion. *Journal of General Psychology, 82*, pp. 3-16.

Lee, C.D. (1953). *The instrumental detection of deception.* Springfield, Ill.: Charles C. Thomas.

Lempert, R.O. (1975). Uncovering "nondiscernible" differences: Empirical research and the jury-size cases. *Michigan Law Review, 73*, pp. 643-708.

Lerner, M.J. (1970). The desire for justice and reactions to victims. In J. Macaullay and L. Berkowitz (Eds.), *Altruism and helping behavior.* New York: Academic Press.

Lerner, M.J., Miller, D.J., and Holmes, J.G. (1976). Deserving and the emergence of forms of justice. In L. Berkowitz (Ed.), *Advances in experimental social psychology* (Vol. 9), New York: Academic Press.

Levine, F.J. and Tapp, J. (1973). The psychology of criminal identification: The gap from Wade to Kirby. *University of Pennsylvania Law Review, 121*, pp. 1079-1131.

Lieberman, J.K. (1970). *The tyranny of the experts: How professionals are closing the open society.* New York: Walker.

Lind, E.A. and O'Barr, W.M. (1978). The social significance of speech in the courtroom. In H. Giles and R. St. Clair (Eds.), *Language and social psychology.* Oxford, England: Blackwell.

Loftus, E. (1974, December) Reconstructing memory: The incredible eyewitness. *Psychology Today, 8* (7), pp. 117-119.

Loftus, G.R. and Loftus, E.F. (1976). *Human memory: The processing of information.* Hillsdale, N.J.: Erlbaum.

Lund, F.H. (1925). The psychology of belief: IV. The law of primacy and persuasion. *Journal of Abnormal and Social Psychology, 20*, pp. 183-191.

Lykken, D.T. (1974). Psychology and the lie detector industry. *American Psychologist, 29*, pp. 725-739.

Lykken, D.T. (1960). The validity of the guilty knowledge technique: The effects of faking. *Journal of Applied Psychology, 44*, pp. 258-262.

Malpass, R.S. and Kravitz, J. (1969). Recognition of faces of own and other race. *Journal of Personality and Social Psychology, 13*, pp. 330-334.

Marquis, K., Oskamp, S., and Marshall, J. (1972). Testimony validity as a function of question form, atmosphere, and item difficulty. *Journal of Applied Social Psychology, 2* (2), pp. 167-186.

Marshall, J. (1969). *Law and psychology in conflict.* New York: Doubleday-Anchor (originally published in 1966).

Maru, O. (1972). *Research on the legal profession.* Chicago: American Bar Foundation.

McCarty, D.G. (1960). *Psychology and the law.* Englewood Cliffs, N.J.: Prentice-Hall.

McGarth, J.E. and Altman, I. (1966). *Small group research: A synthesis and critique of the field.* New York: Holt, Rinehart & Winston.

Means, J.R. and Weiss, M. (1971). Gestural behavior of the courtroom witness. *The Journal of Forensic Psychology, 3* (1), pp. 12-20.

Michotte, A. (1963). *The Perception of Causality.* New York: Basic books.

Mischel, W. (1968). *Personality and assessment.* New York: Wiley.

Mitchell, H.E. and Byrne, D. (1973). The defendant's dilemma: Effects of jurors' attitudes and authoritarianism. *Journal of Personality and Social Psychology, 25*, pp. 123-129.

Miller, N. and Campbell, D. (1959). Recency and primacy in persuasion as a function of the timing of speeches and measurements. *Journal of Abnormal and Social Psychology,* *59,* pp. 1–9.

Mills, L.R. (1973). Six-member and twelve-member juries: An empirical study of trial results. *University of Michigan Journal of Law Reform, 6,* pp. 671–711.

Mills, E.S. (1962, Summer). A statistical study of occupations of jurors in a (Maryland) United States district court. *Maryland Law Review, 22,* pp. 205–214.

Missouri Bar-Prentice-Hall Survey. (1963). *A motivational study of public attitudes and law office management.* Cited in American Bar Association, *ABA Compilation of Reference Materials on Prepaid Legal Services.* (1973). Chicago: ABA.

Mitford, J. (1974) *Kind and Usual Punishment.* New York: Vintage Books.

Monahan, J. (1973). Abolish the insanity defense?—Not yet. *Rutgers Law Review, 26,* pp. 719–740.

Moore, H.A., Jr. (1974, November/December). Redressing the balance. *Trial Magazine, 10,* pp. 29–35.

Mosier, M.M. and Soble, R.A. (1973). Modern legislation, metropolitan court, miniscule results: A study of Detroit's landlord-tenant court. *University of Michigan Journal of Law Reform, 7,* p. 6.

Mossman, K. (1973). Jury selection: An expert's view. *Psychology Today, 6* (12), pp. 78–79.

Munsterberg, H. (1914). The mind of they juryman. Chapter V in *Psychology and Social Sanity.* New York: Doubleday.

Munsterberg, H. (1909). *On the Witness Stand: Essays on Psychology and Crime.* New York: Doubleday, Page & Co.

Munsterberg H. (1909). Untrue confessions. In *On the Witness Stand: Essays on Psychology and Crime.* New York: Doubleday, Page & Co.

Munsterberg, H. (1915). *On the witness stand: Essays on psychology and crime.* New York: Doubleday.

Muscio, B. (1915). The influence of the form of a question. *British Journal of Psychology, 8,* pp. 351–389.

Myers, D.G. and Lamm, H. (1976). The group polarization phenomenon. *Psychological Bulletin, 83,* pp. 602–627.

Myers, D.G. and Kaplan, M.F. (1976). Group-induced polarization in simulated juries. *Personality and Social Psychology Bulletin, 2,* pp. 63–66.

Myslieviec, S.R. (1974). Toward principles of jury equity. *Yale Law Journal, 83* (5), pp. 1023–1054.

Nadar, R. and Green, M. (Eds.) (1976). *Verdicts on lawyers.* New York: Thomas Y. Crowell.

National Advisory Commission on Criminal Justice Standards and Goals. (1973). *Report on Courts.* Washington, D.C.: U.S. Government Printing Office.

Nemeth, C., Endicott, J. and Wachtler, J. (1976). From the '50s to the '70s: Women in jury deliberations. *Sociometry, 39* (4), pp. 293–304.

Nemeth, C. (1977). Interactions between jurors as a function of majority vs. unanimity decision rules. *Journal of Applied Social Psychology, 7* (1), pp. 38–56.

Nemeth, C. and Sosis, R.H. (1973). A simulated jury study: Characteristics of the defendant and the jurors. *Journal of Social Psychology, 90,* pp. 221–229.

Newman, D.J. (1956). Pleading guilty for considerations: A study of bargain justice. *The Journal of Criminal Law, Criminology, and Police Science, 46,* pp. 780–790.

O'Donnell, P., Churgin, M.J. and Curtis, D.E. (1977). *Toward a just and effective sentencing system.* New York: Praeger.

Ostrom, T.M., Werner, C. and Saks, M. (1978). An integration theory analysis of jurors' presumption of guilt or innocence. *Journal of Personality and Social Psychology, 36,* pp. 436–450.

Packer, H. (1968). *The limits of the criminal sanction*. Stanford, Calif.: Stanford University Press.

Padawer-Singer, A., and Barton, A. (1975). The impact of pretrial publicity. In R.J. Simon (Ed.), *The Jury System in America*. Beverly Hills, Calif.: Sage Publications.

Padawer-Singer, A., Singer, A. and Singer, R. (1974) Voir dire by two lawyers: An essential safe-guard. *Judicature, 57* (9), pp. 386–391.

Padawer-Singer, A. and Barton, A.H. (1975). The impact of pre-trial publicity on jurors' verdicts. Chpater 5 in R.J. Simon (Ed.), *The Jury System in America: A Critical Overview*. Sage Criminal Justice System Annuals, Vol. 4. Beverly Hills: Sage Publications.

Patridge, A. and Eldridge, C. (1974). *The Second Circuit Sentencing Study: A Report to the Judges of the Second Circuit*, Washington, D.C.: Federal Judicial Center.

Plutchik, R. and Schwartz, A.K. (1964, May). Jury selection: Folklore or science? *Criminal Law Bulletin, 1* (4), pp. 3–10.

Podlesny, J.A. and Raskin, D.C. (1977). Physiological measures and the detection of deception. *Psychological Bulletin, 84*, pp. 782–799.

Pollack, M. (1975). Pre-trial procedures more effectively handled. *Federal Rules Decision, 65*, pp. 475–484.

Prassel, F.R. (1975). *Introduction to American criminal justice*. New York: Harper & Row.

Prettyman, E.B. (1960). Jury instruction—First or last? *American Bar Association Journal, 46*, p. 1066.

Reid, J.E. and Inbau, F.E. (1966). *Truth and deception: The Polygraph ("lie detector") technique*. Baltimore, MD.: Williams and Wilkins.

Reik, I. (1966). *The Compulsion to Confess*. New York: Wiley Science Editions.

Reiser, M. (1974). Hypnosis as an aid in a homicide investigation. *American Journal of Clinical Hypnosis, 17*, pp. 87–97.

Reynolds, D.E. and Sanders, M.S. (1973). The effects of defendant attractiveness, age, and injury severity on sentence given by simulated jurors. Paper presented at the Western Psychological Association meeting.

Rokeach, M. and Vidmar, N. (1973). Testimony concerning possible jury bias in a Black Panther murder trial. *Journal of Applied Social Psychology, 3*, pp. 19–29.

Rosenthal, D.E. (1974). *Lawyer and client: Who's in charge?* New York: Russell Sage Foundation.

Rosenthal, D.E. (1976). Evaluating the competence of lawyers. *Law and Society Review, 11*, pp. 257–286.

Rosett, A. and Cressey, D.R. (1976). *Justice by consent: Plea bargains in the American courthouse*. Philadelphia: Lippincott.

Rosnow, R. and Goldstein, J. (1976). Familiarity, salience, and the order of presentation of communications. *Journal of Social Psychology, 173*, p. 97.

Rosnow, R.L. and Robinson, E.J. (Eds.) (1967). *Experiments in persuasion*. New York: Academic Press.

Ross, H.L. (1970). *Settled out of court*. Chicago: Aldine.

Sage, W. (1973). Psychology and the Angela Davis jury. *Human Behavior, 2* (1), pp. 56–61.

Saks, M.J. (1977). *Jury verdicts*. Lexington, Mass.: D.C. Heath.

Saks, M.J., Werner, C.M. and Ostrom, T.M. (1975). The presumption of innocence and the American juror. *Journal of Contemporary Law, 2*, pp. 46–54.

Saks, M.J. and Benedict, A.R. (1976). Evaluation and quality assurance of legal services: Concepts and research. In L. Brickman & R. Lempert (Eds.), *The role of research in the delivery of legal services*. Washington, D.C.: Resource Center for Consumers of Legal Services.

Saks, M.J. (1974). Ignorance of science is no excuse. *Trial, 10*, pp. 18ff.

Saks, M.J. (1976). The limits of scientific jury selection: Ethical and empirical. *Jurimetrics Journal, 17*, pp. 3–22.

Saks, M.J., and Ostrom, T.M. (1975). Jury size and consensus requirements: The laws of probability vs. the laws of the land. *Journal of Contemporary Law, 1,* pp. 163–173.

Saks, M.J. (1976). Social scientists can't rig juries. *Psychology Today, 9* (8), p. 48ff.

Sales, B.D., Elwork, A. and Alfini, J.J. (1977). Improving comprehensive for jury instructions. In B.D. Sales (Ed.), *Perspectives in law and psychology.* Vol. I: *The criminal justice system.* New York: Plenum.

Schulman, J., Shaver, P., Colman, R., Emrich, B. and Christie, R. (1973). Receipe for a jury. *Psychology Today, 6* (12), p. 37.

Schum, D.A. (1975). The weighing of testimony in judicial proceedings from sources having reduced credibility. *Human Factors, 17,* pp. 172–182.

Sealy, A.P. and Cornish, W.R. (1973a). Jurors and their verdicts. *Modern Law Review, 36,* pp. 496–508.

Sealy, A.P. and Cornish, W.R. (1973b, April). Juries and the rules of evidence. *Criminal Law Review,* pp. 208–223.

Sears, D.O. (1966). Opinion formation and information preferences in an adversary situation. *Journal of Experimental Social Psychology, 2,* pp. 130–142.

Sellin, I. (Ed.) (1967). *Capital Punishment.* New York: Harper & Row.

Shapley, D. (1974, September 20). Jury selection: Social scientists gamble in an already loaded game. *Science, 185,* pp. 1033–1034, 1071.

Shapley, D. (1974, September 20). Jury selection: Social scientists gamble in an already loaded game. *Science, 185,* pp. 1033ff.

Shaver, K.G. (1975). *An introduction to attribution processes.* Cambridge, Mass.: Winthrop Publishers.

Shaw, L. (1975). Trial by jury: An analysis of the jury's verdict. Unpublished doctoral dissertation. Rensselaer Polytechnic Institute.

Shephard, R.N. (1967). Recognition memory for words, sentences, and pictures. *Journal of Verbal Learning and Verbal Behavior, 6,* pp. 156–163.

Sherif, M., Harvey, O.J., White, E.J., Hood, W.E. and Sherif, C.W. (1961). *Intergroup conflict and cooperation: The Robber's Cave experiment.* Norman, Okla.: University of Oklahoma Book Exchange.

Shure, G., Meeker, R. and Hansford, E. (1965). The effectiveness of pacifist strategies in bargaining games. *Journal of Conflict Resolution, 9,* pp. 106–117.

Sigall, H. and Landy, D. (1972). Effects of the defendant's character and suffering on juridic judgment: A replication and clarification. *Journal of Social Psychology, 88,* pp. 149–150.

Signall, H. and Ostrove, N. (1975). Beautiful but dangerous: Effects of offender attractiveness and nature of the crime on juridic judgment. *Journal of Personality and Social Psychology, 31,* pp. 410–414.

Simon, R.J. (1976). Murder, juries, and the press. *Transaction, 3,* pp. 40–42.

Simon, R.J. (1976). *The jury and the defense of insanity.* Boston: Little, Brown.

Single, E.W. (1972). The consequences of pre-trial detention. Paper presented at the annual meeting of the American Sociological Association, New Orleans.

Skolnick, J. (1966). *Justice without trial.* New York: Wiley.

Slater, P.E. (1958). Contrasting correlates of group size. *Sociometry, 21,* pp. 129–139.

Slovic, P. and Lichtenstein, S. (1971). Comparison of Bayesian and regression approaches to the study of information processing in judgment. *Organizational Behavior and Human Performance, 6,* pp. 649–744.

Smith, A.B. and Blumberg, A.S. (1967). The problem of objectivity in judicial decision-making. *Social Forces, 46,* pp. 96–105.

Smith, B.M. (1967). The polygraph. *Scientific American, 216* (1), pp. 25–30.

Smoke, W.H. and Zajonc, R.B. (1962). On the reliability of group judgments and decisions. In J.J. Criswell, H. Solomon, and P. Suppes (Eds.), *Mathematical methods in small group processes.* Stanford, Calif.: Stanford University Press.

Solomon, L. (1960). The influence of some types of power relationships and game strategies upon the development of interpersonal trust. *Journal of Abnormal and Social Psychology, 61*, pp. 223–230.

Solomon, G.F. (1975). Capital punishment as suicide and murder. *American Journal of Orthopsychiatry, 45* (4), pp. 701–711.

Sommer, R. (1961). Leadership and group geography. *Sociometry, 24*, pp. 99–110.

Sommer, R. (1976). *The End of Imprisonment*. New York: Oxford University Press.

Special Committee to Survey Legal Needs. (1976, January). *Alternatives: Legal Services and the Public*, (Special Issue). Chicago: American Bar Association.

Steiner, I.E. (1972). *Group process and productivity*. New York: Academic Press.

Stephan, F.F. and Mishler, E.G. (1952). The distribution of participation in small groups: An experimental approximation. *American Sociological Review, 17*, pp. 598–608.

Stevens, C.M. (1963). *Strategy and collective bargaining negotiation*. New York: McGraw-Hill.

Strodtbeck, F.L., James, R.M. and Hawkins, D. (1957). Social status in jury deliberations. *American Sociological Review, 22* (6) pp. 713–719.

Strodtbeck, F.L. and Mann, R.D. (1956). Sex role differentiation in jury deliberations. *Sociometry, 19*, pp. 3–11.

Strodtbeck, F.L. and Hook, L.H. (1961). The social dimensions of a twelve-man jury table. *Sociometry, 24*, pp. 397–415.

Sue, S., Smith, R.E. and Caldwell, C. (1973). Effects of inadmissible evidence on the decisions of simulated jurors: A moral dilemma. *Journal of Applied Social Psychology, 3* (4), pp. 345–353.

Thibaut, J.W. and Riecken, H. (1955). Some determinants and consequences of the perception of social causality. *Journal of Personality, 24*, pp. 113–133.

Thibaut, J., Walter, L. and Lind, E.A. (1972). Adversary presentation and bias in legal decision-making. *Harvard Law Review, 86*, pp. 386-401.

Thibaut, J.W. and Kelley, H.H. (1959). *The social psychology of groups*. New York: Wiley.

Thibaut, J. and Walker, L. (1975). *Procedural justice: A psychological analysis*. Hillsdale, N.J.: Erlbaum.

Thomas, E.J. and Fink, C.J. (1963). Effects of group size. *Psychological Bulletin, 60*, pp. 371-384.

Thomas, E.S. (1973-1974). Plea bargaining: Clash between theory and practice. *Loyola Law Review, 20*, pp. 303-312.

Thorne, B. (1973). Professional education in law. In E.C. Hughes, B. Thorne, A.M. DeBaggis, A. Gurin, and D. Williams, *Education for the professions of medicine, law, theology, and social welfare*. New York: McGraw-Hill.

Tivnan, F. (1975, November 16). Jury by trial. *The New York Times Magazine*, p. 30ff.

Tribe, L.H. (1971). Trial by mathematics: Precision and ritual in the legal process. *Harvard Law Review, 84*, pp. 1329-1393.

Ulmer, S.S. (1962). Supreme Court behavior in racial exclusion cases: 1935-1960. *American Political Science Review, 56*, pp. 325-330.

Ulmer, S.S. (1971). *Courts as small and not so small groups*. Morristown, N.J.: General Learning Press.

Valenti, A.C. and Downing, L.L. (1975). Differential effects of jury size on verdict following deliberation as a function of the apparent guilt of a defendant. *Journal of Personality and Social Psychology, 32* (4), pp. 655-663.

Vanderzell, J.H. (1966). The jury as a community cross section. *Western Political Science Quarterly, 19*, pp. 136-149.

Vernon, P.E. (1964). *Personality assessment: A critical survey*. New York: Wiley.

Vidmar, N. (1972). Effects of decision alternatives on the verdicts and social perceptions of simulated jurors. *Journal of Personality and Social Psychology, 22*, pp. 211-218.

Vidmar, N. and Ellsworth, P.C. (1974). Public opinion on the death penalty. *Stanford Law Review, 26* (6), pp. 1245-1270.

Vidmar, N. and Crinklaw, L. (1973, May). Retribution and utility as motives in sanctioning behavior. Paper presented at the Midwestern Psychological Association Convention, Chicago.

Walbert, D.F. (1971). The effect of jury size on the probability of conviction: An evaluation of *Williams v. Florida. Case Western Reserve Law Review, 22,* pp. 529-554.

Walster, E. (1966). Assignment of responsibility for an accident. *Journal of Personality and Social Psychology, 3,* pp. 73-80.

Walster, E., Berscheid, E. and Walster, G.W. (1973). New directions in equity research. *Journal of Personality and Social Psychology, 25* (2), pp. 151-176.

Warkov, S. and Zelan, J. (1965). *Lawyers in the making.* New York: Aldine-Atherton.

Weick, K.E. (1969). *The social psychology of organizing.* Reading, Mass.: Addison: Wesley.

Weiss, W. and Steenbock, S. (1965). The influence on communication effectiveness of explicity urging action and policy consequences. *Journal of Experimental Social Psychology, 1,* pp. 396-406.

Weld, H.P. and Danzig, E.R. (1940, October). A study of the way in which a verdict is reached by a jury. *American Journal of Psychology, 53,* pp. 518-536.

Whipple, G.M. (1909). The observer as reporter: A survey of the psychology of testimony, *Psychological Bulletin, 6,* pp. 153-170.

Whipple, G.M. (1915), Psychology of testimony. *Psychological Bulletin, 12,* pp. 221-224.

Wigmore, J.H. (1935). *A student's textbook of the law of evidence.* Brooklyn: The Foundation Press.

Williams, G.R., England, J.L., Farmer, L.C. and Blumenthal, M. (1976). Effectiveness in legal negotiations. In G. Bermant, C. Nemeth, and N. Vidmar (Eds.), *Psychology and the Law,* Lexington, MA.: D.C. Heath.

Wispe, L.G. and Thayer, P.W. (1957). Role ambiguity and anxiety in an occupational group. *Journal of Social Psychology, 46,* pp. 41-48.

Yale Law Journal (1968). Notes and Comments: On instructing deadlocked juries, *78,* pp. 100-142.

Zadny, J. and Gerard, H.B. (1974). Attributed intentions and information selectivity. *Journal of Experimental Social Psychology, 10,* pp. 34-52.

Zeisel, H. (1971). ". . . and then there were none." The diminution of the federal jury. *The University of Chicago Law Review, 38,* pp. 710-724.

Zeisel, H. and Diamond, S.S. (1974). Convincing empirical evidence on the six-member jury. *University of Chicago Law Review, 41,* pp. 281-295.

Zeisel, H. and Seidman Diamond, S. (1976). The jury selection in the Mitchell-Stans conspiracy trial. *American Bar Association Research Journal, 1,* pp. 151-174.

Zeisel, H. (1963). What determines the amount of argument per juror? *American Sociological Review, 28,* p. 279.

Zeisel, H. (1968). *Some Data on Juror Attitudes Towards Capital Punishment.* Chicago: University of Chicago, Center for the Study of Criminal Justice.

Zeisel, H. (1977). The deterrent effect of the death penalty: Facts v. Faiths. In P.B. Furland (Ed.), *The Supreme Court Review,* Chicago: University of Chicago Press.

Zerman, M.B. (1977). *Call the final witness.* New York: Harper & Row.

Part II: CORRECTIONS

Adler, F. (1975, November). The rise of the female crook. *Psychology Today, 9* (6), pp. 42ff.

Adorno, T., Frenkel-Brunswick, E., Levinson, D. and Sanford, N. (1950). *The authoritarian personality*. New York: Harper.

Alex, N. (1969). *Black in Blue: A Study of the Negro Policeman*. New York: Appleton-Century-Crofts.

Alker, H.A. (1972). Is personality situationally specific or interpsychically consistent? *Journal of Personality, 40*, pp. 1-16.

Allport, G.W. (1961). *Pattern and Growth in Personality*. New York: Holt, Rinehart & Winston.

Argyris, C. (1964). *Integrating the Individual and the Organization*. New York: Wiley.

Armstrong, S. Social irresponsibility in management. *Journal of Business Research,* in press.

Aronfreed, J. (1968). *Conduct and Conscience*. New York: Academic Press.

Aronfreed, J. (1976). Moral development from the standpoint of a general psychological theory. In T. Lickona (Ed.) *Moral Development and Behavior*, pp. 54-69. New York: Holt, Rinehart & Winston.

Ayllon, T. (1975). Behavior modification in institutional settings. *Arizona Law Review, 17*, pp. 3-19.

Badalamente, R.V., George, C.E., Halterlein, P.J., Jackson, T.T., Moore, S.A. and Rio, P. (1973). Training police for their social role. *Journal of Police Science and Administration, 1* (4), pp. 440-453.

Baehr, M.E., Furcon, J.E. and Froemel, E.C. (1969). *Psychological Assessment of Patrolman Qualifications in Relation to Field Performance*. Washington, D.C.: U.S. Department of Justice, Law Enforcement Assistance Administration.

Bales, R.F. (1958). Task roles and social roles in problem-solving groups. In E.E. Maccoby, T.M. Newcomb, and E.L. Hartley (Eds.) *Readings in Social Psychology* (3rd ed.). New York: Holt.

Bandura, A. (1973). *Aggression: A Social Learning Analysis*. Englewood Cliffs, N.J.: Prentice-Hall.

Bannon, J.D. and Wilt, G.M. (1973). Black policemen: A study of self-images. *Journal of Police Science and Administration, 1* (1), pp. 21-29.

Banuazizi, A. and Movahedi, S. (1975). Interpersonal dynamics in asimulated prison: A methodological analysis. *American Psychologists, 30*, (2), pp. 152-160.

Bard, M. (1970). *Training Police as Specialists in Family Crisis Intervention*. Washington, D.C.: U.S. Department of Justice. Law Enforcement Assistance Administration.

Becker, G.M. and McClintock, C.G. (1967). Value: Behavioral decision theory. *Annual Review of Psychology, 18*, pp. 239-286.

Bem, D.J. (1967). Self-perception: An alternative interpretation of cognitive dissonance phenomena. *Psychological Review, 74*, pp. 245–254.

Bickman, L., Lavrakas, P.J., Green, S.K., North-Walter, N., Edwards, J., Borkowski, S., Shane-DuBow, S. and Wuert, J. *National Evaluation Program Phase I Summary Report Citizen Crime Reporting Projects*. Chicago: Applied Social Psychology Program, Loyola University of Chicago (undated).

Bickman, L. (1971). The effect of social status on the honesty of others. *Journal of Social Psychology, 85*, pp. 87-92.

Bickman, L. and Green, S.K. (1975). Is revenge sweet? The effect of attitude toward a thief on crime reporting. *Criminal Justice and Behavior, 2* (2), pp. 101-112.

Bickman, L. and Green, S.K. (1977). Situational cues and crime reporting. Do signs make a difference? *Journal of Applied Social Psychology, 7* (1), pp. 1-18.

Bickman, L. (1975). The social power of a uniform. *Journal of Applied Social Psychology, 4*, (1) pp. 47-61.

Bickman, L. (1976). Bystander intervention in a crime. Chapter 11 in E.C. Viana (Ed.) *Victims and Society*. Washington, D.C.: Visage Press, Inc.

Bickman, L. (1976). Attitude toward an authority and the reporting of a crime. *Sociometry, 39* (1), pp. 76-82.

Boggs, S.L. (1966). Urban crime patterns. *American Sociological Review, 30* (6), pp. 899-908. Reprinted in D. Glaser (Ed.), (1970). *Crime in the City.* New York: Harper & Row.

Brehm, J.W. (1966). *A theory of psychological reactance.* New York: Academic Press.

Byrne, D. (1969). Attitudes and attraction. In L. Berkowitz (Ed.), *Advances in Experimental Social Psychology* (Vol. 4), New York: Academic Press.

Campbell, C. (1976, May). Portrait of a mass killer. *Psychology Today, 9* (12), pp. 110ff.

Campbell, D.T. (1969). Reforms as experiments. *American Psychologist, 24,* pp. 409-429.

Carroll, J.S. (1977). Judgments of recidivism risk: Conflicts between clinical strategies and base-rate information. *Law and Human Behavior, 1,* pp. 191-198.

Carroll, J.S. (1979). Judgments made by parole boards. In I.H. Frieze, D. Bar-Tal, and J.S. Caroll (Eds.), *New Approaches to Social Problems: Applications of Attribution Theory.* San Francisco: Jossey-Bass.

Chaneles, S. (1976, October). Prisoners can be rehabilitated—now. *Psychology Today, 10* (5), pp. 129-134.

Chevigny, P. (1969). *Police Power: Police Abuse in New York City.* New York: Vintage Books.

Christiansen, K.O. (1977). A review of studies of criminality among twins. Chapter 4 of S. Mednick and K.O. Christiansen (Eds.) *Biosocial Bases of Criminal Behavior.* New York: Gardner Press, Inc.

Christiansen, K.O. (1977). A preliminary study of criminality among twins. Chapter 5 in S. Mednick and K.O. Christiansen (Eds.) *Biosocial Bases of Criminal Behavior.* New York: Gardner Press, Inc.

Cloward, R.A. (1968). Social control in the prison. Chapter 5 in L. Hazelrigg (Ed.), *Prison Within Society.* Garden City, N.Y.: Doubleday Anchor Books.

Cole, G.F. (1970). Decision to prosecute. *Law and Society Review, 4,* pp. 331-343.

Coleman, J.R. (1978, March). Prison guard in Texas for a week. *Fortune News,* pp. 8-10.

Cramer, J. (1968). *Uniforms of the World's Police.* Springfield, Ill.: Charles C. Thomas.

Criminal Victimization Surveys in Eight American Cities. (1976). A comparison of 1971/72 and 1974/75 findings. Washington, D.C.: Department of Justice, National Crime Survey Report.

Crosby, A. (1975). Situational testing as an assessment technique in police organizations. Paper presented at convention of the American Psychological Association, Chicago.

Crosby, A. (1976). Implications of police personnel management practices for selection system characteristics. Paper presented at convention of American Psychological Association, Washington, D.C.

Dawes, R.M. (1972). *Fundamentals of attitude measurement.* New York: Wiley.

Dawes, R.M. and Corrigan, B. (1974). Linear models in decision making. *Psychological Bulletin, 81,* p. 95.

Drahams, A. (1900). *The Criminal: His Personnel and Environment.* New York: Macmillan.

Durham, M. (1973). For the Swedes a prison sentence can be fun time. *Smithsonian, 4* (6), pp. 46-52.

Edwards, G. (1972). Commentary: Murder and gun control. *Wayne Law Review, 18* (4), pp. 1335-1342.

Eisenberg, T. and Reinke, R.W. (1973, March). The use of written examinations in selecting police officers: Coping with the dilemma. *The Police Chief,* pp. 24-28.

Erikson, E. (1956). Ego identity and the psychosocial moratorium. In H. Witmer and R. Kotinsky (Eds.) *New Perspectives for Research on Juvenile Delinquency,* Washington, D.C.: U.S. Department of Health, Education and Welfare, Children's Bureau, pp. 1-23.

Festinger, L., Schachter, S. and Back, K.W. (1950). *Social Pressures in Informal Groups: A Study of Human Factors in Housing.* New York: Harper & Row.

Festinger, L. and Carlsmith, J.M. (1959). Cognitive conseqences of forced compliance. *Journal of Abnormal and Social Psychology, 58,* pp. 195–202.

Fink, A.E. (1938). *Causes of Crime: Biological Theories in the United States: 1800–1915.* Philadelphia: University of Pennsylvania Press.

Fleming, A. (1975). *New on the Beat: Women Power in the Police Force.* New York: Coward, McCann & Geoghegan.

Freedman, J.L. and Fraser, S.C. (1966). Compliance without pressure: The foot-in-the-door technique. *Journal of Personality and Social Psychology 4,* pp. 195–202.

Friedlander, K. (1947). *The Psycho-analytical Approach to Juvenile Deliquency.* London: Routledge. Cited in R. Hood and R. Sparks. *Key Issues in Criminology* (1970). New York: McGraw-Hill World University Library.

Friedman, P.R. (1975). Legal regulation applied behavior analysis in mental institutions and prisons. *Arizona Law Review, 17,* pp. 39–104.

Gallo, P., Funk, S.G. and Levine, J.R. (1969). Reward size, method of presentation, and number of alternatives in Prisoners' Dilemma Game. *Journal of Personality and Social Psychology, 13,* pp. 239–244.

Gallo, P. and Sheposh, J. (1971). Effects of incentive magnitude on cooperation in the Prisoners' Dilemma Game: A reply to Gumpert, Deutsch, and Epstein. *Journal of Personality and Social Psychology, 19,* pp. 42–46.

Gelfand, D.M., Hartmann, D.P., Walder, P. and Page, B. (1973). Who reports shoplifters? A field-experimental study. *Journal of Personality and Social Psychology, 25* (2), pp. 276–285.

Gergen, K.J. (1969). *The psychological of behavior exchange.* Reading, Mass.: Addison–Wesley.

Gibbons, D. (1965). *Changing the Lawbreaker.* Englewood Cliffs, N.J.: Prentice-Hall. Cited in R. Hood and R. Sparks *Key Issues in Criminology.* (1970). New York: McGraw-Hill World University Library.

Glaser, D. (1964). *The Effectiveness of a Prison and Parole System.* New York: Bobbs–Merrill.

Glaser, D. (Ed.) (1970). *Crime in the City.* New York: Harper & Row.

Gotkin, J. (1975). New words for an old power trip: A critique for behavior modification in institutional settings. *Arizona Law Review, 17,* pp. 29–32.

Greenberg, M.S. (1976). An experimental approach to victim crime reporting. Paper presented at 84th Annual Convention, American Psychological Association, Washington, D.C.

Hindelang, M.J. (1976). *An Analysis of Victimization Survey Results from the Eight Impact Cities: Summary Report.* Washington, D.C.: Law Enforcement Assistance Administration, U.S. Department of Justice, 1974, Albany, N.Y., Criminal Justice Research Center.

Hindelang, M.J. and Gottfredson, M. (1976). The victim's decision not to invoke the criminal justice process. Chapter 2 in W.F. McDonald (Ed.) *Criminal Justice and the Victim.* Beverly Hills: Sage Publications.

Holland, J.G. (1976). Behavior modification for prisoners, patients, and other people as a prescription for the planned society. *Mexican Journal of the Analysis of Behavior, 1* (1), pp. 81–95.

Homan, G.C. (1961). *Social behavior: Its elementary forms.* New York: Harcourt, Brace, and World.

Hood, R. and Sparks, R. (1970). *Key Issues in Criminology.* New York: McGraw-Hill World University Library.

Horn, J. (1976, April). Portrait of an arrogant crook. *Psychology Today, 9* (11), pp. 76–79.

Hovland, C.I., Janis, I.L. and Kelley, H.H. (1953). *Communication and persuasion.* New Haven: Yale University Press.

Huston, T.L., Geis, G. and Wright, R. (1976, June). The angry samaritans. *Psychology Today, 10,* (1), p. 61ff.

Huston, T.L. and Geis, G. (1976). Public policy and the encouragement of bystander intervention. Paper presented at symposium on Citizen Response to Crime: Behavior of Victims and Witnesses. 84th Annual Convention, American Psychological Association, Washington, D.C.

Inn, A., Wheeler, A.C. and Sparling, C.L. (1977). The effects of suspect race and situation hazard on police officer shooting behavior. *Journal of Applied Social Psychology, 7* (1), pp. 27–37.

Janis, I.L. (1971). *Victims of "Groupthink."* Boston: Houghton Mifflin.

Jericho: Newsletter of the National Moratorium on Prison Construction.

Jones, E.E. and Harris, V.A. (1967). The attribution of attitudes. *Journal of Experimental Social Psychology, 3,* pp. 1–24.

Joseph, N. and Alex, N. (1971). The uniform: A sociological perspective. *American Journal of Sociology, 77,* pp. 719–730.

Kaufman, K. (1976, March 25). Prisoners, all. *The New York Times,* p. 35.

Keith–Speigel, P. (1976). Children's rights as participants in research. In G. Koocher (Ed.), *Children's Rights and the Mental Health Professions,* pp. 53–81. New York: Wiley.

Kent, D.A. and Eisenberg, T. (1972, February). The selection and promotion of police officers: A selected review of recent literature. *The Police Chief,* pp. 20–29.

Kerckhoff, A.C. and Back, K.W. (1968). *The June Bug: A Study of Hysterical Contagion.* New York: Appleton-Century-Crofts.

Kiesler, C.A., Collins, B.E., and Miller, N. (1969). *Attitude change.* New York: Wiley.

Kittrie, N.N. (1973). *The Right to be Different.* Baltimore: Penguin Books.

Kozol, H.L., Boucher, R.J. and Garofalo, R.F. (1972). The diagnosis and treatment of dangerousness. *Crime and Delinquency, 18,* pp. 371–392.

Krasner, L. and Ullmann, L.P. (1973). *Behavior influence and personality.* New York: Holt, Rinehart & Winston.

Kuehn, L.L. (1974). Looking down a gun barrel: Person perception and violent crime. *Perceptual and Motor Skills, 39,* pp. 1159–1164.

Latane, B. and Darley, J.M. (1970). *The Unresponsive Bystander: Why Doesn't he Help?* New York: Appleton-Century-Crofts.

Latane, B. and Darley, J. (1970). Situational determinants of bystander intervention in emergencies. In J. Macaulay and L. Berkowitz (Eds.) *Altruism and Helping Behavior.* New York: Academic Press.

Lefkowitz, J. (1975). Industrial-organizing psychology and the police. *American Psychologist, 32* (5), pp. 346–364.

Lerner, M.J. and Simmons, C. (1966). Observer's reaction to the "innocent victim": Compassion or rejection? *Journal of Personality and Social Psychology, 4,* pp. 203–210.

Levenson, H. (1975). Multidimensional locus of control in prison inmates. *Journal of Applied Social Psychology, 5* (4), pp. 342–347.

Lewis, M. (1970). Structural deviance and normative conformity: The "hustle" and the gang. In D. Glaser (Ed.) *Crime in the City.* New York: Harper & Row.

Livermore, J., Malmquist, C. and Meehl, P. (1968). On the justification for civil commitment. *University of Pennsylvania Law Review, 117,* p. 75.

Lombroso, C. and Ferrero, W. (1915). *The Female Offender.* New York: Appelton.

Love, R.E. (1972). *Nonreactive, nonverbal measures of attitudes,* Doctoral dissertation at the Ohio State University.

Lunde, D.I. (1975, July). Our murder boom. *Psychology Today, 9* (2), pp. 35–42.

Lunde, D.I. (1976). *Murder and Madness.* San Francisco: San Francisco Book Company.

Margolis, R.J. (1971). *Who Will Wear the Badge: A Study of Minority Recruitment Efforts in Protective Services.* Washington, D.C.: United States Commission on Civil Rights.

McDonald, W.F. (1976). Criminal justice and the victim: An introduction. Chapter 1 in W.F. McDonald (Ed.) *Criminal Justice and the Victim*. Beverly Hills: Sage Publications, Inc.

McEvoy, D.W. (1974). Training for the new centurions. Chapter 2 in J.L. Steinberg and D.W. McEvoy (Eds.) *The Police and the Behavioral Sciences*. Springfield, Ill.: Charles C. Thomas.

McGuire, W.J. (1969). The nature of attitudes and attitude change. In G. Lindzey and E. Aronson (Eds.), *The Handbook of Social Psychology* (Vol. 3). (second ed.). Reading, Mass.: Addison-Wesley.

Mednick, S.A. (1977). A biosocial theory of the learning of law-abiding behavior. Chapter 1 in S.A. Mednick and K.O. Christiansen (Eds.) *Biosocial Bases of Criminal Behavior*. New York: Gardner Press, Inc.

Mednick, S.A. and Christiansen, K.O. (Eds.) (1977). *Biosocial Bases of Criminal Behavior*. New York: Gardner Press, Inc.

Meehl, P.E. (1962). Schizotaxia, schizotypy, schizophrenia. *American Psychologist, 17*, pp. 827-838.

Milgan, M.A. and McKee, J.M. (1974). Behavior modification principles and application in corrections. In D. Glaser (Ed.) *Handbook of Criminology* Chicago: Rand McNally.

Milgram, S. (1970, March 13) The experience of living in cities. *Science, 167*, pp. 1461-1468.

Milgram, S. (1974). *Obedience to Authority: An Experimental View*. New York: Harper & Row.

Miller, F.W. (1969). *Prosecution: The decision to charge a suspect with a crime*. Boston: Little, Brown.

Mischel, W. (1973). Toward a cognitive social learning reconceptualization of personality. *Psychological Review, 80*, pp. 252-283.

Mischel, W. (1969). Continuity and change in personality. *American Psychologist, 24*, pp. 1012-1018.

Monahan, J. and Geis, G. (1976). Controlling "dangerous" people. *Annals of the American Academy of Political and Social Science, 423*, pp. 142-151.

Monahan, J. (1978). Prediction research and the emergency commitment of dangerous mentally ill persons: A reconsideration. *American Journal of Psychiatry, 135*, pp. 198-201.

Morris, N. (1974). *The Future of Imprisonment*. Chicago: University of Chicago Press.

Niedehoffer, A. (1967). *Behind the Shield: The Police in Urban Society*. New York: Doubleday Anchor Books.

Nisbett, R.E. and Wilson, T.D. (1977). Telling more than we know: Verbal reports on mental processes. *Psychological Review, 84*, pp. 231-259.

Opton, E.M., Jr. (1974). Psychiatric violence against prisoners: When therapy is punishment. *Mississippi Law Journal, 45*, pp. 605-644.

Opton, E.M., Jr. (1975). Institutional behavior modifications as a fraud and sham. *Arizona Law Review 17*, pp. 20-28.

Osgood, C.E. and Tannenbaum, P.H. (1955). The principle of congruity in the prediction of attitude change. *Psychological Review, 62*, pp. 42-55.

Oskamp, S. (1977). *Attitudes and opinions*. Englewood Cliffs, N.J.: Prentice-Hall.

Police Training and Performance Study. (1969). Report to the New York City Police Department and Law Enforcement Assistance Administration, United States Department of Justice, New York: New York City Police Department.

President's Commission on Law Enforcement and Administration of Justice. (1967). *The challenge of crime in a free society*. Washington, D.C.: U.S. Government Printing Office.

Proshansky, H., Ittelson, W., and Rivlin, L. (Eds.) (1970). *Environmental psychology*. New York: Holt, Rinehart & Winston.

Radzinowicz, L. (1948). *A History of English Criminal Law and Its Administration from 1750*. (Vol. 1). *The Movement for Reform*. London: Stevens & Sons Limited.

Rapoport, A. and Chammah, A. (1965). *Prisoners' Dilemma*. Ann Arbor: University of Michigan Press.

Raven, B.H. and Eachus, H.T. (1963). Cooperation and competition in means-interdependent triads. *Journal of Abnormal and Social Psychology, 67,* pp. 307-316.

Reiss, A.J., Jr. (1971). *The Police and the Public*. New Haven: Yale University Press.

Richardson, J.F. (1974). *Urban Police in the United States*. Port Washington, N.Y.: National University Publications, Kennikat Press.

Robin, G.D. (1963). Justifiable homicide by police officers. *Journal of Criminal Law, Criminology and Police Science, 54,* pp. 225-229.

Roebuck, J. (1965). *Criminal Typology*. Springfield, Ill.: Charles C. Thomas. Cited in R. Hood and R. Sparks *Key Issues in Criminology*. (1970). New York: McGraw-Hill World University Library.

Rokeach, M., Miller, M.G. and Snyder, J.A. (1971). The value gap between police and policed. *Journal of Social Issues, 27* (2), pp. 155-171.

Rosenthal, R. (1966). *Experimenter Effects in Behavioral Research*. New York: Appleton-Century-Crofts.

Rubin, J.G. (1974). Police identity and the police role. Chapter 6 in J.G. Goldsmith and S.S. Goldsmith (Eds.) *The Police Community: Dimensions of an Occupational Subculture*. Pacific Palisades, Calif.: Palisades Publishers.

Rudovsky, D. (1973). *The Rights of Prisoners*. New York: Avon Books.

Saunders, A.G., Jr. (1974). Behavior therapy in prisons: Walden II or Clockworth Orange? Paper presented at 8th annual convention of the Association for the Advancement of Behavior Therapy, Chicago.

Schacter, S. (1951). Deviation, rejection, and communication. *Journal of Abnormal and Social Psychology, 46,* pp. 190–207.

Schelling, T.C. (1960). *The strategy of conflict*. Cambridge, Mass.: Harvard University Press.

Schlesinger, S.E. (1977). Psychotherapists in prison: The emperor's new clothiers? Paper presented at Symposium on Psychology and the Criminal Justice System, 48th meeting of the Eastern Psychological Association, Boston.

Sellin, T. (1928). The Negra criminal: A statistical note. *Annals of the American Academy of Political and Social Science, 140,* pp. 52–64.

Serrill, M.A. (1978, February). A cold new look at the criminal mind. *Psychology Today, 11* (9), p. 86ff.

Shah, S.A. (1976). Dangerousness: A paradigm for exploring some issues in law and psychology. Invited address to 84th annual convention. American Psychological Association, Washington, D.C.

Shaw, L. (1973). The role of clothing in the criminal justice system. *Journal of Police Science and Administration, 1* (4), pp. 414–420.

Sherif, M., Harvey, O.J., White, B.J., Hood, W. and Sherif, C. (1961). *Intergroup Conflict and Cooperation: The Robbers Cave Experiment*. Norman, Okla.: University of Oklahoma Institute of Intergroup Relations.

Sherman, L.J. (1973). A psychological view of women in policing. *Journal of Police Science and Administration, 1* (4), pp. 383–394.

Simon, R.J. (1975). *The Contemporary Woman and Crime*. Rockville, Md.: N.I.M.H. Crime and Delinquency Series.

Skelton, W.D. (1968). Stress and coping in prison. Chapter 1 in *A Handbook of Correctional Psychiatry*, Vol. I, 1968, Washington, D.C.: Department of Justice, U.S. Bureau of Prisons.

Skinner, B.F. (1974, February 26). To build constructive prison environments. Letter to the Editor. *The New York Times*.

Smead, A. (1972). Cooperation and competition. In L.S. Wrightsman, *Social psychology in the Seventies*. Belmont, Calif.: Brooks/Cole.

Smith, A.E. and Maness, D., Jr. (1976). The decision to call the police: Reactions to burglary. Chapter 3 in W.F. McDonald (Ed.) *Criminal Justice and the Victim*. Beverly Hills: Sage Publications, Inc.

Sommer, R. (1971). The social psychology of the cell environment. *The Prison Journal, 5* (1), pp. 15–21.

Staats, A.W. (1975). *Social Behaviorism*. Homewood, Ill.: Dorsey.

Steadman, H.J. and Keveles, G. (1972). The community adjustment and criminal activity of the Baxstrom patients: 1966–70. *American Journal of Psychiatry 129*, pp. 304–310.

Steadman, H.J. and Cocozza, J.J. (1975, January). We can't predict who is dangerous. *Psychology Today, 8* (8), p. 32ff.

Steinberg, J.L. and McEvoy, D.W. (1974). *The police and the Behavioral Sciences*. Springfield, Ill.: Charles C. Thomas.

Stier, S. (1976). Prison research, *APA Monitor, 7* (7), p. 1ff.

Stock, R.W. (1968, October, 28). The XYY and the criminal. *The New York Times Magazine*, pp. 30ff.

Sutherland, E.H. and Cressey, D.R. (1966). *Principles of criminology*. New York: Lippincott.

Suttles, G. (1970). Deviant behavior as an unanticipated consequence of public housing. In D. Glaser (Ed.) *Crime in the City*. New York: Harper & Row.

Tenzel, J.H. and Cizanckas, V. (1973). The uniform experiment. *Journal of Police Science and Administration, 1* (4), pp. 421–424.

Terhune, K.W. (1968). Motives, situation and inter personal conflict within the Prisoner's Dilemma. *Journal of Personality and Social Psychology, 8*, pp. 1–24.

Terhune, K.W. (1970). The effects of personality in cooperation and conflict. In P. Swingle (Ed.), *The structure of conflict*. New York: Academic Press.

Toch, H. and Schulte, R. (1961). Readiness to perceive violence as a result of police training. *British Journal of Psychology, 52* (4), pp. 389–393.

Trotter, S. (1975). Patuxent: "Therapeutic" prison faces test. *APA Monitor, 6* (5), p. 1ff.

Uejio, C.K. and Wrightsman, L.S. (1967). Ethinic group differences in the relationship of trusting attitudes to cooperative behavior. *Psychological Reports, 20*, pp. 563–571.

Wall, C.R. and Culloo, L.A. (1973). State standards for law enforcement selection and training. *Journal of Police Science and Administration, 1* (4), pp. 425–532.

Weiss, K. (Ed.) (1976). *The Prison Experience: An Anthology*. New York: Delacorte Press.

Whipple, G.M. (1918). The obtaining of information: Psychology of observation and report. *Psychological Bulletin, 15*, pp. 217–248.

Whyte, W.H., Jr. (1956). *The Organization Man*. New York: Simon and Schuster.

Wicker, A.W. (1969). Attitudes versus actions: The relationship of verbal and overt behavioral responses to attitude objects. *Journal of Social Issues, 25*, pp. 41–78.

Williams, W. and Miller, K.S. (1977). The role of personal characteristics in perceptions of dangerousness. *Criminal Justice and Behavior, 4* (3), pp. 241–252.

Wilson, J.Q. (1975). *Thinking about Crime*. New York: Basic Books.

Witkin, H.A., Mednick, S.A., Schulsinger, F., Bakkestrom, E., Christiansen, K.O., Goodenough, D.R., Hirschhorn, K., Lundstean, C., Owen, D.R., Philip, J., Rubin, D.B. and Stocking, M. (1976). XYY and XXY men: Criminality and aggression, *Science, 193*, pp. 547–555. Reprinted as Chapter 10 in S.A. Mednick and K.O. Christiansen (Eds.), (1977). *Biosocial Bases of Criminal Behavior*. New York: Gardner Press, Inc.

Wolfgang, M.E. (1958). *Patterns in Criminal Homicide*. Philadelphia: University of Pennsylvania Press.

Wolpe, J. (1973). *The Practice of Behavior Therapy*. Pergamon Press, Inc.

Wrightsman, L.S., Davis, D.W., Lucker, W.G., Bruininks, R., Evans, J., Wilde, R., Paulson, D. and Clark, G. (1967). Effects of other person's race and strategy upon cooperative behavior in a Prisoner's Dilemma game. Paper presented at the meeting of the Midwestern Psychological Association, Chicago.

Wrightsman, L.S., O'Connor, J. and Baker, N.J. (Eds.) (1972). *Cooperation and competition: Readings on mixed-motive games.* Monterey, Calif.: Brooks/Cole.

Yochelson, S. and Samenow, S.E. (1976). *The Criminal Personality Volume I: A Profile for Change.* New York: Jason Aronson.

Zimbardo, P.G., Haney, C., Banks, W.C. and Jaffe, D. (1973, April 18). A Pirandellian prison: The mind is a formidable jailer. *The New York Times Magazine,* pp. 38–60.

Zimbardo, P.G., Haney, C., Banks, W.C. and Jaffe, D. (1972). *Stanford Prison Experiment.* Stanford, California: Philip G. Zimbardo, Inc. (slide and tape program).

Zimbardo, P.G., Haney, C., Banks, W.C. and Jaffe, D. (1971). *The Stanford Prison Experiment: A Slide Show.* Stanford, Calif.: Philip G. Zimbardo, Inc.

Zimbardo, P. and Ebbesen, E. (1969). *Influencing attitudes and changing behavior.* Reading, Mass.: Addison–Wesley.

Zimbardo, P.G. (1966). The psychology of police confessions. Paper read at 74th annual convention American Psychological Association, New York.

INDEX

INDEX